THE POLITICS OF WOMEN AND WORK
IN THE SOVIET UNION
AND THE UNITED STATES

RESEARCH SERIES

No. 50

The
Politics *of*
Women & Work
in the
Soviet Union & *the* United States

*Alternative Work Schedules
& Sex Discrimination*

JOEL C. MOSES

INSTITUTE
OF INTERNATIONAL
STUDIES
University of California, Berkeley

Library of Congress Cataloging in Publication Data

Moses, Joel C.
  The politics of women and work in the Soviet Union
and the United States.

  (Research series/Institute of International Studies,
University of California, Berkeley, ISSN 0068-6093;
no. 50)
  Includes bibliographical references and index.
  1. Hours of labor—Soviet Union. 2. Hours of labor—
United States. 3. Women—Employment—Soviet Union.
4. Women—Employment—United States. I. Title. II.
Title: Alternative work schedules and sex discrimination.
III. Series: Research series (University of California,
Berkeley. Institute of International Studies); no. 50.
HD5195.M63 1982   331.4'0947   82-23307
ISBN 0-87725-150-9

CONTENTS

Preface   vii

Acknowledgments   xi

1. INTRODUCTION: ALTERNATIVE WORK SCHEDULES AS A
   POLICY ISSUE   1

2. ALTERNATIVE WORK SCHEDULES IN THE SOVIET UNION   10
   Policy Context   10
   Policy Tendencies and All-Union Policy   22
   Economic and Political Determinants of Policy   32
   Economic and Political Constraints   42

3. ALTERNATIVE WORK SCHEDULES IN THE UNITED STATES   54
   Economic Determinants of Policy   57
   Political Determinants of Policy   69
      Feminists and Federal Policy   69
      Unemployment and Equality as Determinants of Policy   88
   Sociocultural Determinants of Policy   104
   Economic and Political Constraints   119

4. CONCLUSION: WOMEN, WORK, AND POLITICS IN THE USSR
   AND UNITED STATES   133

Abbreviations Used in References   144

Notes   147

Index   171

Preface

The origin of this monograph can be traced to a four-day national conference on Russian women in May 1975 at Stanford University. I was invited to participate because of a paper I had recently written on the political recruitment of women in the Soviet Union; the paper was a by-product of my ongoing research on the regional policy-making process and leadership recruitment in the Soviet Union since 1953. The conference aroused my interest in the substantive social, economic, and political issues surrounding women in the Soviet Union, and I have redirected my research efforts over the last few years to focus on the role of women in the context of major issues confronting the Soviet Union. From these research efforts, not only have I begun to comprehend facets of the Soviet Union from a sharpened perspective, but also a logical and natural turn has led me to understand and contrast the role of women in the context of major policy issues and problems confronting the United States. The cross-national scope of this monograph represents an analytical exploration of comparable problems and policy considerations relative to working women in both nations.

The monograph may appear to be overly ambitious in scope and pretensions, and these are unlikely to please either Western Sovietologists, with whom I primarily identify myself by research interests, or scholars of American or comparative public policy, who will probably resent this intrusion on their analytical "turf" by a novice and outsider. However, the intention of the monograph has been essentially to build upon the excellent studies by scholars on women in the Soviet Union and United States which have been written over the last decade. My indebtedness to these scholars is best reflected in my frequent citation of their studies and the integration of their insights into my analysis.

Nevertheless, as a Western student of contemporary Soviet politics, I believe that the deliberate cross-national and cross-systemic focus of this study represents a relevant and important new methodological approach among Western studies to explain and comprehend the policy context of issues in the Soviet Union. Prominent Western Sovietologists like Jerry Hough and Thomas Larson and scholars of American and comparative policy-making like Valerie Bunce and Charles Lindblom have challenged their fellow researchers in recent years to reexamine some of their conventional interpretations of Soviet politics and evaluations of Soviet policies framed from an isolated and narrow inquiry on the reality of the Soviet Union alone. For Hough in *The Soviet Union and Social Science Theory* (1977) and Larson in *Soviet-American Rivalry* (1979), the realities of Soviet political power, elite-mass linkages, mass political participation, welfare policy, and foreign policy may appear less negative and lead to quite different interpretations when compared and contrasted to similar realities in other industrialized nations like the United States. For Bunce in *Do New Leaders Make a Difference?: Executive Succession and Public Policy under Capitalism and Socialism* (1981), the impact of leadership change on policy-making in the Soviet Union and East European socialist systems over recent decades has followed a cyclical pattern closely parallel to its impact in the United States and Western capitalist democracies. For Lindblom in his award-winning *Politics and Markets: The World's Political-Economic Systems* (1977), the performance and failures of Western market systems can be better understood by comparing their properties and political dynamics to those in authoritarian command systems like the Soviet Union. While not ignoring the uniqueness of the Soviet political system, a cross-national and cross-systemic study may sensitize Western Sovietologists (like myself) to latent anti-Soviet biases by forcing us to evaluate Soviet policy responses relative to similar policy responses in nonsocialist nations.

In broadening our scope of inquiry into Soviet policies to consider identical problems and issues in Western capitalist nations, our final judgment of the Soviet situation may be no less critical; nor should the comparison of problems in the Soviet Union with those in the United States be interpreted as an implicit apologia for the Soviet system. Indeed the path-breaking study which first realized the usefulness of comparing the Soviet Union and the United States— Zbigniew Brzezinski and Samuel Huntington, *Political Power: USA/USSR* (1964)—reinforced the impression of profound differences in policy performance and political processes between the two political systems. But times have changed since 1964, and it is highly significant that by the end of the 1970s the two nations were confronting similar problems associated with the role and status of working women and attempting to address some of those problems with similar reforms—such as alternative work schedules. At a minimum, a comparative analysis of such similar policies in the Soviet Union and the United States may alert us to the limitations and potentials for responsiveness and political change in the Soviet political system by forcing us to ask similar questions about the American political system.

J. C. M.

February 1983

Acknowledgments

I am greatly indebted to Iowa State University for providing me financial support and granting me a faculty leave for the winter and spring quarters of the 1979-80 academic year to undertake the research for this monograph. I was able to conduct extensive interviews with American policy participants concerned with the issue of alternative work schedules (and with the general problems of sex discrimination in the labor force) in Washington, D.C., New York, and Detroit during a ten-week period from February through April 1980. While I promised complete anonymity to the participants, their contribution to the monograph is evident—particularly in Chapter 3 on alternative work schedules in the United States. I bear any responsibility for unintentional distortions or misinterpretations of their comments. During the time that I was completing my research on the Soviet Union at the Library of Congress, I was affiliated as a visiting scholar with the Kennan Institute for Advanced Russian Studies of the Woodrow Wilson International Center for Scholars of the Smithsonian Institution. To Dr. Abbott Gleason, Executive Secretary of the Institute, to Sabrina Palmer, assistant to Dr. Gleason, and to numerous fellows then in residence at the Institute, I owe particular thanks for providing me with the intellectual environment and support by which I was able to complete my research. A final and not insignificant contribution has been made by Bojana Ristich, who as senior editor at the Institute of International Studies skillfully wrought a very polished final monograph from a rough first draft, and whose own evident talents employed in something of an alternative work situation several thousand miles from Berkeley eloquently personify the advantages for all of us in American employers' flexibly adjusting their terms of employment to meet the needs and tap the potentials of many working women.

Chapter 1

INTRODUCTION:
ALTERNATIVE WORK SCHEDULES AS A POLICY ISSUE

It may be symptomatic of the growing interdependence of the world and our consciousness as a global village that apparently identical problems have come to be recognized and apparently identical solutions offered for problems in the policy realms of nations otherwise seeming to have little in common. Most nations in one way or another have been forced to address such priority issues as environmental pollution, food, energy, and inflation, and international conferences in these areas throughout the 1970s focused worldwide attention on the need to arrive at mutually compatible solutions (although they failed to develop consensus among capitalist, Communist, industrial, and preindustrial nations on the sources of their common problems).

Parallel to the international context of policy formation, social scientists in recent years have been drawn to the cross-national comparative study of public policy and have sought explanations of the reasons that nations perform differently in meeting common policy problems. The hybrid subfield of comparative public policy has produced an impressive number of studies ranging from aggregate quantitative analyses of the policy performance of many nations to qualitative case studies of comparable policy areas among a few nations.[1] Both the quantitative and qualitative approaches attempt to determine the relative influence of different causal factors on policy formation—socioeconomic conditions, political structures, political "input" variables (interest groups, political parties), and national ideologies have been the most prevalent and logical—and to explain national variations in policy outcomes. One important result has been that in comparing the impact of causal factors on public policy, these studies have provided evidence that political differences among nations better explain policy variation than do socioeconomic

1

differences. For example, nations with similar socioeconomic conditions vary in their commitment to identical policies on comparable problems depending on their ideologies, political structures, and the relative influence of social classes and interest groups in their political systems.*

Within the subfield studies have pointed out that the emerging international context of policy-formation is an important factor in the evolution of policy within nations. Recognition of this factor has been particularly evident in studies concerned with issue areas directly affecting women and with explaining national variations in improving their status and condition as a distinct group. One clear example is a comparative study of equal employment policy for women in seven advanced industrialized nations—Austria, Canada, the Federal Republic of Germany, France, Sweden, the United Kingdom, and the United States—in which case studies disclosed not only that women's equality had emerged as a priority policy consideration in all seven nations, but also that proposals to reduce sexual discrimination in the labor force more frequently were shared by government officials and academic specialists.[2] As a by-product of the emerging international women's movement, decision-makers in one of these nations had often consciously modeled their programs after those in another, and policy specialists on women's issues had interacted to formulate common approaches to problems.[3]

Thus women's issues and the formation of policy to resolve the problems of women reflect the changing international context of public policy as an interrelated phenomenon cutting across national-

---

*From aggregate analysis Wilensky (in *The Welfare State and Equality*) shows that economic growth and its demographic and bureaucratic correlates have been dominant in the emergence of the welfare state over the last hundred years, but he finds divergence in welfare commitment among the richest nations depending on such political and organizational variables as the responsiveness of central governments to working classes, the perception of tax burdens and tax equity to fund welfare among middle-income groups, and the size of private welfare and the military establishment. Adams and Winston deemphasize socioeconomic conditions as determinants of policy toward women, but they find interesting similarities in policy between the quite different political systems of Sweden and China based on similar political orientations toward the family and women's support programs—in sharp contrast to these orientations in the United States, which otherwise closely approximates Sweden in many political characteristics and socioeconomic conditions.

cultural boundaries and developing priorities and approaches from universally shared experiences. The formation of policy to deal with women's issues has implicitly brought together a loose coalition of like-minded policy specialists, whose views and concerns identify them as a worldwide reformist policy "tendency" or potential political group.[4] Indeed these specialists have recognized that only through more systematic cross-national studies of women's issues can we hope to identify and understand similar constraints among nations and limiting political assumptions within nations which have prevented significant improvements in the condition of women in advanced industrialized nations.[5] In comparative cross-national studies of women's issues, theory has united with reality: many scholars drawn to a systematic comparative inquiry of these issues have become participants in shaping the international political context of women's issues and the cross-national influence on policy formation.

Over recent years a subtle and unmistakable indication of the global policy convergence on issues directly affecting women has been an increased interest in several industrialized nations in the policy reform of alternative work schedules. Simply defined, alternative work schedules encompass any modification of labor policy requiring that all regular employees adhere to the same prescribed times and number of hours worked daily or weekly. Thus they represent any departure from the conventional work mode of a five-day, eight-hour schedule typical of many industrialized nations.

The most common types of alternative work schedules include staggered work hours, flexible work hours (or "flexitime," as it has become popularly termed worldwide), compressed work weeks, permanent part-time employment, and work-sharing.[6] Under staggered work hours, regular full-time employees are permitted to start and end their daily shifts at slightly varying times, as long as they all work the same total number of hours daily. Under flexitime, all employees work during a prescribed "core time" during the day and then choose from a range of optional plans ("flexitour," "gliding time") to determine their additional hours so that the total number of hours adds up to the prescribed daily salaried period. (In some instances, employees on flexitime work under an honor system, in which management trusts them to put in the prescribed hours without direct monitoring; in other instances, they may be monitored by a time clock.) Compressed work weeks allow employees to compile or "bank" the standard norm of weekly work hours in less than the standard number of workdays per week. Under four-day compressed work weeks, employees work a standard weekly norm of hours in four days; under two-week compressed work schedules, employees bank work hours or days during a two-week span and receive equivalent off-hours or off-days as compensation within that span.

Permanent part-time employment—which, as defined by the International Labor Office (ILO) in Geneva, includes "regular voluntary employment carried out during working hours distinctly shorter than normal"—is not considered an alternative work schedule unless the reduction in work hours distinguishes the part-time employees from the rest of the national labor force in terms of wages and benefits.* Work-sharing is a derived form of part-time employment in which employees are compensated for off-time in either state transfer payments or vacation time. Under revised work-sharing programs in several Western European nations since the 1960s and in new experimental programs such as that in California since 1978, employees voluntarily work fewer days weekly or monthly and receive partial compensation for their sacrificed wages through some form of unemployment compensation or state furlough.[7] In Western Europe, where some nations have experimented with work-sharing programs since the 1920s, work-sharing gained prominence during the latter 1960s, when several nations were experiencing labor shortages and attempted through work-sharing to attract gainfully employable strata of their domestic labor pools (like homemakers) who were reluctant to work eight-hour days. The program has been highly praised by some Europeans both for its achievements and for a number of unintended positive consequences—for example, it has been credited for the high per capita labor productivity of European labor forces during the 1970s and for holding down the unemployment rate among workers who otherwise would have been completely laid off. In the Federal Republic of Germany one economist reported that work-sharing reduced potential full-time unemployment by one sixth during the 1975 economic recession.[8] Others remain less sanguine about the

---

*As it has evolved in many industrialized nations, permanent part-time employment includes any work mode in which employees work a predetermined number of hours daily or weekly fewer than the norms established by labor law or practice. Part-time workers (or "part-timers") do not receive pay for the hours or days they do not work.

European experience; some employers and labor economists have criticized work-sharing for increasing labor-unit costs and thus holding back long-term expansion in output and productivity. Yet following his election in June 1981, French President François Mitterand endorsed thirty-five-hour work weeks and related work-sharing reforms as part of his Socialist Party's platform to stem the high rate of unemployment among French workers.[9]

In California the passage of Proposition 13 entailed (among other things) the reduction of local revenues from property taxes. However, as a result of the work-sharing program, 37,475 employees in 840 firms (all but 8 in the private sector) by June 1980 were able to keep their jobs despite the restrictions of both Proposition 13 and (more important) a national economic recession in 1979-80.[10] In something of a novel California twist to work-sharing termed "leisure-sharing," since the mid-1970s employees in certain local government departments have voluntarily accepted a reduction in work hours and salary increases up to 20 percent in exchange for a commensurate number of vacation days covered by health and retirement benefits.[11] Nonetheless, the most prevalent forms of work-sharing in all industrialized nations are uncompensated and include the equal sharing of one full-time position by two employees and the voluntary reduction in hours without unemployment compensation or vacation benefits. In the United States, for example, over one third of all union contracts allow for uncompensated work reductions to thirty-two hours a week in order to prevent layoffs.

It is important to point out that the various types of alternative work schedules have become universally similar enough departures from conventional work modes that a common terminology has evolved and statistics on them from industrialized nations have been gathered and reported by the ILO.[12] National policy clearing-houses in particular nations have been formed to undertake research and monitor the international trends of these work patterns; for example, for the United States in 1978 the National Council for Alternative Work Patterns listed and described 290 private and public enterprises which employed workers on some type of alternative work schedules.[13] As noted, the internationalization of workplace reforms has resulted in a cross-national pooling of expertise and experiences, and multinational corporations noted for their innovative management have introduced alternative work schedules for their employees in several industrialized nations.[14] Thus alternative work schedules as a series of related workplace reforms could be characterized as an emerging global policy tendency in many industrialized nations during the latter decades of the twentieth century.

The internationalization of alternative work schedules as a global policy tendency not only has shown increasing attempts by national governments to monitor and regulate these reforms, but it has also revealed that similar concerns motivate governments and private employers to endorse the expanded options of alternative work schedules for their labor forces. Advanced industrialized nations confront somewhat parallel economic, social, demographic, and cultural problems and concerns which have increased their awareness and interest in workplace reforms. Among the most common have been the following: labor shortages (as noted above for Western Europe); transportation costs and traffic congestion at peak hours of regular shift changes; the humanization of the workplace and a trend away from the rigid assembly-line production process to forms more conducive to the physical and emotional well-being of employees; the democratization of the workplace and a trend to spur employee morale and productivity through increased employee participation in the terms of their employment; a more efficient utilization of labor input among regular employees in the production cycle; and the purported reduction in unemployment rates and higher per capita labor productivity from employees on alternative work schedules. Many of these nations have perceived alternative work schedules as a short-term solution—irrespective of their national ideologies or political systems.

Even more prevalent in prompting governments and employers to consider alternative work schedules has been their concern with the particular needs and demands of working women. In all industrialized nations the proportion of working women has increased sharply over the last few decades,[15] and women have had to confront a growing conflict between their comparatively new work roles and their still dominant family roles of child-rearing and homemaking. As the economies of industrialized nations have become more dependent on their working women, the conflict has directly limited the numbers of women who could work and the kinds of jobs they could perform, and it has indirectly constrained the potential for economic growth in nations which have failed to utilize their female labor

6

reserve effectively. For reasons of equity and economic efficiency, some direct modifications of the conventional work modes through flexitime or permanent part-time employment to accommodate women have become more frequently supported in the policy realms of industrialized nations. So predominant have been the problems of working women in forcing increased consideration of alternative work schedules in several industrialized nations that it would be fair in some respects to identify the policy of alternative work schedules as a global "women's issue."

Yet although similar problems and concerns have led more industrialized nations to expand alternative work schedules in the latter decades of the twentieth century, their record in encouraging and implementing workplace reforms has varied, and enactment of these reforms has symbolized profoundly different kinds of fundamental political change given the varying political economies of the nations in which they have been introduced. The political-ideological differences among nations must be considered a major factor in explaining how, why, and to what effect similar workplace reforms have been enacted and implemented. The impact of political-ideological factors on alternative work schedules is perhaps most strikingly apparent in the national policy agenda of the Soviet Union and the United States since 1970. On the one hand, as a result of common socioeconomic problems and underlying changes in both countries and despite their quite different political economies, decision-makers in both nations since 1970 have committed themselves in varying degrees to greater experimentation with and implementation of alternative work schedules; and they have commonly identified their commitment with a basic concern over the problems and status of working women. In addition, policy specialists and government officials in both nations have advocated alternative work schedules as a means to remedy long-term economic problems of falling labor productivity and underemployment, as well as sociocultural changes associated with a perceived transformation or breakdown of traditional family life. On the other hand, while similar arguments have been advanced favoring or opposing similar types of alternative work schedules, the tenor of the policy controversy and the implications of the reforms differ profoundly between the Soviet Union and the United States.

In a microcosm the similarities and differences in the policy controversy reveal much about the relative political priorities of the two nations, the impact of their political structures on policy formation, the underlying assumptions of their national policy toward working women, and the extent to which similar problems have resulted in different responses. Because the problems and concerns appear very similar and the workplace reforms appear formally identical, alternative work schedules as a policy issue provide us with a particularly salient case study for comparative analysis of policy responses between the Soviet Union and the United States.

In this monograph we shall attempt to compare and analyze the origin and substance of alternative work schedules as a major contemporary issue in the Soviet Union and the United States by considering four major policy questions:

(1) Why have alternative work schedules as a policy issue become so salient on the national policy agendas of both nations over the last decade? We shall assess the social, economic, cultural, and political factors which have generated increased awareness and interest in workplace reforms.

(2) What major interests and policy tendencies have supported an expansion of alternative work schedules? By comparing the issues and concerns to which alternative work schedules have been linked by policy advocates, we shall attempt to provide some insights on the scope of political conflict within which the issue has become defined in both nations.

(3) What political factors in the decision-making processes account for the specific programs enacted over recent years? The political decisions on alternative work schedules can be appreciated only in comparison to other major controversial issues and against the background of differing institutional frameworks. Despite the generally authoritarian and ideocratic nature of the Soviet policy-making process, our analysis will disclose that decisions in both the Soviet and American systems have been made pragmatically, following a somewhat similar open and pluralistic debate among government and academic specialists on the practical merits of the reforms and devoid of attempts to force changes through administrative fiat.

(4) What interests and policy tendencies have emerged in opposition to alternative work schedules? In both nations we shall find some striking similarities among resisters who consider workplace reforms a threat to their economic positions, although in the Soviet Union (unlike in the United States) the definition of the issue and the

8

nature of the reforms proposed have evoked widespread resistance from working women. With some nuances the nature of the interests opposing alternative work schedules in both nations has led to the symbolization of workplace reforms as forms of politically progressive change, and most supporters have come to be identified as egalitarian reformers even within the widely different ideological spectrums of both political systems.

In essence, the framework of analysis in our case study will examine the underlying factors which have conditioned the emergence of the policy issue, the cross-cutting issues and problems to which the workplace reforms have been closely linked in the public policy debate evolving in both nations, and the interests and tendencies advocating and opposing expansion of the workplace reforms in both nations. While similar conditions may have prompted similar workplace reforms, the question remains whether the surface appearance of policy convergence between the two nations is borne out by a qualitative analysis of alternative work schedules as a substantive policy response in both nations. There is no more important theoretical concern in comparative public policy than the relative impact of socioeconomic conditions or political factors on national policy responses. Thus we shall attempt to determine whether political differences between the Soviet Union and the United States are significant in distinguishing the manner in which the two systems have advanced similar workplace reforms in response to similar socioeconomic conditions.

Chapter 2

ALTERNATIVE WORK SCHEDULES IN THE SOVIET UNION

POLICY CONTEXT

In the Soviet Union the most visible commitment to alternative work schedules has long focused on the alleged advantages of permanent part-time employment for women, by which full-time workers would be granted the option of working fewer hours daily or weekly than the prescribed full-time Soviet norm of a forty-one-hour week extended over five or six days. Four-hour daily shifts for full-time workers were first instituted on a trial basis during the early 1960s among some female sewing machine operators in selected textile factories of Moscow, Kishinev (Moldavia), and Tallinn (Estonia). The experiment appeared to be prompted by Soviet economic planners still unquestionably committed during the Khrushchev regime (1957-64) to a national investment strategy centered on extensive capital expenditures, with the related need to mobilize all potential labor reserves from the adult population into the labor force. In the 1970s most party-government leaders were to denounce this investment strategy as economically wasteful both of capital and labor, but in the context and perspective of planning during the 1960s reduced work shifts allegedly proved successful. Job opportunities were provided for unemployed women and for those who, with young infants or sick children at home, would have been compelled to drop out entirely from the labor force. The reduced work shifts not only alleviated chronic labor shortages in these urban locales, but they also raised labor productivity among women formerly employed full-time on regular shifts. For one thing, the part-time employees were reported to be less tired when they arrived to work. For another, labor productivity normally declined for one worker operating a machine over an eight-hour period; thus two part-time operators of the same

10

machine had a higher rate of productivity and total output than one full-time employee.[1]

A reform on part-time employment was endorsed in 1969 in a memorandum of the Russian Republic State Committee on Labor Resource Utilization as a valid means to induce full-time homemakers with young infants to reenter the labor force and to reduce labor shortages in the republic,[2] but it remained in the experimental stage until January 1971, when new national labor legislation went into effect throughout the USSR. Article 26 of the new national labor code (paralleled by identical articles in the codes adopted at the same time by the Union republics) included reduced work shifts as a legal "right" guaranteed to all Soviet workers. Subsequent interpretations of the article qualified that "right" to more of a "privilege" for women, pensioners, and invalids, whose unique employment problems or outside burdens merited adjustment of their work schedules.[3] Nevertheless, state ministries were instructed to devolve discretionary authority to managers in industrial enterprises, retail outlets, and public facilities, who (with the approval of ministerial officials, local trade union committees, and the employees concerned) could institute reduced work shifts on a weekly or daily basis for the employees requesting them.

Regulations adopted after the new labor legislation stressed that part-timers would not be treated as second-class employees by either managers or local trade-union committees. They would be guaranteed the same pro rata hourly wages for their skill-wage category (*razriad*) or the same piece-rate salary they would have earned if employed full-time, and they would retain the same length of service (*stazh*) privileges accorded full-time employees in the work collectives. For cumulative length of service in the collectives, part-time work would be considered equivalent (not just on a pro rata basis) to full-time work in determining eligibility for pensions, vacations, maternity leaves, or priority positions on waiting lists for apartments, resorts, and automobiles—all of which were under the aegis of local management and trade-union officials.[4]

In addition to wage and service guarantees, the emphasis has always been on the completely voluntary nature of part-time employment—i.e., employees had the right to return to full-time work once part-time employment was no longer beneficial to them. Thus by 1977 over a third of all part-time employees in Estonia—the national

11

innovator for the reform since the early 1960s—alternated their daily work shifts between four and eight hours or worked several eight-hour shifts consecutively, followed by an additional number of off-days to accumulate a total bank of hours below the forty-one-hour norm for full-time employees, and the overwhelming majority of part-time employees remained in reduced work shifts only between one month and a few years before transferring back to full-time shifts.[5]

While part-time work has been primarily endorsed for its benefits to women with young infants, advocates have emphasized its applicability to other groups as well: students in universities and technical institutes, who could supplement their incomes while gaining invaluable practical experience related to their studies; invalids, who might otherwise have to withdraw from the workforce because of a physical incapacity to work full-time; and—most important—pensioners, who, by transferring gradually to reduced work shifts in the years immediately preceding and subsequent to their retirement, could transmit their expertise and enthusiasm to younger employees, supplement their pensions, ease their emotional adjustment into full retirement, and exercise their physical and mental faculties and extend their life expectancy by remaining active in work collectives.[6] With these advantages in mind, recent Soviet pension reforms have allowed those past retirement in certain occupational groups to work and retain up to 100 percent of their pensions, and there are plans to extend these reforms to include collective farmers past retirement age by the twelfth five-year plan of 1986-90.[7] Attracting and retaining pensioners on a part-time basis has become a top priority. In the service sector—in which approximately one fourth of the Soviet labor force is employed—economic investment has been increasing in the 1970s, and a need for more employees has become critical, particularly in large cities like Moscow and Leningrad, where help-wanted notices are posted in service establishments everywhere.* The youngest and most educated workers continue to desert the collective farms; thus an extension of work benefits to retired collective farmers is necessary to shore up a very inefficient agricultural economy which

---

*As implied by several Soviet economists, major contributing factors to long-term increases in investment for the service sector and the related need for additional pensioners to supplement expanded employment in this sector are the aging of the population in the Western European republics and declining labor productivity. With an older population past retirement more dependent than a

is eight times more labor-intensive than its American counterpart and unable to satisfy growing consumer demands for meat products.

Part-time employment in addition has been closely linked with other reforms in work scheduling presently being introduced in preliminary stages. Experiments in flexitime and compressed work schedules have been initiated in selected industrial enterprises, and their results have been reported and debated in the media. Mothers of young children, who have difficulty arriving at work when daycare facilities open after their work shifts have begun, have been allowed to adopt a flexitime alternative in which they begin and end their shifts outside of the normal scheduled times.[8] In some instances women have been allowed to bank extra work-hours on certain days or weeks to make up for off-days used to care for ailing children over a prolonged period not covered by sick leave.[9] Particular attention has been given to the so-called practice of "homework" (*nadomnichestvo*), by which industrial enterprises contract out piece-work to women and pensioners to complete at home and return to the enterprises in almost a throwback to a cottage-industry work format.[10] Indeed by the time the Twenty-Sixth Party Congress convened in Moscow in early 1981, part-time employment had become formally linked with the flexitime and homework options as interrelated reforms for working women. In a final draft of the "Basic Guidelines" adopted at the end of the Party Congress, a program was endorsed to expand short-day or short-week work options for women in which they could be employed "on a flexible schedule as well as working at home";[11] furthermore, in a joint resolution of the CPSU Central Committee and the USSR Council of Ministers, passed a few weeks after the Party Congress, Union republic Councils of Ministers and relevant national ministries and departments were instructed to work out and implement wide-ranging measures to employ more women on part-time schedules in flexitime or homework options.[12] (Proceedings of the congress are discussed on pp. 52-53 below.)

younger population on services, from medical care to government-administered benefits, the proportion of Soviet workers servicing these needs must increase. With declining productivity attributed in part to the lack of consumer services and relatedly low material incentive of Soviet workers to work hard, it is argued that increased investment and personnel in service outlets are necessary to re-stimulate worker enthusiasm.

A number of Soviet sociologists and economists have endorsed part-time shifts to humanize the work environment for women and reduce the unfairness and strain of their dual burden of salaried jobs and housework. (The latter is still nonchalantly unloaded almost entirely on women by the typically unliberated Soviet husbands.) In addition, they have advocated comparable reforms—e.g., a significant reduction of women in night shifts and in difficult and hazardous occupations,[13] and a reduction of output norms for women relative to men with the retention of the same salaries and privileges as compensation for women's housework and childcare burdens.[14] On one hand, part-time employment has generally been equated with the granting of partially paid maternity leaves of up to one year (a policy formally adopted in 1976 and supposedly implemented during the 1976-80 plan period) and leaves without pay of up to three years, with the inclusion of leave times in cumulative length-of-service records. On the other hand, some academicians have argued that part-time shifts would be preferable to lengthy maternity leaves for highly skilled women, whose extended absence from work would cause them irreversible losses in skills and advancement opportunities.[15]

Some Soviet proponents of reduced work shifts have viewed them as a solution to underemployment and low vocational mobility among women in the industrial labor force—i.e., women could take advantage of their free time to upgrade their vocational skills and potential for career advancement. For example, M. Ia. Sonin, a prominent labor economist and demographer in the Academy of Sciences Institute of Economics, has championed part-time employment for women over the last two decades. In articles which have thrown light on the inequities still suffered by working women, Sonin has urged that concurrent with reduced work shifts, women be guaranteed "reserved quotas" (*broni*) in vocational-technical institutes and be paid their normal salaries while enrolled there full-time. From a perspective of macroeconomic efficiency, Sonin has advocated that women who have been retrained be placed in sectors where their per capita productivity would far exceed the dismally low levels characteristic of many female-dominant and labor-inefficient sectors. Sonin has contended that these measures must be undertaken to correct the present situation in which only one third of Soviet institute graduates are women, the female graduates are overconcentrated in female trades, and women sorely lag behind men in skills, wages, and productivity.[16]

14

Others have gone beyond Sonin's concerns with inequities in the home and the workplace to link the issue of part-time employment with a comprehensive package of reforms aimed at stemming a breakdown in Soviet family life. Significant declines in family size — especially among Slavic and Baltic ethnic groups — have been partly related to the high percentage of women employed full-time. With reduced work shifts or homework (promoted as a means of encouraging women to have more children and reorient their lifestyles more to their homes),[17] women would have an incentive to have more than one or two children and could devote both more and better time in raising them,[18] while they would remain in the labor force and retain their skills and sociopolitical involvement in their work collectives until they could return to full-time employment. (Pronatalist views are discussed in detail below, pp. 22-25.)

From an experimental reform premised on expanding the labor force in the early 1960s to inclusion in the 1971 national labor law, reduced work shifts received a further boost in the mid-1970s, when the Soviet leadership at the Twenty-Fifth Party Congress endorsed an extension of part-time employment as a primary goal of the tenth five-year plan to "improve the conditions of labor and everyday life for working women."[19] Following the formal party endorsement, reduced work shifts for women became a universal civil right and a subject of debate for inclusion in a new constitution drafted in 1977. By the end of the debate, women with young infants were formally guaranteed the right of a "gradual reduction of working time" in an amendment to Article 35 of the ratified constitution (specifying the supposedly equal rights of women and men in the USSR).[20] By April 1978 at a prestigious national round-table conference of a thousand scientists and government and party leaders on raising labor-force effectiveness, the participants unanimously concurred that expanded part-time employment would be a positive step to correct a number of interrelated labor deficiencies in the Soviet economy.[21]

Despite the attempts of the 1970s to endorse part-time work as an unquestionable benefit for working women and other designated groups, it has never generated much enthusiasm or support within the Soviet labor force — especially among women who are employed full-time. By 1974 only 2-2.5 percent of all workers had transferred to part-time work in the Russian republic, which had endorsed it since 1969.[22] In Estonia only 1.4 percent of the labor force was on part-time shifts by 1976.[23] Throughout the USSR by 1978 less than one half of one percent of all workers were employed part-time, and only one half of these were women.[24] Furthermore, by 1978, 80 percent of Estonian pensioners who chose to work after retirement were working full- rather than part-time shifts—apparently because of economic necessity: there had been no pension reforms since 1956, and old-age pensions had fallen to less than half of average salaried earnings.[25] (Alastair McAuley, a prominent Western student of Soviet welfare policy, estimates that perhaps as many as one fourth of all Soviet citizens past retirement do not qualify for old-age pensions and are therefore solely dependent on their earnings or help from relatives.)[26]

It is important to note that surveys conducted in various republics in the 1970s after the passage of Article 26 revealed that 80-94 percent of women employed full-time would have strongly opposed a transfer to reduced work shifts.[27] Later surveys—among workers in selected industrial enterprises of the Moldavian republic in 1974 and in 120 light-consumer industrial enterprises nationwide in 1977—have shown much more enthusiasm among women, with up to three fourths of those polled in the 1977 survey expressing a willingness to go on some limited form of part-time.[28] However, in both surveys, most of those willing to transfer to part-time were willing to accept a maximum reduction of only one or two hours a day.[29] Furthermore, among the women willing to transfer, part-time was more a necessity than a freely chosen option—e.g., there were not adequate daycare facilities in which they could confidently place preschool infants, or they did not have older children and relatives who could babysit.[30] Many of these women are low-skilled and low-salaried—i.e., they can justify saving the expense of childcare (averaging probably a minimum of 100 rubles per year even when state subsidies pick up 80 percent of the costs) and consumer outlays for prepared foods and washing by taking care of their children and households by themselves, while retaining at least part of their monthly salary for the family income.[31] At the opposite end of the income spectrum, the small number of women in high-income families with few if any children indicate that they would enthusiastically welcome part-time work, and they could justify a loss of income in terms of the additional free time they would have.[32]

In the republics surveyed the workers most resistant to part-time employment have been a vast majority of professional and skilled women and mothers in single-parent families in which they are the sole breadwinners. Professional and skilled women perceive severe career liabilities in part-time work. Furthermore, advocates of the reform have conceded that under current Soviet production constraints reduced work shifts could be provided only to women in less skilled factory or consumer outlet jobs whose absence would not disrupt the production cycle and for whom foremen or odd-job "reserve workers" could subsitute when necessary.[33] Excluded would be professional-technical and managerial personnel, whose work days and expected job performance are not tied to prescribed hours or piecerate output quotas.

A fear among many professional and skilled women—which may be well founded—is that reduced work shifts would establish an unwelcome precedent. If part-time work were extended to them (and recent articles in the Soviet press on the supposed advantages of part-time employment for female research scientists imply an intent to include professional women under the reform), their salaries would be reduced, but they would still be expected to put in the same long hours or maintain the same performance levels as before.[34] In industrial enterprises skilled women forced to work part-time could be at a severe career disadvantage relative to men unless there were an overhaul of the criteria used to determine length-of-service records, on-the-job training, salaries, and promotions. In the articles which have noted an association between unskilled jobs and part-time shifts, the impression has been left that professional and skilled women would be required to sacrifice their higher status careers and assume unskilled jobs in order to qualify for part-time shifts. Thus concern with the effects of part-time shifts on the overall job status of Soviet women has evoked charges that the reform is patently discriminatory against women.[35]

A reduction in salaries would cause particular hardships for single mothers and mothers in two-spouse families living at the poverty line—women who constitute a growing segment of Soviet families. Since the liberalization of divorce laws in the Soviet Union in 1967, the number of single-parent families headed by working women has dramatically increased to an estimated one seventh of Soviet families—a phenomenon approximating that in the United States.[36] Many single Soviet mothers suffer from poverty, as do many single mothers in the United States, where 36 percent of families headed by women have a family income below the official poverty line defined by the U.S. Department of Labor.[37] In the Soviet Union child-support and alimony laws are inadequately enforced, and special income maintenance programs for the children of single mothers have never provided more than a marginal percentage of family needs, which must be supplemented by the full-time employment of the mothers.[38] In 1974 a child-support subsidy for "underprovided" (*maloobespechennyi*) Soviet families was adopted, implicitly recognizing the extent of poverty in the country; it guaranteed a cash transfer of twelve rubles per month for each child up to the age of eight years in families whose per capita income fell below fifty rubles per month.* However, the age limitation and low per capita ceiling excluded many millions; to some extent it seems that the subsidy was prompted as a pronatalist reform to encourage low-income women to have more children.[39]

Even the cash transfers provided by the 1974 reform have not always been readily forthcoming. Reports have appeared in the press of foot-dragging by local officials, and their foot-dragging may have been prompted by signs of behind-the-scenes opposition to the reform among some key party and government decision-makers who are alarmed that such "give-aways" are likely to contribute to the undisciplined and nonchalant attitude of many Soviet workers toward their jobs.[40] Those attached to government institutes have been equally concerned by the anti-feminist bias implicit in the reform. Indicative of the controversy surrounding the reform, two prominent sociologists, V.P. Piskunov and V.S. Steshenko, have criticized the 1974 reform and other such subsidies for undermining the workforce commitment and social equality of women in the USSR and for encouraging a welfare mentality among Soviet workers contrary to the work ethic and the material incentives of paid employment basic to Soviet socialism. Their criticism apparently had sufficient political backing to require repeated rebuttal by highly placed Soviet academicians in the Academy of Sciences four years after the passage of the 1974 subsidy and four years after Piskunov and Steshenko first raised their objections.[41]

---

*Two-spouse families could qualify for this subsidy — unlike the Aid to Families with Dependent Children program in the United States, which is available only to single-spouse families with underaged children.

The controversy over the 1974 reform was not surprising. As McAuley contends, the prevailing policy bias in Soviet welfare programs over many decades has been to grant cash transfers only to those who meet certain minimum criteria of continuous employment and income earnings. Intended to reinforce the work ethic and therefore more workfare than true welfare, cash transfers are designed only to supplement earnings for those experiencing extraordinary hardships which pull their incomes below a minimum standard. With the exception of the 1974 child-support subsidy and other minimal family income supplements, entitlement to cash transfers in the Soviet Union has been based not on need or the promotion of egalitarianism, but on the provision of a minimal equality of opportunity.[42]

Given the uncertain political climate in the Soviet Union since 1974 and the policy of prorating cash transfers in part to income earnings, single working mothers have been extremely reluctant to rely on the state to make up the income they would lose if employed part-time. The 1974 Moldavian survey disclosed that at most 20 percent of single working mothers would be willing to accept part-time employment—and only then because they had adult working children at home who could supplement the family income. Without such children, the mothers willing to accept part-time employment dropped to 5 percent.[43]

Some opponents of part-time employment have been troubled by the inequities and double standard which the reform would legitimate. Despite passing allusions by proponents that reduced work shifts would apply equally to men (who would therefore presumably assume household and childcare responsibilities) and assertions that the reform represents only the first stage in reducing hours for all Soviet workers in the 1980s,[44] the reform has clearly been designed for women.* In an experiment in Taganrog (in the Rostov province of the Russian republic) during the early 1970s, only working mothers

*Kuleshova begins her article by referring to part-time shifts as appropriate "for women, who combine work in production with housekeeping and raising children, and for men" (p. 54). This is the only reference to men in the entire article, which elaborates at great length on the advantages of the reform for working mothers. Similarly, in her study, Shishkan at one point surveyed both male and female workers in Moldavian enterprises to assess their interest in part-time shifts, but she cites findings only for male students concerned with shifts which would allow them to continue their studies, not husbands concerned with equalizing responsibility for childcare and housekeeping (p. 176).

19

were granted a paid hour off daily to measure the effect on workers' time budgets; results showed that husbands simply unloaded additional responsibilities for the home and children on their wives.[45] As disclosed in the Taganrog study and consistently in surveys of women who have transferred to reduced work shifts since the 1971 reform, women have not utilized their off-time for vocational retraining, cultural pursuits, or other forms of personal enhancement, but for cleaning house and caring for their children.[46] Under the circumstances, altering work shifts only for women would further legitimate the already inequitable division of labor in housework and childcare. In addition, part-time shifts could enhance what a prominent Western analyst of Soviet women has termed an underlying view among some Soviet decision-makers—i.e., women should fit into a rigidly traditional female role in which motherhood and housework are the only prescribed sources of role identity and satisfaction.[47]*

Part-time work as advanced in the Soviet Union has a further discriminatory potential: it can create the impression that women's paid employment is a secondary and supplementary source of family income—i.e., that it is "pin money." One critic of reduced work shifts (in an as yet unpublished candidate dissertation) has countered the argument that more women could enter or remain active in the workforce with part-time shifts by noting that the positions offered to substantiate the argument have been those of salesclerks, cashiers, dishwashers, nannies, and mail carriers.[48] Soviet part-time work almost seems intended to result in the same temporary work phenomenon prevalent in many Western countries, where the occupational segregation of many women is compounded by their part-time employment in low-paying and unskilled sales and clerical jobs. For example, women in the United States hold 70 percent of all part-time jobs, and 30-40 percent of all working women are employed as temporaries in marginal clerical and sales jobs, underemployed relative to their education and potential, and without job security, pension benefits, or health insurance.[49] Although the Soviet state assures pension and health benefits to part-timers under the provisions of the 1971 reform, not only would a

---

*Kanaeva distinguishes three "models" or "orientations" (*napravleniia*) among Soviet family policy specialists, one of which includes those favoring part-time shifts for women. She criticizes their support on the grounds that it is "at the expense of women themselves and at the expense of infringing on their equal rights with men in public-sector production" (p. 153).

woman's contribution to total household income fall—and currently only 15 percent of Soviet working women earn as much as their husbands—but so would her status in the family and workplace.[50]

Proponents of part-time labor in the Soviet Union have done little to dispel the impression that it would replicate the temporary work phenomenon evident in the West. In studies comparing the status of Western and Soviet women and part-time female employment in both systems, they have resorted to a convoluted reasoning remarkable even by Soviet standards of ideological double-talk. On the one hand, part-time work is castigated as capitalist exploitation of women, while on the other, the Soviet part-time reform is praised as symbolic of the benign concern of the Soviet state for its working women—even though both Western and Soviet women have been similarly described as holding unskilled and low-paying part-time jobs.[51] So contrived have been the distinctions made by some Soviet journals between the Western and Soviet phenomena that their editorial position could be characterized as almost schizophrenic. In 1975—the International Year of Women—*Rabochii klass i sovremennyi mir* [The working class and the contemporary world], a bimonthly publication of the International Workers' Movement Institute in the Academy of Sciences (and reputedly a refuge of liberal sociologists purged from the Institute of Sociology during the 1970s), published articles uniformly supportive of part-time shifts as a progressive change for women in the USSR. At the same time, it published an article condemning reduced work shifts in capitalist countries as discriminatory against women and indicative of their lower status in the Western workforce.[52]

The article condemning Western reduced work shifts may have represented an Aesopean critique of the Soviet reform by academicians in the institute constrained by censors from openly attacking state policy. However, proponents of part-time shifts have also undermined their case by offering examples of "progressive" reforms in other Leninist regimes—e.g., they have frequently referred to East Germany, although (as they themselves concede with unintended irony) most female part-timers under the "progressive" East German reform work as cleaners and janitorial aides in factories and plants.[53] Such examples are unlikely to still what proponents contend are unfounded beliefs among some Soviet women that part-time shifts "represent some kind of discrimination against women."[54] In addition, opponents of part-time shifts have not been indifferent to the ranking of alleged advantages for Soviet women from the reform. Although proponents make pro-forma references to women remaining active in the workforce and developing their skills, the increased time available for housework and children has always headed the rank order of justifications for part-time shifts. No less alarming to opponents of the reform have been consistent findings of a high inverse correlation between the desire of Soviet women to select part-time shifts and the availability of adequate daycare and consumer services (see p. 16 above).[55] The far from subtle implication in such findings (and the openly advocated position of certain Soviet economists like Novitskii and Babkina) has been that the state could defer costly capital expenditures for daycare facilities (particularly nurseries) and consumer services by subsidizing women indirectly to bear the burdens.[56]

As we have noted, there is a strong pronatalist tenor among some supporters of part-time shifts, and it has been so apparent that the reform has often seemed to be advocated more for its consequences in raising birthrates than in resolving national labor problems. Prominent demographers like V.A. Perevedentsev and B.Ts. Urlanis have persistently urged that the highest priority of Soviet economic policy should be a higher birthrate, in order that a sufficient labor pool can be guaranteed for the last two decades of the twentieth century; in addition, they have linked declining birthrates to the predominance of women's work roles over their aspirations to bear more children. Relegated to marginal part-time jobs, women would have greater incentives to have more children—especially if the state extended maternity leaves and made it economically irrational for women to rely on underfunded daycare facilities and consumer services. Perevedentsev and Urlanis have distinguished between part-time shifts and maternity leaves and painstakingly denied wanting to reduce female employment merely for the sake of increasing birthrates; nonetheless, as a result of such linkages, some proponents have associated both part-time shifts and extended maternity leaves as alternative pronatalist rather than work reform policies.[57]

POLICY TENDENCIES AND ALL-UNION POLICY

The association of part-time shifts with a pronatalist orientation has complicated the debate over work reforms. To an extent, the issue mirrors the broader policy divisions or different policy tendencies pertaining to central, long-term economic issues among Soviet policy advisers as those divisions or tendencies have polarized into distinct positions in recent years. Thus among those who have at least tentatively questioned the desirability of part-time shifts for women have been prominent policy advisers in the community of governmental-academic institutes directly concerned with labor policy, like L.E. Darskii (Section Chief of the Population Reproduction Laboratory of the Central Statistical Administration) and T.V. Riabushkin (Director of the Academy of Sciences Institute of Sociological Research). They and other like-minded advisers in posts of economic and sociological institutes (V.T. Boldyrev, A.A. Tkachenko, T.N. Medvedeva, G.I. Litvinova, A. Ia. Kvasha, and A.G. Vishnevskii) have objected not so much to part-time shifts per se but to what they consider overly simplified assumptions about population shortages and inevitable declines in economic growth rates for which part-time shifts and extended maternity leaves have been offered as solutions. In particular, such reforms have been advocated by those like Perevedentsev and Urlanis, with their doomsday projections that the current low fertility rates of Slavic and Baltic women will create grave labor shortages for the next two decades and limit labor productivity, national income, and economic expansion.

While the group of advisers identified with the position of Darskii and Riabushkin concede that only a few hundred thousand new workers may be entering the labor force by the mid-1980s, they counter that real future economic growth cannot be projected solely on the size of the labor pool, but that "qualitative" dimensions of future labor reserves must be considered as well. Basic to their meaning of "qualitative" is an optimum reproductive rate—a less rapidly growing population, but one with a higher proportion of skilled and educated workers, whose per capita labor productivity will not only be higher, but will also be accelerated by scientific-technological advances and labor-saving automation in the workplace. They contend that alarmist predictions about grave population shortfalls and economic stagnation derive from economically erroneous and irrational extrapolations from present manpower requirements. For Darskii and the others, these present requirements have locked the Soviet economy into a false dependency on a surplus of unskilled and underutilized workers, which in turn has dragged down potential labor productivity,

23

thwarted the introduction of new technology and automation, and discouraged rational innovations and labor efficiency at the enterprise level.[58]

Some of these policy advisers (particularly Riabushkin, Tkachenko, Kvasha, and Litvinova) depart in principle from pronatalists on the highly controversial and sensitive issue of differential demographic policy among ethnic groups in the Soviet Union. They contend that demographic policy should differentiate in its goals according to the socioeconomic and reproductive requirements of these groups— for example, Central Asian women in rural areas should be encouraged to reduce their large average family sizes through regional modernization and a related increase in their education and workforce participation, while Slavic and Baltic women should be encouraged to increase their average family sizes to achieve a Union-wide optimum replacement level of two to three children per family. They have defended this differential demographic policy with supporting claims that the health, life expectancy, and actual years of work in the public sector, Russian language competency, and vocational skills of Central Asian rural populations (upon reaching workforce entry ages) lag "qualitatively" behind those of non-Asian populations. In essence, the economy suffers not just from a gross population shortage and labor deficit, but from the related capabilities and cumulative labor contribution in life-years of ethnic groups (such as the large number of Central Asians still living in rural locales) who may have maintained very high birthrates but have undersupplied skilled and educated new generations for the labor pool. They claim that the proportion of skilled and educated workers within a population and their cumulative labor contribution in life-years are more accurate measures of the "active" real labor reserve which can be employed for meaningful economic growth than are absolute size or reproductive rates.[59]

Given the potentially explosive nature of ethnic relations between Asians and non-Asians, other advisers reject the differential demographic policy even though they and the policy's supporters share similar views on the surplus of unskilled workers inefficiently utilized in the labor force. Some (like Manevich), uncomfortable with the racially discriminatory overtones of a policy geared toward a reduction of birthrates among rural Asians and an increase among Slavs, have proposed a more feasible and ideologically defensible policy: workers in rural regions with underemployed labor surpluses, such as Central Asia, should be encouraged to migrate to regions (European and Siberian) which are labor-deficient.[60] Supporters of a differential demographic policy (including the pronatalist Urlanis) have tried to strike a middle ground by calling for a complex and broad approach to demographic policy in which demographers, sociologists, economists, jurists, psychologists, and medical researchers could contribute their particular insights and balance their own policy concerns within a realistic framework of dealing with the general population problem. Such a scientific approach could generate feasible and rational reforms to stimulate birthrates, whereas scientifically unfounded reforms could not only fail to accomplish even the one-sided goal of a larger population, but could also cause unforeseen and irreparable socioeconomic damage—a decrease in the proportion of skilled and educated labor reserves in the population; a limit to the per capita increases in national income, which would have to be redistributed among a larger total population; a reduction in the quantitative and qualitative employment of Slavic and Baltic women; and an excess of unskilled, immobile, and less employable Asians. Critics of the one-dimensional goal of a larger population have urged that the broader definition and goals of demographic policy include an enhancement of qualitative dimensions of the workforce and an improved quality of life for Soviet citizens, and that such measures as extended maternity leaves or part-time shifts for women be considered in terms of these goals under the broadened meaning of a Union-wide demographic policy.*

Although these advisers are opposed to the underlying assumptions of pronatalists, some of them have supported part-time shifts for women. But their support stems from quite different immediate concerns and premises about what part-time shifts should accomplish. Ineffective labor-force utilization has been their most prevalent concern, and they have persistently criticized the unnecessarily large surplus of unskilled workers underemployed at the enterprise level which has resulted in declining rates of labor productivity over recent years. This surplus has stymied efforts since 1965 to rationalize

---

*Kvasha, for one, argues that the Soviet government in its approach to problems of population should make policy decisions based on what he labels in Russian as "KDPRN"—a "Complex Long-Term Program of Developing the Population"—consciously derived from overall comprehensive socioeconomic development of the USSR for the rest of the century (pp. 191-99).

economic growth through increased technology and automation in the industrial sector. Thus these advisers have generally endorsed part-time shifts as a positive step to correct labor inefficiencies at the enterprise level. Explicitly, they have been optimistic that part-time shifts would alleviate the work and home responsibilities of many women, give them an opportunity to have additional children, and provide them the time and incentives to upgrade their skills in vocational-technical institutes and better realize their true productive potentials.[61] Implicitly, they cannot but have noticed that part-time shifts would effectively achieve the same or higher production outputs through a reduction of the surplus unskilled workforce— equivalent to the fewer number of hours worked every week by the total number of women transferred to part-time shifts.

Among those who have apparently been persuaded that part-time shifts are a spur to labor efficiency are officials in GOSPLAN, the state economic planning committee. At least one could make that preliminary judgment based on a 1978 article in *Planovoe khoziaistvo* [Planned economy], the monthly journal of GOSPLAN and a mirror of political leanings among central planners. In the article detailed statistical analysis and economic rationale were presented to prove that great workforce efficiencies resulted from part-time shifts: an increasing number of "real" workdays completed by part-timers, more motivation and commitment on the job, and lowered rates of absenteeism and tardiness compared to full-time workers.[62] Other articles in the journal over recent years had consistently underscored the constraints that a surplus of unskilled women in the labor force had placed on effective economic growth.[63]

The emphasis on the labor efficiencies of part-time shifts leaves the distinct impression that for central planners and economists the reform is primarily a calculated means to speed up production, extract higher outputs from workers, and discipline all workers expected to match the higher hourly production levels of part-timers— an interpretation which would be vigorously denied officially. In essence, part-time shifts directed solely to women would serve to accomplish these ends while maintaining the ideologically unassailable commitment to de facto full employment for all Soviet citizens under Marxism-Leninism. Women are a segment of the labor force least likely to resist a change that in truth would increase their real unemployment rate, speed up their workplace, raise their output

26

norms, and reduce their take-home wages. Yet supported by the appropriate arguments, an otherwise controversial policy to cut back the labor force can be promoted by central planners and economists as a progressive step to "liberate" Soviet women from the inordinate physical-emotional strains of full-time employment.

Related reform proposals closely identified with some advocates of part-time shifts reenforce suspicions that they have ulterior motives in sponsoring reforms ostensibly advantageous to working women. For example, some (like Kotliar and Turchaninova) have persistently urged limits to the number of women employed in night shifts. Despite vague promises of limitation in the past, women in some republic and Union-wide industries make up over half of those working night shifts, and their physical and emotional stress has become of increasing concern among Soviet economists and sociologists.[64] On the surface the reform appears quite progressive in that it places priority on the needs of workers over the needs of production. Yet the elimination of women from night shifts has become a major labor priority during recent years at the same time wage supplements for night-shift workers in several Soviet industries have been substantially raised. The contradiction has not gone unnoticed by some analysts, who have urged a compromise reform in which women would not be discriminated against financially for accepting this alleged privilege of reduced night shifts.[65]

A second reform proposal urges that women be removed from so-called "difficult" and "hazardous" occupations. However laudatory such a reform would be for the health of working women, there has been no attempt to revise the criteria by which base salary rates are formulated Union-wide—and, as in most industrialized countries, much higher salaries and pension benefits go to employees in the very same difficult and hazardous occupations. Some analysts have noted that Soviet women have generally resisted the attempts to "improve" their work conditions which would involve reassigning them to lower paying jobs.[66] Others have proposed a fundamental reevaluation of wage criteria in industry. While ostensibly sex-neutral, the criteria have penalized women by undervaluing such factors as the complexity and emotional strain associated with certain occupations and overvaluing such male-biased factors as physical endurance. In essence, women have received equal pay for equal work in Soviet industry, but they have yet to receive "just" pay for the quality and contribution of their work to the overall economy.[67]*

Nor does the removal of only women from difficult and hazardous occupations—particularly those which expose them to toxic substances, intense machine vibrations, and carcinogens—address the more basic problems of obsolete and dangerous plant facilities and processes in many Soviet enterprises. Many workers are needlessly exposed to these health hazards because plant renovation has a low priority and there is little economic payoff for managers to reinvest in old plant equipment.[68] Soviet analysts have been increasingly alarmed by poor safety and health conditions in industry. Demographers and medical researchers have been disturbed by the deleterious effects of poor work environments on the childbearing potential of working women,[69] and labor economists have noted both that the equivalent of millions of workdays annually is lost as a result of health-related absenteeism and that worker productivity is reduced by physical-emotional illnesses contracted in poor work environments.[70] However, in this area too their consideration seems dictated by ulterior concerns about inefficient labor resource utilization and future labor pool shortages.

Currently several research institutes in the USSR are studying the effects of the work environment on women's health and safety, but historically low priority has been assigned to the health and safety of workers relative to the meeting of production quotas. Given the inadequacy of research and the absence of scientifically based health norms for the workplace, existing legislation intended to protect the health and safety of women has been enforced in a senseless fashion. For example, the law requires pregnant women to be transferred to work environments or other jobs considered healthy for the unborn children; however, at times they have been transferred to settings exposing them to chemicals whose effects had not been tested and which could prove dangerous to them and their fetuses.[71] Thus inadequate medical research may be a contributing factor to the rising infant mortality rate in the Soviet Union over recent

*"Just pay" (rather than the traditional Soviet term "equal pay") suggests a similarity to "comparable pay," a term used by Western feminists (particularly in the United States), who have argued that salaries in occupations dominated by women need to be increased in order to provide comparable pay for work of comparable value to work done by men in traditionally male occupations.

years.[72] At a minimum, a Union-wide campaign to reassign women to occupations defined as healthy more by administrative fiat than by substantive research has had dubious success.*

In addition to their careless enforcement, labor protection laws for women in the USSR have often been violated, unenforced, under-funded, worded vaguely (giving broad exclusionary discretion to managers), and generally sacrificed to economic expediency by managers in concert with male secretaries, trade union officials, and labor safety inspectors.[73] Some female Soviet academicians particularly concerned with the problems of working women recently concluded that protective labor laws for women have long remained unenforced at the enterprise level, and that managers have been more willing to pay the fines (which are minimal) if caught breaking the law or pay women wage supplements to work under unsafe or hazardous conditions than disrupt the production process and provide special dispensations for them.[74] Furthermore, if the laws were implemented conscientiously, the researchers warned that it could reinforce occupational segregation and exclude women from better paying jobs.[75] The warning came in April 1978—just as the USSR State Committee on Labor and the Central Council of Trade Unions passed a newly amended list of occupations prohibited to women for reasons of health and safety. Perhaps anticipating widespread resistance by women, who were relegated by the new list to lower paying jobs, the State Committee on Labor and Social Questions rushed to minimize the negative impression of the reform: it emphasized that severance pay would be provided for women in occupations

---

*Advanced research in the West has revealed that the exposure of men to certain toxic substances has as harmful an effect on their reproductive organs as it does on the ability of women to bear healthy children. For a summary of findings, see Jane E. Brody, "Sperm Found Especially Vulnerable to Environment—Miscarriages, Defects, Infertility Linked to Damage by Toxins," *New York Times*, 10 March 1981, pp. 15 and 17. In the United States, findings by the Occupational Safety and Health Administration of the Department of Labor were compiled in "Interpretative Guidelines on Employment Discrimination and Reproductive Hazards," *Federal Register* 45, 23 (1 Febuary 1980): 7514-17. The guidelines, which were adopted in February 1980 by the Equal Employment Opportunity Commission and the Labor Department's Office of Federal Contract Compliance Programs, proscribed arbitrary transfers of women to lower paying jobs because of their exposure to certain chemicals which were found equally harmful to male and female reproductive organs and fetuses.

now prohibited to them, and that retraining or reassignment would be offered to them, with up to six months' average salary from their previous jobs during their retraining or temporary layoffs.[76]

The issues of lower salaries and special safety and health provisions for women have raised questions which represent a subtle departure in Soviet policy discussions of the "woman question" and which have direct relevance to the debate over part-time shifts. Since the 1920s a one-sided "social feminist" logic has underscored all reforms for Soviet women. The underlying assumption has been that female and male roles are by nature asymmetrical and that the state's principal responsibility in advancing sexual equality is to rebalance that asymmetry by granting special privileges to women to compensate for their burdensome family duties. Explicit in the questions now raised by contemporary policy advisers is a challenge to this social feminist logic: whatever its good intentions, does the Soviet policy orientation toward women not actually debase them by channeling them into lower status jobs and thus contribute to their greater factual inequality both at home and at work? In Western countries like Sweden and the United States policy clashes even among otherwise like-minded passionate supporters of greater equality for women have historically reflected the differences between advocates and opponents of social feminism as a philosophical point of departure.[77] In the Soviet Union the emergence of a counterpoint to social feminist logic cannot be minimized, however subtle or limited to questions about current policies affecting women.

One consequence of the challenge to social feminist logic has been that some advocates of part-time shifts for women openly concede that Soviet women have justifiable grounds to suspect the intent and impact of the reform. Indeed many of them have contributed to a growing public awareness of and debate on the problems holding back the attainment of full equality for women in Soviet society.[78] Their studies have introduced a new policy orientation toward women's issues and have raised serious doubts whether isolated reforms like part-time shifts would improve the status of women or help the Soviet economy. A consensus has emerged in these studies that the problems and solutions should be approached from a rational and comprehensive perspective which would first carefully project the costs, benefits, and unintended possible consequences from various policy alternatives and would then evaluate them against explicit goals of status and role for women in future Soviet society.

The most explicit endorsement of the rational-comprehensive approach has surfaced among some Soviet academicians in various research institutes and government officials whose overlapping functional areas of specialization have commonly and prominently identified them as the policy specialists for women's issues on the national decision-making level. During the April 1978 round-table colloquium (mentioned above),* they proposed the establishment of a national scientific center to coordinate cross-disciplinary research for policy recommendations affecting working women and the incorporation in all five-year and long-range economic plans of programmatic measures (with funding implied for them) to improve their socioeconomic condition. As an example of what such an explicit programmatic approach could avoid, they specifically criticized reduced work shifts, which had not increased free time for working women but had instead increased the time they spent on housework.[79]

Not only would proposals for a rational-comprehensive approach halt the rush to implement isolated reforms based on an unquestioned social feminist logic, but they would also tie in with the policy proposals of the economists, sociologists, and demographers who (as we observed) have argued for a more rational and broadened perspective of population problems which would consider goals and consequences beyond the absolute growth of Soviet society. Evidence that the position of the policy specialists for women's issues is beginning to appeal to the mainstream of reform-minded Soviet economists, sociologists, and demographers can be seen in *EKO*. Following the round-table colloquium, over half the pages of the journal were devoted to articles analyzing various unresolved problems and inefficiencies in utilizing female labor to its optimal potentials in the Soviet economy.**

*The colloquium was cosponsored by the Scientific Research Department of the Central Trade Union Council and the journal *Ekonomika i organizatsiia promyshlennogo proizvodstva* [*EKO*— Economics and organization of industrial production].

**EKO* and its parent institute by the same title in the Novosibirsk Academy of Sciences have long been renowned as the cutting edge of reformist economic thinking in the nation. Publishing translated articles from Western business journals, *EKO* has consciously oriented itself to what may be an emerging

From the perspective of the policy specialists on women's issues in the round-table colloquium and perhaps some reform-minded economists like A. G. Aganbegian, a rational-comprehensive approach to the problems of Soviet working women must begin with an appreciation of the role they play in the economy. Over one half of the entire labor force and 49 percent of the industrial labor force is female; nine out of ten women between the ages of sixteen and fifty-five either work full-time most of their lives (averaging 37.4 years overall—only five years less than men, despite an earlier retirement age), or are enrolled in educational training programs which will qualify them eventually for full-time employment.[80] The one exception is in Central Asia, where policies to induce Asian women (particularly in rural areas) to leave their households and work in the public sector are resisted. An estimated 25 percent of Asian women nationwide still do not work in the public sector, and as few as 3 percent of women enrolled in vocational-technical institutes in some of the Asian republics are native.[81] However, from a Union-wide perspective, the pool of unemployed women available as additions to the labor force had been effectively exhausted by 1981. Given the heavy dependency of the Soviet economy on women, these policy specialists have contended that the problems of the

stratum of younger industrial managers and economists—less committed to rigidly centralized planning and the inefficiencies of the Soviet command economy, less tolerant of petty party interference in their decision-making prerogatives, and more inclined to consider Western-type reforms with greater entrepreneurial initiative in production and price-determination. (For a perspective on this new breed of managers by a former Soviet free-lance political writer and journalist, see Alexander Yanov, *Detente after Brezhnev: The Domestic Roots of Soviet Foreign Policy* [Berkeley: Institute of International Studies, 1977], pp. 22-42.) Since its founding in 1970, the journal has consistently served as a forum for the somewhat unorthodox views of its editor A. G. Aganbegian, one of the youngest persons to receive a doctorate in economics in the USSR and considered by Soviet and Western economists as a relatively free thinker and reformer in the context of Soviet economic circles. (Impressions conveyed to author by Western scholars somewhat privy to the opinions of Soviet economists and knowledgeable on the policy divisions within Soviet economic circles. Also see Richard W. Judy, "The Economists," in *Interest Groups in Soviet Politics*, ed. H. Gordon Skilling and Franklyn Griffiths [Princeton: Princeton University Press, 1971], pp. 214, female labor force can almost be equated with the major inefficiencies of the entire economy, and the underutilized potential of that labor force with the limitation of long-term growth prospects.

National aggregate figures on wages by sex and economic sector are either not compiled or not published in the Soviet Union (although some labor economists have urged that they be both compiled and published). Nonetheless, it is apparent that women in the public sector are concentrated in the most unskilled occupations, and even conservative estimates by Soviet economists indicate that the total percentage of women in unskilled labor Union-wide is 2.4 times higher than that of men, and that the total percentage of women in skilled labor is 1.8 times lower than that of men.[82] Publication of Union-wide wage averages by sex would probably only fuel political controversy and prove embarrassing to officials who insist that women under socialism have achieved an equality not achieved by their sisters under oppressive capitalism. The best information available

230, and 237-51, and Aron Katsenelinboigen, *Soviet Economic Thought and Political Power in the USSR* [New York: Pergamon Press, 1980], pp. 83-85 and 133-34.) Aganbegian is somewhat isolated in Novosibirsk, but allegedly he has political links to the major planning institutes and to establishment economists through his relationship to a former Politburo member, A. I. Mikoian, and through his collaboration on articles in *EKO* with economists and ministerial officials in Moscow. In recently stating the editorial position of the journal, Aganbegian may have echoed the leanings of some of these economists and officials. He appeared to stretch the limits of Soviet censorship by advocating a frank exchange on a wide range of economic problems and viewpoints: "I think that in the long-range future the discussion of economic problems on the pages of our publication will be more open, more involved, and mass-oriented, and that as a rule representatives of different points of view will participate whose position academic science will bring forth for the widest discussion by Soviet public opinion. We are attempting to realize all these principles in our journal today, relative to our abilities and objective possibilities" ("Stranichka redaktora—zhurnal stanovitsia yezhemesiachnikom," *EKO*, no. 5 [September-October 1978]: 208. "Discussions and analyses in 'round-table' forums of *EKO* usually demonstrate not only diverse points of view but show that not just one is obligatorily correct and all the others are mistaken. All depends on the criteria, on the goals. Demonstrating such an approach, we also hope to see it in the articles submitted to our editorial staff for publication" ("Stranichka redaktora—den' otkrytykh dverei . . . k 10-letiiu *EKO*," *ibid.*, no. 1 [January 1980]: 203). Thus it may have been far from accidental that Aganbegian's journal served as the outlet for the very frank and extensive analysis of problems confronting Soviet women in 1978.

on skill and wage disparities by sex, reconstructed by outsiders from isolated published Soviet studies of selected industrial enterprises or regions, reveals a consistent pattern of sexual discrimination closely resembling that in Western capitalism and points to wide disparities between Soviet women and men in skills, wages, and general career opportunities:

(1) Of the six skill-grade categories by which industrial occupations and basic wage rates are classified in the Soviet economy, women predominate in the lowest, averaging at least one skill grade less than men nationally.

(2) Women more often remain in the lower skill grades throughout their careers; they show much lower rates of upward mobility, even when they have the same formal vocational-technical training as men.

(3) The percentage of women enrolled in vocational-technical institutes is disproportionately low, and those enrolled tend to prepare for traditionally female trades and occupations.

(4) Women are overrepresented in industrial branches which have the lowest prestige in economic planning and pay the lowest salaries.

(5) Women earn 30 to 40 percent less than men; on the average, their take-home wages are probably two thirds of those of men among all white- and blue-collar employees and the so-called "intelligentsia"; at least part of that wage differential is attributable to outright discrimination.

(6) Despite education and training equivalent to men, women are grossly underrepresented among industrial managers, engineering-technical officials in industrial enterprises, shop and departmental foremen, collective and state farm heads, and farm brigade leaders because of discriminatory attitudes and practices.[83]

In all fairness—as Soviet analysts would hasten to point out (particularly those who have studied the role of women in the labor force)—some of these disparities reflect generational differences among Soviet women: those in the older age groups generally have less education and more traditional attitudes. Many of them had been homemakers who became unskilled manual workers in the public sector during the late 1950s, when minimum wages and pension benefits were raised for the least skilled workers and when then

Premier Nikita Khrushchev proposed to reduce the size of private farm plots and the personal household incomes of collective farmers. The vast majority of women over fifty have remained unskilled manual workers. Younger working women have wages, skills, and career mobility records more similar to men in their age cohorts. Nonetheless, disparities in skills and wages exist despite the fact that women equal or surpass men in the average number of completed years of formal education and constitute 59 percent of those employed in white-collar—or what Soviet statisticians classify as "mental"—occupations in the labor force.[84]

Thus generational differences are not a completely satisfactory explanation—as even some Soviet analysts would concede. For one thing, equity in wages and skills among younger male and female workers seems to disappear once the women marry and begin to raise children. A large percentage of highly educated married women in industrial enterprises hold lower skill-grade rankings and earn much less than men in these enterprises with less than a secondary school education, and married women will more frequently experience reduced career mobility as they take time to have children.[85] Furthermore, aggregate figures for educational attainment among white-collar workers can be highly misleading. Women entering the labor force who equal or surpass men in formal education have an initial advantage, but it often soon disappears. With or without additional domestic burdens, they typically fall behind men in their skill upgrading, formal vocational training, and career advancement because they must contend with stereotyped prejudices that male industrial managers hold about their low career potential.[86] A high proportion of women are employed in low-salaried and low-status positions (e.g., clericals, doctors, lawyers, and teachers) which for statistical purposes are classified as "mental"; such a classification overstates women's overall accomplishments in the workforce and understates the very high percentage in unskilled manual occupations in both industry and agriculture.[87]*

*In an historical and sociological analysis of social stratification, Walter D. Conner concludes that the hidden feminization of lower level white-collar positions probably explains the semblance of income equality between skilled blue-collar and white-collar workers in the countries studied—i.e., the low average wages of white-collar women pull down the average earnings of all white-collar workers, a broad category that ranges from clericals to elite professionals (see *Socialism, Politics, and Equality in Eastern Europe and the USSR* [New York: Columbia University Press, 1979], pp. 215-66).

In the industrial workforce women are somewhat better proportionally distributed in almost all branches than they have been in the past. Over the 1960s and 1970s in particular they have broken out of the traditionally female branches like textiles, clothing, and food processing into higher status and previously male-dominated branches like machine-building (metal-working), which now employs the largest absolute number of all women in industry. Nonetheless, women still predominate in the least mechanized and unskilled jobs on the assembly line and in auxiliary positions like loaders and freight operators. Thus in machine-building 65 percent of the women are unskilled workers, and over half of the female machine operators earn salaries at the lowest skill-grade category for machine operators.[88] Indeed new machine-building subdivisions like radio, electronics, and automobile assembly plants have attracted many women, and managers seem to prefer them, considering them more suited to the monotonous and intense pace of the assembly-line processes;[89] an estimated 80-90 percent of all mounters-assemblers on machine-building conveyor lines are women.[90] In construction, the absolute number of women increased one and one half times between 1959 and 1970; by 1975 there were approximately three million — 28 percent of all construction workers. However, 60 percent of women in earthwork construction are manual laborers (compared to 18 percent of the men), and only 12 percent of all construction foremen are women.[91] In agriculture, in a long-term and "progressive" trend (from the perspective of Soviet analysts) the proportion of women has steadily declined. They now constitute 55 percent of collective farm workers, but they hold fewer than one percent of the skilled positions (tractor drivers, combine operators), and in some republics they make up 90-98 percent of the manual laborers (e.g., field workers or livestock growers).[92]

These shortcomings and limitations of Soviet working women must be addressed in resolving the long-term barriers to economic growth. Among the policy specialists on women, economists especially (like Sonin) have urged a sober recognition of the fact that women's low skill levels put a drag on general economic growth. In Soviet economic parlance, women have reduced the "effective utilization" of real human capital and the so-called "qualitative" dimensions of labor input in the industrial production cycle. Some analysts have gone so far as to conclude that a major reason for declining productivity among construction and agricultural workers during the 1970s can be directly traced to a large influx of unskilled female workers.[93] Others have drawn a broader indictment, contending that women's lower skill levels and prevalence in the industrial labor force have kept down growth rates in labor productivity for the entire industrial sector and have been a major obstacle to the incorporation of sophisticated new technology on the assembly line and in auxiliary industrial operations (74 percent of which are still performed manually and mostly by women). This contention was apparently considered serious enough to require an open rebuttal, lest the wrong policy implications be derived from singling out women as barriers to scientific-technological progress.[94]

Soviet economists have calculated that industry lacks 60 percent of the skilled personnel needed to operate machinery currently installed, and that in 1978, 67 percent of newly commissioned plants in the Russian republic alone lacked the skilled personnel to make them fully operational.[95] Compounding the shortage of skilled personnel, new machinery has failed to produce even a marginal increase in output. There are frequent breakdowns, and the machinery is improperly operated and serviced by unskilled workers or by supposedly skilled workers in formal grade classifications who actually lack essential training. Given the increasing interdependency of production processes, automation, and advanced technology, and given the increased time lags between the installation of new machinery and the adequate training of personnel, such breakdowns have become more the rule than the exception in Soviet industry; they slow down the production cycle, cause a substantial underutilization of plant capacities, and reduce total production outlays for long periods of time.[96] While women are not the only ones who improperly operate machinery, undue emphasis on their lower skill levels may have made them easy scapegoats.

Debate over the comparable labor productivity of women and men in the Soviet workforce has become a legitimate outlet for disagreement among Soviet analysts during recent years and has led to conflicting findings and implications for policy. Some have concluded that women have lower rates of productivity and output than men in identical industrial settings because of lower skill levels, as well as the physical-emotional burdens of domestic responsibilities. Others have countered that differences between male and female workers are insignificant once labor productivity of workers is controlled for such intervening factors as the number of years of service in the same job, the age composition of the workforce, and the rate of real capital investment in industrial branches employing varying proportions of male and female workers.[97] Still others have determined that women are the most "stable," "disciplined," and "effective" segment of the workforce.

Supporting evidence for the positive attributes of working women in the USSR seems obvious to their defenders. Soviet women remain for longer periods in the same jobs and have up to a 50 percent lower turnover rate than men Union-wide.[98] They commit only about one twelfth of the labor violations committed by men and are much less likely to be dismissed for violating rules.[99] Despite their option to take sick-leave to care for ailing children, their annual rate of absenteeism averages one third that of men.[100] Women show up enthusiastically for the periodically convened national Saturday workdays (*subbotniki*) to volunteer their labor—even if they are on formal leaves of absence—while men typically remain home.[101] Eighty percent of women in textile factories may express serious dissatisfaction about having to work frequent night shifts (compared to a 20 percent rate of dissatisfaction among men), but all the women will show up for the shifts, while men will frequently be absent without cause.[102] Finally, fewer than one of eight women who voluntarily leave an industrial enterprise will cite inadequate wages as the reason, even though many women are concentrated in the lowest paid jobs.[103]

The attributes of "stable," "disciplined," and "effective" might indicate that women are compliant, acquiescent, trapped in their work situations, and more easily manipulated by plant management, but without national statistical breakdowns of worker productivity and output by sex, accurate conclusions are not possible. In any case, these attributes contrast with problems increasingly associated with young male workers (and to some extent conceded by Soviet analysts): absenteeism, frequent job turnover, apathy, alcoholism, theft and sabotage of equipment, and spontaneous challenges to institutional authority.[104] In this regard, the director of a flax combine with a predominantly female workforce may have been typical in stressing the advantages from a managerial perspective of working women. After noting that prestige is low for workers in a flax combine, the difficulties of modernizing equipment in the combine to reduce the arduous physical demands on workers, and the necessity for workers to put in several night shifts every month, the director nonetheless buoyantly concluded:

> I am often asked whether the leadership of a women's work collective doesn't present particular difficulties. I want to respond: on the contrary, work with a women's work collective brings me great satisfaction. In all probability, I would simply not have been able to have been supported for so long in a similar work collective made up of men.[105]

The implication from those who contend that women are more "stable" and "disciplined" is that the state should capitalize more fully on this human resource by upgrading their skills and labor input. It is probably not coincidental that at least one female economist (Tatarinova) who concludes that women evidence these positive labor attributes also urges part-time shifts primarily as a means of providing working women free time for retraining.[106]

Some central planners and economists are unimpressed by the allegedly positive attributes of working women but rather are concerned with the low levels of economic growth in Soviet industry. As a solution they have proposed that career promotions be awarded only after workers have taken some formal training in and been certified by a vocational-technical institute. They cite studies which have consistently shown more predictable and substantial increases in labor productivity for workers promoted after such training. In contrast, after training on the job or in vocational shops within enterprises, workers are often promoted even though they lack pertinent skills. In addition, these planners have proposed that base rates for engineers and the highest skill-grade workers be raised significantly to encourage constant formal reschooling and grade mobility.[107]

If implemented, such proposals would negatively affect the work status of many women in Soviet enterprises who have had only brief on-the-job apprenticeships in which they learned to run a machine or perform simple repetitive tasks on a conveyor line. For several reasons women cannot compete with men for upgrading via formal vocational-technical training: they have a generally low self-esteem; their husbands and male bosses resent and are insensitive toward their career aspirations; and their household responsibilities would prevent them from attending night and weekend classes in vocational-technical institutes. An increase in wage differentials between the highest and lowest skill-grade categories would mean an increase of the wage disparity between men and women Union-wide. Thus it might not be coincidental that both proposals have received backing at the same time that part-time shifts for women would further reduce the dependency of the economy on their high work-force participation and reduce the contribution of their salaries from unskilled jobs to their relative family income.

It is interesting to note that political support for these proposals seems to have mounted in recent years among a segment of top Soviet decision-makers in the party and government at the same time as has support for part-time shifts for women. The economic problems of the nation since 1976 have increasingly frustrated decision-makers, and the political climate appears to be less tolerant of unskilled workers and labor inefficiencies and less committed to relative wage equality in the workforce than in the past. By late 1979 Soviet economists committed to optimal planning and labor reforms were stressing that the rate of growth in industrial labor productivity for 1976-80 would fall at least 9 percent short of the targeted figure (27 percent). At the same time, at least one million more new industrial workers would enter the labor force than had been targeted by a 1976 policy aiming at the production of more and better goods with a reduced influx of new workers.[108]

By 1979 stagnancy was rampant in the economy, increasing sums were being diverted from domestic investment for the military budget, and the costs for fixed capital and energy had increased considerably, eliminating the option of stimulating growth by extensive capital expenditures. General Secretary Leonid Brezhnev evidenced the concern and frustration within the political establishment in his annual economic report to the Central Committee Party Plenum in November 1979. With unusual candor for that type of speech, he lashed out personally at several ministry heads for their failures to meet construction-transportation deadlines and production targets even after they had been revised downward, and he berated officials, managers, and workers alike for their indifference in all sectors of industry and agriculture.[109] In January 1980 a joint resolution of the Council of Ministers, the CPSU Central Committee, the Supreme Soviet Presidium, and the USSR Council of Ministers placed strict limitations on the freedom of Soviet workers to transfer jobs and established stiff penalties for violations, reversing a trend over the last two decades to remove the psychological climate of draconian Stalinist work laws. In its timing and interpretation by Politburo members, the resolution appeared to represent a watershed in a more hardline approach toward workers, whose freedom to change jobs was condemned as a sign of weakening discipline and a major cause of declining rates of productivity and output.[110]

On the one hand, Soviet women, with their 50 percent lower turnover rate than men, may benefit from the resolution, which grants bonuses to workers with long tenures in their enterprises. On the other hand, women have made up over 60 percent of new entrants into the labor force during a time when it was being suggested that large numbers of new entrants were dragging down growth in labor productivity. Thus the argument for placing more women on part-time shifts seems to have become more attractive. Based on explicit or implied points raised in published articles defending part-time shifts, the promises of this argument as it may well have been presented to Soviet decision-makers would include the following alleged advantages of part-time shifts.

First, more part-time shifts for women would effectively reduce the size of the inefficient labor force by the absolute number of women working even one or two fewer hours per day. At the same time, they would not formally violate Article 40 of the 1977 constitution which guarantees all Soviet citizens the right to work because an amendment to Article 40 qualified that right to mean work "not below the minimum amount established by the state."[111] Second, total labor productivity would be spurred not only by a reduced labor input, but also by the higher hourly output of part-timers.[112] Third, a reduced female labor force would only logically follow from the conclusions of certain Soviet central planners and economists, whose contention that women lag behind men in productivity and output unintentionally may have provided decision-makers a rationale to forego expenditures seemingly wasted in retraining the many unskilled women. Fourth, chronic labor shortages in the expanding but unmechanized and labor-intensive service sector would be eased by transferring women (as well as pensioners) from basic industry into consumer outlets and public eating establishments, where peak demand times and workflows vary during the day and can be better regulated through the hiring of part-timers. Fifth, fixed capital and energy costs could be held down by investing less in new machinery for fewer full-time workers, while marginal growth rates in total output would not be affected because the same absolute number would be in the workforce. In addition, hidden inflationary pressures within the economy would be contained; these have been mounting as disposable income has increased and not been spent owing to an insufficient quantity and quality of durable goods.[113] Sixth (following from the fifth advantage), pay raises granted to the highest brackets of skilled workers would be offset by the lowered aggregate salaries of part-timers.

A final and perhaps most appealing argument is political. Experts predict that the increased trend toward automated technology will result in the displacement of hundreds of thousands of unskilled manual workers.[114] Although Soviet economists are optimistic that the displaced workers will be retrained for jobs in newly expanding sectors (like the energy extraction industry), Soviet leaders may fear widespread discontent in the interim from the hundreds of thousands of workers laid off through automation. Increasing part-time shifts for women, who are politically more passive, could delay or entirely put off such displacements—i.e., it would be equivalent to laying off full-time unskilled male workers. One Soviet female economist has hinted at the political advantage of part-time shifts not only in the Soviet Union but also in other Comecon countries. In addition, she has proposed transfers of surplus workers among Comecon countries (particularly women in border areas) to labor-deficit regions to ease the problems of providing jobs for unskilled manual workers without precipitating the "complex socioeconomic problems" attendant upon the displacement of unskilled workers through automation.[115]

ECONOMIC AND POLITICAL CONSTRAINTS

Before part-time shifts for women could be fully implemented, the immediate problem of skilled labor shortages in several industrial branches of the USSR would have to be overcome. If women constitute a vital segment of the industrial workforce, career mobility should be encouraged for skilled women and upgrading and retraining for the unskilled. If part-time shifts could provide incentives for women to retrain, absolute declines in labor growth during the 1980s would eventually be compensated with increased labor productivity and output. However, part-time shifts that would redirect women only into unskilled service jobs or increased childbearing would cause even graver shortages of skilled workers.

According to the most conservative estimates, a reduction of eight hours monthly in the work shifts of half the women in the USSR would be equivalent to an annual loss of 950,000 full-time workers.[116] Implicit in such a reduction would be the economic gamble that growth could be sustained with combined increases in new technology and in the productivity of part-time workers. However, such increases presume fundamental changes in the rigid planning and pricing of the Soviet command economy and a major reorientation of managerial incentives at the enterprise level. Reforms extant since 1965 to stimulate efficiency and rapid technological infusion have dismally failed owing to the very nature of the command economy: the tautness of economic plans, the fetish with short-term production quotas, and the arbitrary setting of prices below actual costs and potential payoffs to induce enterprise managers to introduce new technology and automation in the production process. Central planners have been reluctant to slow down economic growth or allow market forces even a limited determination of the real economic value of products manufactured from new technology, and enterprise managers have not had sufficient risk-taking and risk-bearing incentives to undertake technological innovations in product mixes and production processes.[117]

Not only does it not pay to innovate at the enterprise level, but also it has never been profitable for Soviet managers to employ workers efficiently. As a rule, managers have opposed part-time shifts or related reforms (like the celebrated "Shchekino" reform introduced experimentally in 1967 to encourage managers to meet their quotas with fewer employees but the same enterprise wage fund) premised on their cost-effective utilization of a reduced labor force in enterprises. The reasons for their opposition appear to be both pecuniary and practical. First, in certain industries like machine-building, salaries and bonuses for managers (not to mention perquisites like dachas and automobiles) are directly pegged to the absolute

43

size of a manager's workforce.[118] Central planners have yet to devise statistical conversions to calculate part-time work in terms of full-time. Second, workforce ceilings apply only to the total number of employees in an enterprise rather than the total number of full-time positions which could be filled by either part-time or full-time employees. As a consequence, managers must meet the same production quotas regardless of whether or not they have a reduced workforce on part-time. Seemingly less convinced than central planners and economists that part-timers have higher hourly output and productivity rates than full-time employees, managers would fear that their overall indices for profitability and labor productivity would decline in hiring part-timers. Illustrative of the problem was an experiment with student part-time work detachments assigned to different industrial enterprises in the Leningrad region in the early 1980s.[119] While cost-effective for the enterprises (students were paid only one ruble per hour—much less than regular full-time employees working overtime), the experiment has not proved successful because managers are penalized by standardized workforce ceilings and judged on overall performance indices. As the authors of the *Pravda* article on the subject concluded, counting only the total number of employees allowed in an enterprise rather than the total number of equivalent full-time positions provides very little incentive for managers to hire student part-timers on a wider basis.

Third, managers have long been in the habit of padding enterprise payrolls with "reserve workers" in order to cope with the frenzied pace of taut plans imposed on them by central officials, the constant uncertainties and breakdowns in supply shipments, the bureaucratic delays involved in contracting with new suppliers, and the periodic upward revisions of production quotas. "Reserve workers," squirreled away in payrolls in addition to the employees on official quotas (which do not set limits on the number of nonproductive auxiliary workers allowed in enterprises), allow managers to meet quotas and give them some operational maneuverability—especially because managers must contend with high turnovers of skilled workers, as well as periodic absences of skilled workers who are reassigned to collective farms in the planting and harvesting seasons. Thus a labor reserve in enterprises has become a functional and rational microeconomic practicality; at the same time, however, it engenders gross inefficiencies from the macroeconomic perspective of central planners who must assess labor needs and reassign workers to areas experiencing genuine labor shortages.[120]

Such managerial practices reflect the inherent futility of Soviet decision-makers trying to correct economic flaws with isolated measures which fail to consider the fundamental irrationalities and problems of a command economy. As the system itself cannot be openly challenged, reformers are limited to chipping away at some of its most glaring problems and finding scapegoats in particular segments of the bureaucracy. Thus if consensus can be found among the supporters of part-time shifts for women, it is that industrial managers are the major obstacle to implementing the reform. They claim that many managers have refused to accept the very concept of part-time shifts, obstinately contending that such shifts would undermine their authority and limit their flexibility, require them to set aside special production areas for part-timers, further underutilize plant capacities and waste start-up and shut-down times, and involve the submission to Moscow of additional reports and forms.[121]

One apparent sign that part-time shifts would limit managerial autonomy is that advocates of the reform (among others) support an expansion of the authority of state "bureaus of labor placement and information" to coordinate the hiring of enterprise workers. Established in the late 1960s, the bureaus represent a first attempt to reclaim some central oversight in the assignment of labor resources Union-wide. Managers have been urged to submit job openings to the bureaus, which would screen and refer suitable applicants from the local communities to the enterprises. Managers have resisted doing so, but the advent of part-timers, whose uniqueness justifies more systematic clearance and control through the placement bureaus, may be a first step in taking hiring authority completely away from managers.[122] The trend toward central control became more apparent in an economic mechanism reform announced in July 1979. Ostensibly intended to reduce irrational pressures on managers and shift more emphasis on five-year rather than annual production indices, the reform included a provision to speed up implementation of a 1976 decision to place absolute ceilings on all employees (including auxiliary personnel) to induce more efficient workforce utilization.[123]

Industrial managers so far have been successful in rejecting part-time shifts for their employees—owing to what some policy advocates refer to as managerial "inertia." Moreover, they retain the right to refuse part-time shifts if they determine their particular enterprise cannot function with part-timers in a particular specialization or under general production conditions.[124] Apparently managers have liberally made such determinations, thus retaining wide discretion in the employment of part-timers. Furthermore, as long as managers retain final hiring authority, they can neglect to inform present or potential employees of their privilege to request part-time shifts.[125]

That Soviet managers typically refuse part-time shifts to women even under extenuating circumstances has been confirmed by Fyodor Turovsky, former chairman of the legal committee of the Moscow Construction Workers' Union (now an émigré in London). For example, Turovsky cites the case (which he defended) of a woman engineer with three sons handicapped from birth who requested a part-time shift in the planning and technology department of her organization. The manager refused the request with the rationale that "if I allow you to shorten your working day, hundreds of other women will want to follow suit [half of the engineers in the department were women], and then we will have to close the department."[126] However, one woman in the department was allowed to leave work every day at noon—the manager's wife. According to Turovsky, this case simply reinforced the impression among women in the department that the law establishing part-time shifts as a right for women was a sham intended to benefit the wives of the elite.[127]

Indeed industrial managers have probably been far from disappointed that central officials have failed to change the rigid workforce ceilings and performance indices for managers from criteria based on the total number of employees to those based on some full-time equivalency of positions which could be filled at managerial discretion by a combination of full- and part-time employees. Any such changes would eliminate the one incontrovertible rationale against hiring part-timers—namely, that hiring part-timers would reduce enterprise efficiency under current workforce ceilings and performance indices. Furthermore, changes might force managers to account formally for the "reserve workers" until now excluded from the formal reports on compliance with workforce ceilings submitted to the central ministry.

The continued resistance of both local industrial managers and many working women may yet prove to be the crucial constraints for central Soviet decision-makers. Despite the deteriorating economic situation in the Soviet Union, decision-makers so far have appeared wary of implementing the part-time reform without careful projections of its likely long-term economic and social impact. This caution is consistent with the general tenor and policy orientation of the Brezhnev era (which began in 1965), whose defining characteristics have been a systematic approach to socioeconomic problems and a more active involvement of policy specialists in the formulation of responses to problems openly admitted to be complex.[128] At least since the round-table conference on women's issues in 1978 (discussed above), some advocates of part-time shifts have been proposing a more modest and gradual phasing-in of the reform. For example, under some of their proposed revisions, only women with very young infants would be eligible for part-time shifts, and they would qualify according to marital status, with the single and widowed having preference over the married. From time to time additional categories of women would be added to the eligibility list, so that eventually women with children up to the age of fourteen would be included. Mothers of children with particular problems would have to submit documents from doctors or school directors attesting to their need for part-time shifts.[129] Other policy advocates—apparently discounting the twenty-year experience with part-time shifts in Estonian enterprises—have suggested that a more extensive testing of the reform's effects is needed on a regional scale.[130] Moreover, there have been second thoughts about partially paid one-year maternity leaves (projected as an attainable goal in the 1976-80 plan). Advocates now contend that part-time shifts for women during the leave might be preferable; the state would not have the expense of full welfare payments if women worked at least part-time, while the women retain their labor-force attachment and skills.[131] To overcome the resistance of industrial managers, advocates cite projections of the Central Labor Resources Research Institute showing that only 5 percent of the industrial workforce would be transferred to part-time employment under given economic constraints; some foresee either that part-time employees will be excluded from the calculations of labor productivity in an enterprise (and thus from a determination of managerial bonuses), or that ministries will set up special enterprises staffed predominantly by part-timers whose performance (and that of the ministries) will be evaluated differently.[132]

Some policy advocates have suggested that women in very demanding jobs with high turnover rates (e.g., in the textile industry) retain their regular salaries if they reduce their work shifts by no more than two hours daily. The state could allegedly make up the differences by eliminating the earlier retirement and pension benefits for women in such industries.[133] Gosha has gone further: she has proposed that reduced work shifts be granted to all women in the Soviet Union—with special considerations for those raising families.[134] Critical of demographic policies which would encourage women to have more children at the expense of their economic contribution to society, she has concluded that the current part-time labor option has been resoundingly rejected by many women because they receive only a portion of their regular salaries. Under her proposal, women with infants under 1.5 years would receive their regular salaries if they reduced their work shifts by two hours daily, while those with children from 1.5 to 7 years would receive regular salaries with a reduction of one hour daily. Gosha considers that such a reduction of work hours and labor input in the short term will stimulate the economy in the long term. She argues that under her proposal, with the removal of the salary penalty, more women would voluntarily accept reduced work shifts; furthermore, they would be expected to use at least part of their free time to continue their education, upgrade their vocational skills, and generally focus on their intellectual growth. In turn, better educated and vocationally mobile women would increase labor productivity. Gosha points out that the levels of labor productivity and output of many Soviet women suffer once they begin to raise families; some drop out of the labor force entirely until their children begin school. A loss in productivity can neither be recouped nor counterbalanced by underutilized aggregate skills in the labor force. Thus the increased labor skills and eventual productivity resulting from mothers on reduced work shifts would more than compensate the state economy over the long term for the temporary short-term losses of paying the mothers for one or two hours of time not worked.

These various proposed revisions for the original part-time reform statute of 1971 clearly suggest a political accommodation to the concerns of many working women as well as industrial managers. Soviet decision-makers no longer have the luxury of pumping large capital investments and unskilled labor into selected high-growth sectors; instead they must wrestle with hard choices which may lead to lower short-term employment levels and slower growth rates in order to spur long-term economic efficiency and facilitate technological modernization. Politically the easy choice would have been to implement part-time shifts full-scale for women, with the immediate reduction of superfluous unskilled workers and the growth of labor productivity. That Soviet decision-makers and the policy specialists whose advice they may heed have not opted for the politically expedient choice argues as much for the complexity of economic problems which they confront as it does for the cautious pragmatism of the current leadership.

As much as its cautious pragmatism, a hallmark of the Brezhnev leadership has also been a general commitment to reducing class inequalities — often at the expense of greater economic efficiencies — and decision-makers may be reluctant to arbitrarily reverse the limited but important advances toward equality that women have made as a consequence of their high participation in the labor force. Despite the recent anti-worker climate in which job transfers have been restricted and proposals made to increase wage differentiations for the most highly skilled workers, the leadership has shown little inclination to adopt "market socialism" types of reforms (as in Hungary) which would grant increased autonomy to industrial managers and could lead to high inflation, unemployment (particularly among the unskilled and less productive workers let go by managers solely preoccupied with their efficiency and profit margins), and increased class divisions by earnings. In the commitment to relative class equality some Western analysts see an indication of the benign authoritarian "corporatist" or "welfare state" policy orientation of the Brezhnev regime — an implicit social compact with the lower working class to ensure their political support and reduce the kind of discontent evident in Polish workers' riots throughout the 1970s.[135] The emergence in 1980 of Solidarity, the independent trade union movement in Poland (with the equal appearance of militant Polish female trade unionists demonstrating at factories) probably served as a further reminder to the Brezhnev regime not to take the Soviet working class and the supposedly apolitical women within that class for granted and not to undertake policies solely on the basis of whether they are justified from a perspective of macroeconomic efficiency.

As should by now be clear, the participants in the complex debate on part-time shifts for women defy simple interest-group classification. The overriding concerns of advocates and opponents alike have been for the long-term state of the economy and long-term solutions to correct deficiencies, and they have differed less in their reformist views than in their immediate priorities and economic projections. Advocates have been more willing to concede the short-term interests of working women for long-term economic efficiency and growth and have been less convinced that significant payoffs in increased productivity would come from training unskilled women. Opponents and fence-straddlers have been troubled by the reform's discriminatory implications in treating women differently from men and have worried that without comprehensive additional measures part-time shifts would lead to more critical shortfalls in output and skilled personnel. Rather than an issue whose advocates and opponents can be paired off as real and distinct interest groups, part-time work has emerged on the national level as a highly divisive political symbol condensing the broader disputes and priorities over socioeconomic policy which constitute the differing tendencies of interest articulation among Soviet decision-makers and policy advisers. As a divisive political symbol, part-time work has quite a different meaning depending on the positions of either advocates or opponents relative to these broader differences of viewpoint over current socioeconomic problems and desired future changes.

One subtle but important distinction between certain advocates and opponents of part-time work rests in the differing priorities they derive from common policy concerns with optimal utilization of the labor force. For advocates, optimal utilization would seem to require a reduction in the economy's dependency on unskilled and inefficient workers, who drag down per capita labor productivity and blunt the absorption of labor-saving technology and automation; part-time shifts for the many unskilled women in the labor force would accomplish this. In the Soviet context their advocacy of part-time shifts may be the closest they can openly come to espousing selective unemployment under socialism as a solution to economic stagnancy; according to unconfirmed rumors in the West, some of the labor economists advocating part-time shifts publicly have at times run into political difficulty for drawing out the logical conclusions of their analyses and proposing (in unpublished papers) some selective unemployment in the Soviet Union.

For opponents and fence-straddlers who remain troubled by various aspects of the reform, however, optimal utilization of the labor force would seem to involve an increase in skill levels among the currently employed. In essence they advocate part-time shifts not as a measure to reduce the size of the labor force but as a needed handicap for unskilled women to upgrade their skills in order to maximize their productive potential for the economy. Thus for advocates, part-time shifts would reduce the *demand* of the current economy for unskilled workers as a first priority toward effective labor force utilization, while for opponents and fence-straddlers, they would increase the *supply* of skilled workers in the 1980s as a first priority toward effective labor force utilization. Both positions have been alternatively—and even simultaneously—taken by individual policy specialists who have not recognized, or not been able to admit openly, that each position would have a quite different significance for the general status of Soviet women. In the complex political debate over part-time work, policy specialists have projected into their advocacy or opposition to the reform only those meanings consistent with their overall vision of current problems in the economy and the most viable solutions to them.

Labor shortages, projected for the 1980s and 1990s by all Soviet economists as a result of declining birthrates, have further complicated the debate and the widely variant symbolic meaning of part-time work as either a progressive or regressive change for women and their overall status in Soviet society. Pronatalists have consistently allied themselves with the advocates of part-time shifts; however, their support stems not from the promised labor force efficiencies of the reform but from its consistency with an overall population policy to encourage higher birthrates among Slavic and Baltic women. The part-time policy advocates seem almost embarrassed by support from the pronatalists. Such support places them on the defensive with opponents and fence-straddlers, whose suspicions of the reform's discriminatory impact appear more credible in view of the justifications for part-time shifts put forth by the pronatalists.

Given the differences among policy advisers and the uncertainties arising from too hasty a full-scale implementation of the reform, a more rational reassessment of the reform's limitations may prevail over the normal penchant of some Soviet decision-makers to force through administrative changes without careful forethought. However, to judge by statements and resolutions in early 1981, concurrent with the convening of the Twenty-Sixth Party Congress, the policy direction of the national leadership was not very clear.

On one hand, support for a scaled-down version of part-time work seemed evident in Brezhnev's Central Committee report at the beginning of the congress. Brezhnev struck a generally pragmatic note in assessing the problems confronting Soviet women and the difficulties in moving too hastily to resolve them.[136] While several changes—including the provision of part-time work and one-year maternity leaves—had been formally promised for 1976-80, "no real appreciable change had taken place."[137] Endorsing the part-time and extended leave provisions outlined in the "Basic Guidelines," Brezhnev at the same time succeeded in placating those concerned with the potentially negative effects of the reform on the labor force participation of women. According to him, the reform would be introduced beginning in 1981—but only gradually, on a selective, region-by-region basis, with "careful consideration to the special features of the situation in the various republics and regions." In sum, pragmatism and caution would dictate that in implementing the reforms "we cannot accomplish everything that we would like at once."[138]

On the other hand, Brezhnev signaled that the leadership (aging and all male) had been won over by those who projected a more traditional and pronatalist meaning to the reform. Both Brezhnev's references at the congress and a subsequent joint resolution of the Party Central Committee and USSR Council of Ministers directly and unambiguously linked part-time work for women with supposedly related measures to encourage higher birthrates.[139] With the introduction of part-time shifts on a regional basis, the leadership included the gradual inception of lump-sum allowances to mothers at the birth of their first, second, and third child; increased annual leaves for women with children under the age of twelve; special privileges in housing, vacation centers, and retail consumer outlets for pregnant women and families with infants; and an expansion in the number and quality of day-care centers and kindergartens. While more and better preschool facilities—particularly the extended-day facilities singled out in the resolution—presumably would help more women to remain active in the labor force, the provision in the resolution seems intended as much to satisfy pronatalists who have contended that the shortage and poor quality of such facilities have discouraged many women from having more children.

It is important to note that neither the "Basic Guidelines" nor the joint resolution maintain even a formal pretense that the part-time work reform is related to improving the career opportunities and status of women. In the contesting symbolic meanings attributed to part-time work, the more traditional meaning has apparently prevailed—at least among the national Soviet leadership. Lumped together with state allowances for bearing children, it seems to have been legitimated solely as a "family" issue to encourage higher birthrates and a more stable family life centered around the traditional role of women as mothers and homemakers, not as a "women's issue" to enhance the equality of working women in a more modern assimilationist female role.

Chapter 3

ALTERNATIVE WORK SCHEDULES IN THE UNITED STATES

Given the cautious reassessment of part-time shifts among Soviet policy advisers, two of the most ardent supporters of part-time shifts in the Soviet Union—A. E. Kotliar and S. Ia. Turchaninova—have urged a careful study of "foreign experience" in part-time work before it is fully implemented in the Soviet Union.[1] Whether intentionally or not, they failed to qualify "foreign experience" with "in other socialist countries," a normal Soviet qualifier in such phrases. If their recommendation were literally followed by Soviet decision-makers, the United States would seem a particularly appropriate model for study.

As in the Soviet Union, interest in alternative work schedules in the United States has surfaced over the 1970s, and the issue has evolved in a highly complex policy setting. As in the Soviet Union, alternative work reforms have been promoted not solely as a "women's issue"—although working women have both prompted increased serious consideration of the reforms and been viewed (along with senior citizens) as one of the groups that would benefit most directly from them—but have been linked with broader policy concerns with family life and a declining economy.

In terms of analysis, the issue of alternative work schedules also poses less of a methodological problem and allows for some comparative generalizations to be drawn for two such vastly different political systems as the Soviet Union and the United States. In labor policy, for example, the highly centralized Soviet government administering all economic resources in the nation obviously sets and implements policy affecting all workers as it is their sole employer, while labor policy in the politically fragmented American political system flows from government actions at the federal and state levels and from uncoordinated and independent initiatives throughout the private sector. Yet in 1978 the United States Congress passed

54

legislation authorizing the option of permanent part-time employment for all civilian federal employees through grade levels up to GS 16 (equivalent to deputy assistant secretary)—2.2 million people—and established a three-year experiment with flexible and compressed work schedules in selected federal agencies. In addition, 600,000 postal workers have long had alternative work schedules. (Details of the legislation are presented below.) The policy for federal civil servants in the American labor force can be compared to policies for the entire labor force in the Soviet Union, where the national government is the sole employer and regulates all terms of employment. Moreover, the proposed adoption of the flexible, compressed, and part-time legislation for federal employees served to crystallize into a national debate on the merits and limitations of alternative work schedules for the entire American economy during Congressional hearings on the subject, and the issues and concerns raised by policy advisers and government officials paralleled those raised in the USSR.

Another comparable policy dimension is that distinctions in the policy-making processes of the USSR and United States (i.e., the generally elitist and authoritarian Soviet process vs. the more open American process in which decision-makers are accountable to mass group influences) do not constitute an important differential factor in explaining alternative work schedule policies in the two nations. Despite the important influence of American feminists and organized women's advocacy groups (which we shall discuss in this chapter), policy decisions on alternative work schedules in the United States—like on other social programs for women—have evolved in a relatively narrow, isolated, and depoliticized policy environment, in which decision-makers have interacted with an activist corps of advocacy group leaders, government officials, and academic policy advisers to formulate programs perceived to be consonant with their major policy goals.[2] Policy on alternative work schedules has been made in the absence of mass-initiated demands for reforms or political controversy. (Indeed—as we shall show below—the 1978 federal legislation passed successfully because advocates maintained a noncontroversial and depoliticized aura around the bills without stimulating public debate.) The predominant role of a relatively small group of government and academic specialists in shaping alternative work schedule policy in the United States somewhat parallels that of the Soviet government and academic specialists, whose views define the parameters of policy participation over part-time work in the Soviet context. In both nations the policy could be characterized as a "trickle-down" response formulated by specialists with a relatively low level of participation by the segments of the public which the policy would affect.

In contrast to the Soviet Union, however, the principle lines of division in the debate over alternative work schedules in the United States have been more clear-cut and consistent. Where reforms in the former have almost seemed to be promoted by some to increase the birthrate and reduce the labor force commitment of women, reforms in the latter have clearly been sponsored by those most concerned with expanding the labor force attachment and options of women, enhancing their role and quality of participation in it, and eliminating sex discrimination in employment. Where alternative work schedules have alarmed many Soviet working women as signaling a possible reversal of egalitarian trends and a move to sacrifice them for economic expediency into a more traditional female role, in the United States they symbolize a feminist tendency in public policy and a movement toward the reduction of inequities for women in both the workplace and the family.

To understand the underlying differences in the significance of alternative work schedules as a policy issue in the United States, we shall analyze the cumulative effects of three major determinants which have apparently conditioned increased support for alternative work schedules in the American policy context:

(1) *Economic determinants*: There has been a rapid growth of women in the labor force over the 1960s and 1970s; they now constitute 42 percent of it. In consequence, officials recognize that national economic policies must consider their role in the labor force and their particular needs and demands.

(2) *Political determinants*: The rising numbers of working women and their advocacy groups and supporters in government have brought an increased awareness of sex discrimination and inequality to the American political conscience; a political stalemate over the implementation of a national full-employment policy and failure to reduce unemployment below 7 percent have been aggravated by the increasing numbers of women entering the labor force and their competition for a limited number of new jobs; and there have been difficulties

in reconciling the competing objectives of equality and equity in hiring as demands for affirmative action by women and racial minorities have clashed with the seniority rights of white males—and all are caught in a recessionary economy and a tight job market.

(3) *Sociocultural determinants*: Management and labor have begun to cooperate in reforming and democratizing the workplace and making jobs more meaningful for employees, while Americans have expressed a mounting dissatisfaction with conventional lifestyles, in which work has been given an overly prominent role and individuals have been needlessly and unrewardingly lock-stepped into a linear pattern of schooling-marriage-work-childrearing-retirement.

ECONOMIC DETERMINANTS OF POLICY

Advocates of alternative work schedules have long urged a change in the conventional American forty-hour work mode—for women in particular because of its inherent liabilities and unfairness for many women. Daycare facilities have either been very costly or unavailable, and women often have been forced to accommodate their work options to the needs of their infants or preschoolers. Frequently the choice has been between either a full-time job and reliance on neighbors, relatives, or older children to care for their "latch-key" infants during the day, or no job at all. Women dependent on their own earnings who could not adjust their schedules to accommodate their infants have had to take temporary part-time jobs with low wages, often fewer health-care benefits than they could receive as single mothers on welfare, few advancement opportunities, and few opportunities to demonstrate their skills or potential. Nationwide statistics still showing a high proportion of women employed part-time in low-paying and low-status clerical and sales positions reflect the prevalence of these accommodations and the discriminatory impact of forty-hour weeks on the work options available to many women. The pattern has not changed appreciably with the significant recent expansion of female employment (see p. 61 below). Since 1966 part-time employment of women has increased almost twice as fast as full-time employment, and the vast majority of female part-timers—approximately one third of working mothers in the United States—are in low-paying and low-status clerical and sales positions.[3]

Allegedly sex-neutral, the conventional work mode in the United States with its rigidly prescribed forty-hour week has subtly reinforced the occupational segregation of women into a narrow sphere of occupations and has further contributed to the vast underutilization of women in the labor force. In addition, part-time employment carries the negative connotation of applying only to low-skilled jobs; few employers in the public and private sectors have been willing to hire skilled or professional employees on part-time or flexitime schedules for positions which are assumed to require full-time work.[4]

As emphasized by prominent American policy advisers on family issues like Urie Bronfenbrenner, women have not been the only ones penalized by the conventional work mode and the reluctance of employers to hire skilled and professional workers part-time.[5] "Latchkey" youngsters, whose mothers work full-time, have been denied a normal upbringing and important emotional contact with their mothers by a work mode slanted to male wage-earners and forcing women to choose between a regular job and their children. In turn, the low status and pay of female part-timers serve to legitimate a subordinate status for them in the family. Husbands employed full-time have easily rationalized a division of family labor in which they bear little responsibility for housework and childrearing when their wives are employed only part-time and contribute only a small percentage of the total family income.

From the perspective of social critics and policy advisers like Bronfenbrenner, a lack of male involvement in parenting has stunted the emotional growth not only of children but of the men themselves, for whom work situations have assumed an emotional importance greater than that of their families. Sociologists have only begun to study the long-term effects of increasing female labor-force participation on the quality of family life and childrearing, and some have refuted the conventional wisdom of those like Bronfenbrenner who claim that the American nuclear family is in crisis and that childrearing has deteriorated as a result of the increasing labor-force participation of married women. However, even critics of the conventional wisdom agree that requiring women to work standard full-time shifts may increase the pressures on both spouses and exacerbate family stress at particular periods of the family "life cycle."[6] Bronfenbrenner (among others) draws a wider (if unprovable) indictment against conventional work modes, claiming that the conflict between family responsibilities and such work modes in families where both spouses work full-time has over the long term led to increasing family stress, divorces, heart attacks, early death among men, and juvenile delinquency among children.

Whether or not Bronfenbrenner's indictment is valid, as female employment has increased, it has become apparent on the national political level that the economy is suffering from underutilized human resources and labor productivity as the pattern of female employment in the American labor force has fundamentally altered over the last two decades. By 1978 half of all American women sixteen years and over were working (an increase of 18 percent since 1947), as were 42 percent of all married women with children under six; 75 percent of all women were either working at least thirty-five hours per week or seeking regular full-time jobs in which they could work at least thirty-five hours per week (considered the minimum for a full-time job). Indeed some researchers at the Urban Institute consider that the most significant changes in what they have characterized as the "subtle revolution" of rising female employment lie in the increased proportion of working women who are married and have infants and the predominant majority of women seeking quality careers.[7]

The reasons for the changes in female employment are complex.[8] In the short term a spiraling rate of inflation throughout the 1970s and the uncertainties of a volatile economy have made the salaries of married women essential to their households, not only to maintain minimal living standards, but also to provide a salary fallback in the case of periodic job layoffs for their husbands. In the long term the number of single women and women who are the sole breadwinners of their families has increased owing to (among other things) changing societal values, increased education for women, and rising divorce rates. As a correlate long-term phenomenon, jobs which have increased most rapidly with a transformation from productive industry to service employment in the United States have been exactly those low-productive and low-paying "dead-end" positions for which women have been preferred over men in hiring. Thus the service and retail trade sectors, traditionally employing the largest proportion of women in the labor force, accounted for more than 70 percent of all newly created jobs in the private sector from 1973 to mid-1980 and employed 43 percent of all Americans in the private nonagricultural economy.[9]

Perhaps the major reason for the increased labor force attachment of women—and one which stems more from sociocultural rather than economic changes—is a fundamental transformation in their values and role identities. Surveys reveal that American women no longer view work merely as a means to supplement family income or reduce boredom, but as a full-time vocation and life commitment essential to their self-esteem and self-worth and their family's well-being. As a consequence, their life-work expectancy has increased to twenty-two years, and statisticians in the Labor Department's Bureau of Labor Statistics predict that 90 percent of women reaching the age of sixteen by 1979 will work at least several years during their lifetimes. Furthermore, the proportion of working women with infants under six or children between six and seventeen will rise 56 percent between 1978 and 1990.[10]

American public officials and private employers, who otherwise could have remained indifferent to the human and societal costs of the role conflict confronting working women emphasized by policy advisers like Bronfenbrenner, have been less able to overlook its effect on a faltering American economy. The vast increase in the proportion of women seeking jobs in the United States over the last two decades has been accompanied by a downturn in the growth rates of the gross national product and labor productivity—parallel to that experienced by the Soviet Union in the same time.

Obviously many complex factors unique to the different Soviet or American situation have accounted for the economic stagnation in each country. However, the problems of a faltering economy cannot be attributed solely to too many women adding to an overcrowded job market, pulling down growth and productivity rates as a consequence, and increasing inflation and unemployment rates. As one prominent labor economist has pointed out, such a simplistic "lump of labor" explanation falsely assumes the availability of a finite amount of work, a fixed number of jobs to be redistributed among contending labor groups, and the necessity of accepting larger unemployment rates as normal to stimulate long-term growth and hold down inflation.[11] Moreover (as we observed in Chapter 2), economic stagnation cannot be blamed on the supposedly lower work potentials or labor productivity of women. In the United States women have reached parity with men in educational attainment (an average of 12.6 years of schooling); by 1979 the number of women enrolled full-time in colleges surpassed the number of men (5.90 vs. 5.48 million); and more women than men per capita participated in all forms of vocational education (except for women in the peak childbearing ages between twenty-two and thirty-four).[12]

From a macroeconomic perspective, the problem can be best understood as the qualitative failure of the American economy to integrate women into occupations which would optimize long-term economic growth. As they have enlarged the labor pool seeking jobs over the last two decades, women have continued to be crowded into the same limited range of occupationally segregated female positions, which have underemployed their potential talents as workers and been among the least productive and lowest paid in the American labor force. Irrationally from a macroeconomic perspective, 80 percent of working women (33 million) are concentrated in pre-dominantly female jobs—clericals (42 percent), service personnel (19.1 percent), salespersons (6.6 percent), and low-skilled factory operatives (10.5 percent).[13] Even in the ten years between 1968 and 1977, when female jobholders increased by 8.9 million in the United States, 3.3 million of them entered low-skilled clerical positions.[14] Of the women employed by the federal government, 77 percent are concentrated in the lowest grade levels (GS 1-3). In 1977 the median income of women with four or more years of college in year-round full-time jobs was below that of male high school dropouts; the proportion of women enrolled in sex-stereotyped vocational courses (to be office workers, health-care specialists, home economists, and homemakers) ranged from 75 to 84 percent, while men made up 98 percent of those enrolled in technical, industrial, and trade courses.[15] Therefore it should come as little surprise that with their increased proportion of the entire labor force, the jobs into which women have been placed have failed to generate labor-productivity advances and economic growth with absolute increases in the entire American labor force over the 1970s.

The waste of human resources stemming from limited job opportunities for women was forcefully revealed in a national survey of 150,000 American working women by the National Commission on Working Women and summarized in testimony before the Senate Committee on Labor and Human Resources during its 1979 hearings on women.[16] Forty percent of the women surveyed felt their jobs were boring and failed to utilize their real skills. Nearly half said that they had no opportunity to train for better jobs. One third had received no counseling about other jobs or training. Because of their perceived inability to advance in their careers, one fourth lacked the self-confidence even to try. And 55 percent had no leisure time and 39 percent no time at all to continue their education for career mobility.

With the number of women seeking jobs increasing so rapidly in the United States, the cumulative labor pool of men and women has far exceeded the commensurate demand for labor, but also—and more important—sex-stereotyped prejudices about the "appropriate" work for women have been perpetuated which do not match the reality of a changing job market. Technological breakthroughs have created or expanded the need for new skilled occupations, and automation and mechanization in industry and construction have eliminated rational physical barriers to female employment in traditionally male sectors.

The long-term economic consequences of a failure to provide realistic vocational counseling to women entering the job market and match their placement distribution to a changing market have become evident to labor economists like Isabel Sawhill, Barbara Reagan, Nancy Barrett, and Ralph Smith, who undertook extensive research during the 1970s on trends in American female employment and the impact of women on the American economy.[17] Affiliated in Washington with liberal research "think-tanks" on public policy like the Urban Institute or directly advising government decision-makers particularly during the Carter administration (for example, Sawhill and Smith served as executive directors of the National Commission on Employment Policy, a quasi-governmental agency advising Congress on labor policy and trends, and some served as assistant secretaries in federal agencies), these labor economists have increased the awareness of decision-makers to the link between low economic growth and productivity and the underemployment of women. (In the latter 1970s their policy role to some extent paralleled that of advisers like Sonin, Tatarinova, and Aganbegian in the Soviet Union, affiliated with Soviet government research institutes or agencies, who stimulated debate over the interrelated problems of under-employment of Soviet women and a Union-wide economic downturn.)

For these labor economists several disparities stand out. For example, as the number of female job claimants has increased, the average yearly earnings of women employed full-time and year-round have declined to less than 60 percent of those of men so employed. In the 1970s even with women making up 60 percent of all new job entries in the job market, their absence from male occupations has limited the influx of job claimants for these male positions and thus failed to stimulate labor productivity through a normal supply competition for work in these occupations. The predominance of women in low-skilled and labor-surplus female occupations has further dragged down labor productivity by underutilizing the potential skills of women, whose total output of goods and services on the job has failed to exceed the equivalent expenditures in real economic terms for their wages.

Parallels in the work status of women in the Soviet Union and the United States should be evident. In both countries a surplus of unskilled women in a narrow range of occupationally segregated positions has prevented the economy from utilizing capital and labor inputs in the most efficient and optimal manner. In the Soviet Union industrial managers have resisted the optimal utilization of the female labor force, while in the United States corporations have resisted it because of sex-stereotyped prejudices and because it has been profitable to use low-wage and unskilled female labor instead of making costly outlays in capital investment and employee retraining. Federal and state officials have accepted the status quo because of their adherence to a free enterprise ideology, which proscribes government interference in the private sector, and because of a reluctance to intervene in the perceived normal functioning of a free labor market in which it is assumed that women freely choose their occupations.

Recent evidence in the United States has pointed to the immense difficulties involved in rectifying the underemployment of women in the labor force and their depressive effect on economic growth and labor productivity. The difficulties stem from interrelated systemic and structural dimensions of the problem. Systemically, to find secure and meaningful employment, many women directly depend on a rapidly expanding growth rate stimulated by a full-employment macroeconomic policy at the federal level. As a peripheral segment of the labor force, women (like racial minorities) are more likely to be laid off, find job reentry extremely difficult, and suffer increasing occupational segregation with low wages and little vocational mobility

63

in a slow-growth economy. The irony of the employment situation confronting women and their critical dependence on a high-growth economy for meaningful job opportunities have been forcefully argued by Ralph Smith. In a detailed macroeconomic analysis of the 1973-77 U.S. recession and partial recovery in late 1977, Smith concluded that although women were maldistributed in such occupations as retail trade, service, and public administration, they lost fewer jobs than men overall during the recession for the very reason that they were concentrated in peripheral sectors of the economy less affected by major business cycles.[18] At the same time, they lost a disproportionate number of jobs in male-dominant sectors like manufacturing, in which they had just begun to make inroads; only with the partial recovery were they able to recoup some of their losses in these sectors. While Smith emphasized the economic arguments for a high-growth economy to reduce the crowding of women in low-productive and low-mobility feminized occupations, he was also cognizant that the problem has important political dimensions. More sensitive to the anguished mood of a white electorate, elected federal officials have seemingly been more concerned about holding down prices with a slack economy than risking inflationary pressures by stimulating the economy to create jobs for the structurally unemployed and underemployed like women and racial minorities.

Even were federal officials willing to initiate policies to stimulate economic growth and create jobs, such policies would only increase the pool of jobs available but would have no selective effect on the kinds of jobs in which women would be hired. Full employment is a necessary but not a sufficient precondition to improve the status of women and regain some of the losses in labor productivity and output associated with their crowding into occupationally segregated sectors. As Smith found, the past experience has been that when labor demands have been stimulated by the federal government, women have been channeled even more intensively into traditionally female occupations. Thus without a simultaneous correction of the structural problem of female occupational segregation, anticipated increases in economic growth and labor productivity would be cancelled out by inflationary macroeconomic stimulants—i.e., the continued maldistribution of even more women in a narrow range of unskilled occupations would not serve to generate a sufficient increase in goods and services to offset the increased outlays from government spending and wages.

The liberal economist Lester Thurow has pointed out another facet of the structural quandary: a nondiscriminating macroeconomic policy to stimulate growth would further cost-push inflation by driving up wages artificially in white male-dominant occupational sectors, where (owing to negligible competition from women) aggregate demand for white males would increase over their labor supply in these sectors. These sectors (such as steelworks) strongly determine overall wage levels in the economy (other sectors peg their wage demands relative to theirs), so that an increase in salaries in these sectors would drive up wages and prices nationally in a continuing cost-push inflationary spiral.[19]

In attempting to correct the structural dimension of the problem, particularly during the latter 1970s the federal government instituted a number of selective employment programs and administrative changes designed in part to "mainstream" women into nontraditional male-dominant occupations. To increase the supply of skilled women for nontraditional jobs, amendments in 1978 to the reauthorized Comprehensive Employment and Training Administration Act (CETA) for the first time targeted women as an economically disadvantaged group who (with racial minorities, the handicapped, veterans, and the aged) should be actively recruited and trained under local CETA programs for occupations in which they make up a small percentage of the workforce.[20]* Women—whose participation rates in all titled programs under CETA since the act's inception had never reached the proportional levels of women in the population—would now no longer be trained just for predominantly female occupations; instead a deliberate good-faith effort would be made to train them for skilled positions in nontraditional occupations. In addition, innovative apprenticeship outreach and pretraining programs would be offered to encourage and prepare women to enter

---

*Since 1973 CETA has consolidated programs at the federal level for disadvantaged, unemployed, and underemployed groups in the labor force. Funding is administered by the Employment and Training Administration in the Department of Labor and enforced by "prime sponsors" (that is, state and city governments and nonprofit employment organizations).

nontraditional joint apprenticeship programs in industry and construction still dominated by men.*

To stimulate a demand for women in nontraditional occupations in the labor pool, in April 1978 the Office of Federal Contract Compliance Programs (OFCCP) in the Department of Labor (DOL) consented to issue and enforce specific regulations with explicit goals and timetables for the number of women who must be employed in construction work contracted by the federal government. (However, it did so only in response to suits which had been filed against the DOL by women's advocacy groups since 1976.) In May 1978 the DOL's Bureau of Apprenticeship and Training (BAT), authorized to oversee and register apprenticeship programs in the private sector, issued similar regulations and goals on the number of women who must be admitted to federally sanctioned joint apprenticeship training programs under goals and timetables for affirmative action compliance. Failure of contractors to meet these goals and timetables would constitute prima facie evidence of sex discrimination and require the federal government to cancel its contract with them and undertake no future business with them until the situation had been remedied. In essence the contractors' good-faith record in reducing sex discrimination would now be weighed as much as their record in reducing racial discrimination in determining their eligibility for government work, while union and employer records in recruiting women to apprenticeable trades would be as important as their record in attracting racial minorities in determining their compliance with the new federal criteria.

Significant as these changes could have been over the long run in reducing female occupational segregation and its costly economic effects, they had little immediate impact, even during the height of commitment to sexual equality during the Carter administration; they were watered down during the latter 1970s as a result of conflicting political priorities, political compromises, and administrative inertia by otherwise well-meaning federal and local administrators.[21] Most CETA programs at the city level are run out of the offices of

*One example of an apprenticeship program is the Employment Project of the Iowa Commission on the Status of Women, sponsored indirectly through a CETA grant to the Iowa State Employment and Training Council; the author is familiar with this program because it was directed by Louise Lex, on leave from the Political Science Department at Iowa State University.

mayors, and the city directors of CETA programs have been confronted by Congress with a multiplicity of targeted disadvantaged groups whose employment and training needs they are legally bound to meet under CETA guidelines, but funds are limited. Thus city directors must exercise discretion in determining how to appropriate the funds and at the same time adhere to the overall spirit of CETA regulations. Many city directors were affiliated with the civil rights movement and Great Society programs of the 1960s and thus have empathy with the employment problems of urban black and Hispanic males. When CETA funds have not been expended solely to keep minority workers on city payrolls from being laid off, such directors, as a result of their backgrounds, have rationalized using the funds to reduce the threat of urban violence stemming from a 40-50 percent unemployment rate among young inner-city black and Hispanic males—at the expense of programs for women.

In certain states like West Virginia and Texas, CETA employment and training programs for women were eliminated by the late 1970s on the grounds that jobs for other groups had priority and because of political pressure against the allegedly "radical" preparation of women for nontraditional occupations.[22] In these and other states there has been a conspicuous absence of women's organizations on local CETA planning and private industry councils, which oversee the compliance of the prime sponsors with Congressional mandates in the programs; as a result, the problems of female occupational segregation have failed to receive serious attention by local directors. Between 1977 and the end of 1979, an estimated four hundred of the six hundred CETA programs for women at the state and local levels throughout the United States were abolished.[23]

Concerned with public criticism of mismanagement and corruption in the CETA programs and anxious to counter it by a good job placement ratio, local CETA directors were reluctant to promote training and employment opportunities for women in nontraditional occupations, rationalizing that most women in such occupations would soon become discouraged and quit. Most women in the CETA program come from lower-class backgrounds and have little formal education or prior job experience; they would lack the self-esteem and emotional fortitude to stick with a job when subjected to subtle or overt forms of sexual harassment by their male coworkers. Rather than showing a high failure ratio and stigmatizing the very regulations on placing and training women in nontraditional occupations, local directors reasoned that it would be better to train most women first for traditional female occupations in which they would more easily be acclimated, accumulate some work credentials, and perhaps build up their self-esteem for future work in nontraditional occupations.

During the latter years of the Carter administration OFCCP and BAT officials did little to stimulate the demand for women in nontraditional occupations. Black male administrators in OFCCP were reluctant to push an elimination of sex discrimination in hiring among federal contractors and in apprenticeable trades as vigorously as they pushed an ending of racial discrimination. Under what one highly placed observer characterized as "black male paranoia," black male administrators feared that emphasizing sex quotas and timetables in contract compliance or apprenticeship rulings would politically undercut their long-term concerted effort to convince trade unions and employers to open up previously all-white crafts and trades to racial minorities. The regulations on the minimum number of construction jobs and apprenticeable trades which had to be filled by women were contiuously reduced and the timetables extended by male officials in the OFCCP in 1978-80—even before the election of a Reagan administration totally unsympathetic with the need to institute affirmative action through federal regulations.

In all fairness it must be noted that OFCCP officials during the Carter administration had been subjected to indirect lobbying pressures from construction contractors and unions (through Congress) who claimed that it was not possible to find and train a sufficient number of women to meet federal criteria. Furthermore, in 1979 the OFCCP was given the additional responsibility of enforcing the compliance of schools with equal employment provisions in hiring and promotion. (Until then this responsibility had rested with the Civil Rights Office in the Department of Health, Education, and Welfare, which had been successful in obtaining court rulings occupying much of the efforts and attention of the OFCCP in 1979-80.) The OFCCP was already overloaded by its mandated priorities to reduce sex discrimination in the banking and coal mining industries, where some successes were achieved in 1979 and 1980.*

*As if these responsibilities were not enough, the OFCCP had long been notorious as a dumping ground for less competent administrators in the DOL and for temporary placements from other executive departments.

It has been observed that the general failures of CETA and OFCCP programs to reduce sex discrimination essentially resulted from traditional male biases and insensitivity. With a scarcity of resources, time, and available jobs, male officials did not tackle the problem of job opportunities for women with the same seriousness and concern they devoted to finding jobs for men denied meaningful career opportunities because of racial discrimination. They readily interpreted urban crime rates of racial minorities as a social pathology which could be corrected through training and employment for males. However, not even liberal male officials recognized that widespread pregnancies among unwed thirteen-year-olds were the female equivalent of the same pathology, rooted in a lack of meaningful life and career opportunities for many young women in American society because of poverty.

POLITICAL DETERMINANTS OF POLICY

FEMINISTS AND FEDERAL POLICY

The biases against occupational equality of male DOL officials (who were conceded even by ardent feminists to be well intentioned, accessible, and cognizant of the reasons for de facto sex discrimination) may point up on the national political level the types of psychological barriers working women must overcome throughout society. With the election of the Reagan administration and a conservative takeover of the Senate in 1980, policy advocates concerned with occupational sex discrimination could not even hope to have well-intentioned and aware administrators in policy-making positions. By the first half of 1981, there had been severe cutbacks in CETA funding, and bills had been introduced in the Senate which would preclude government enforcement of affirmative action programs and guidelines, thus signaling an abandonment of the policy premises which had prompted the Carter administration to attempt to rectify the occupational segregation of women.[24]*

*All the difficulties associated with CETA programs and funding under the Carter administration seemed insignificant in retrospect by the fall of 1982: CETA was eliminated entirely by the Reagan administration, and a new jobs training program funded at only $2 billion was approved by Congress with no provisions for affirmative action or even placement of targeted disadvantaged groups in actual jobs.

Yet the feminists in and out of American government even during the latter 1970s did not despair of their ability to bring about at least partial changes. Instead they focused their efforts on short-term and more immediately obtainable measures to reduce the extent of female occupational segregation. It is in this context that they have urged a widespread adoption of alternative work schedules throughout the private and public sectors of the American economy. In essence they have advocated a qualitative change in the conventional terms of employment that would make employment more compatible to the dual roles of many married women and to the equal entry of women into skilled and professional vocations. Indeed regulations adopted subsequent to the reauthorized 1978 CETA legislation and at the special pleading of women's groups explicitly encouraged employers to devise flexitime and work-sharing alternatives for female CETA participants to reduce one major artificial barrier to their employment in nontraditional vocations.

Rather than eliminating irregular work patterns, causally linked to the occupational segregation and underemployment of many women, advocates of equal opportunity urge the universal adoption of alternative work schedules as a policy in the American labor force.[25] The very meaning, mobility potential, and status of temporary work would be fundamentally altered by opening up and encouraging permanent part-time employment in highly skilled and professional vocations as normal. Women would have a greater genuine choice in the quality of their temporary jobs, a greater opportunity to display their aptitudes and skills, and real equality in consideration for full-time jobs matched to their abilities and with start and stop times (under flexitime and compressed schedules) allowing them to care for their children or continue their education.

It is important to note that advocates have neither singled out an increase in alternative work schedules as a privilege for women (as has been done in the Soviet Union), nor limited their value concerns to the economic advantages of widespread alternative work schedules. On the contrary, they have emphasized both their equity and economic efficiency and have urged that women and men alike be given the option and encouraged to select them. If a policy on alternative work schedules were not made universal and applied to both sexes, part-time work would retain the stigma of dead-end and low-status temporary work for women despite the good intentions of utilizing it to break down occupational segregation in the labor force.

Advocates maintain that alternative work schedules for both women and men would alleviate a situation in which many skilled and professional women lose vocational credibility by dropping out periodically during their childbearing years (between the ages of twenty-five and forty) while their male counterparts remain full-time employees and accumulate the skills and work continuity which is translatable into a future advantage in career promotions. In addition, women would suffer less de facto discrimination from employers who, anticipating the women's periodic absences during childbearing years, have been reluctant to hire, train, or advance part-time employees. A wider availability and acceptance of permanent part-time jobs would allow women involved with childbearing and childrearing to earn income, develop or maintain their professional skills, and build up their self-confidence and a work resume while having sufficient time for their families. If they wanted to assume a full-time career after their children entered school (or if full-time wages become a necessity as the result of a divorce, for example), they would be qualified. They would avoid the problem confronting many highly educated women who became homemakers after they graduated from college and attempted to find a job for the first time twenty years later. Lacking a work record and unfamiliar with changes in their professions over the interim, these women cannot qualify for anything but semi-skilled clerical work.

As they view the future American home, feminist advocates anticipate that if it were typical for American husbands to be employed on alternative work schedules, they would be more willing to share household and childrearing responsibilities equally with their wives. In addition, they would feel less inhibited about expressing suppressed nurturing and nonaggressive "feminine" traits and giving freer rein to the evolution of their personalities. In this light, some feminist supporters have identified alternative work schedules with attempts to transcend artificial sex roles in American society and induce a gradual acceptance of a more truly egalitarian and androgynous society in which both women and men feel free to break out of rigid sex-role behaviors and in which inherently male or female traits would receive equal value at home and at work.[26]

The model frequently cited by American advocates has been Sweden. As part of an overall attempt to reduce de facto sex roles and discrimination, the Swedish government in 1974 passed (and in 1978 amended) legislation eliminating the concept of maternity leaves and instituting a nine-month"parental leave" subsidy for childcare. Considering a husband and wife to be a family unit jointly responsible for childcare, the state pays a subsidy to the family commensurate to its reduction of work hours by the employers of the husband or wife until their child reaches the age of eight. Unlike maternity leave, childcare is not assumed to be the responsibility of just the mother: during parental leave either a husband or wife by their choice can alternate periods when either one reduces his or her work hours and stays home to care for a newborn infant.[27]

The Swedish experiment with parental leaves has proven disappointing for some feminists in that in most instances it has been wives who have reduced their shifts. Others have deduced from the Swedish failure that in the United States alternative work schedules must be introduced on a gradual and long-term basis. One supporter of alternative work schedules concluded that an environment must be created over an extended period in which both sexes—and especially men—come to accept permanent part-time employment and work-sharing as natural. A cultural predisposition toward regular full-time employment cannot be changed by administrative fiat or the establishment of arbitrary quotas for the number of jobs which must be set aside for permanent part-time employment or work-sharing. If this is attempted, as in Sweden—where parental leaves were enacted without a gradual preparation of the populace—men will resist alternative work schedules as a loss in work status; women primarily will assume them, and occupational segregation will continue.[28]

The proposed expansion of alternative work schedules provides feminist advocates with the political advantage of supporting what appears to be only an incremental policy change in an established labor practice. Temporary jobs have always been an accepted facet of employment in the United States, and as projected by these advocates, alternative work schedules would not involve a radical redistributive change which would ostensibly threaten powerful interests and force government and business to bear the costs of social engineering. While women and sexual equality have been central concerns of these advocates, they have (as noted above) carefully guarded against the identification of alternative work schedules as a "women's issue" and have structured public debate over the proposed expansion to emphasize its broad-based advantages for employers, employees, and—most important—the society and economy as a whole.

Advocates have emphasized that flexitime has become accepted and proven economically successful in several Western countries since its introduction in 1967 in the Messerschmidt Research and Development Center in Munich. In his 1977 macroeconomic study, Owens concluded that one third of the Swiss labor force, 5-10 percent of the white-collar workforce in West Germany, and at least one million employees in Great Britain, France, and the Scandinavian countries combined worked some flexitime mode.[29] In the United States by 1977, an estimated 2.5-3.5 million employees (approximately 5.8 percent of the workforce) had been transferred to flexitime modes— 12.8 percent in nongovernmental organizations with 50 or more employees and 200,000 federal employees. An additional million workers were employed on compressed work schedules, and 17 percent on part-time shifts (although the majority of these were women employed as temporaries in unskilled and seasonal work).[30]

A 1978 microeconomic survey of public and private employers in the United States revealed that in 290 firms flexitime, compressed work schedules, work-sharing, and permanent part-time employment were the norms, while a 1977 questionnaire of personnel practices in 34 state governments disclosed that 18 made some allowance for alternative work schedules.[31] Innovative state governments like those of Wisconsin, Massachusetts, and California—long in the forefront of initiating policy reforms only later emulated by the other states—have led the way with alternative work schedules as well.[32] Since 1972 they have passed laws establishing flexitime and compressed work options and work-sharing experiments for state employees (Wisconsin), mandating part-time employment and quotas for all state agencies and grades of state personnel (Massachusetts), or (as we already noted in Chapter 1) authorizing partial unemployment compensation for private- and public-sector employees who adopt work-sharing as an alternative to layoffs (California). Perhaps nothing more clearly indicates the feminist projection of alternative work schedules as unradical and incremental than the close financial and organizational association of such mainstream corporations, trade unions, and business interest groups as McDonald's, the Communications Workers of America, and the Chamber of Commerce with the major clearing-house supporting an expansion of alternative work schedules— the National Council for Alternative Work Patterns (NCAWP) in Washington, D.C.[33]

The success of advocates in structuring public debate over alternative work schedules as simply a noncontroversial and incremental change with broad-based benefits is perhaps best demonstrated in the passage of two public laws by the United States Congress in April 1978 mandating a formal expansion of alternative work schedules as programmatic goals for the 2.2 million civilian employees in the federal workforce.[34]

One law, the Federal Employees Flexible and Compressed Work Schedules Act, established a three-year experiment through 1981 on flexible and compressed work schedules in agencies desiring them. While a considerable number of federal employees already worked on flexitime informally prior to the passage of the law, the law for the first time specified flexitime as a discrete administrative management option and program for all federal agencies; in addition, it mandated that during the experiment the Office of Personnel Management (OPM; formerly the Civil Service Commission) evaluate the effects of flexitime on specific goals concerning government efficiency, agency availability to the public, transportation and energy usage, and general employee morale. Although agencies would voluntarily opt to introduce flexitime (with the consent of their trade union representatives), a broad sample of agencies differing by size, activity, location, and personnel composition would deliberately be included as control groups for measuring the achievement of the goals specified. The provision for compressed work schedules in the federal workforce was the only source of controversy during House and Senate hearings on the bill. Union leaders questioned how compressed times would affect standard overtime guarantees for employees; the law consequently provides for the temporary suspension of overtime guarantees for employees working compressed shifts of eighty-hour biweeks in which the total number of hours worked in one week exceeds forty.

Congress subsequently failed to appropriate sufficient funds for the OPM to carry out the evaluation. However, a nongovernmental survey conducted by Halcyone Bohen and Anamaria Viveros-Long compared respondents in one federal agency transferring to flexitime under the 1978 law with a control group in another agency remaining under regular work schedules. It found that by 1981 over 90 percent of the respondents in the flexitime agency were very satisfied with the reform and wanted the program to become permanent; the subgroup of married couples without children showed a particularly high level of satisfaction. Yet other results of the survey proved disappointing for the authors' principle hypotheses about the broader socioeconomic benefits of flexitime. Respondents in the flexitime agency did not differ significantly from those in the control agency in sharing domestic responsibilities with their spouses, reducing stress on women from the dual burdens of work and family, improving women's career opportunities, or markedly improving the quality of parenting and childcare.[35] No similar surveys have been conducted for federal employees on compressed work schedules, but the general impression among administrators in the program in 1980 was that ten-hour four-day weeks had become extremely popular among many grades of personnel in different Washington-based agencies and—like the Bohen and Viveros-Long survey for flexitime would suggest—seemed to have contributed to the goal of raising employee morale.

The other law, the Federal Employees Part-time Career Employment Act, provided for a part-time option of sixteen to thirty-two hours per week for federal employees through grade GS 15 (a grade just below that of deputy assistant secretaries in federal agencies and averaging an annual full-time salary of $50,112 in 1980). Like flexitime, part-time employment had been informally used in the federal workforce prior to the passage of the law, but part-timers— or "intermittents," as one OPM official characterized them—were actually temporary workers in the worst sense of the term "temporary." In most instances they were low-skilled female clericals hired for short periods; their employment was not formally sanctioned by the OPM, and it did not provide them retirement, health, or job security benefits normally available to all regular full-time federal employees. Indeed this type of employment (along with the practice of agencies in contracting out work to consulting firms in the private sector) had become a standard agency subterfuge over recent years to get around the stringent personnel ceilings for all federal agencies imposed by the Office of Management and Budget (OMB) in the Executive Office of the White House. These ceilings pertain only to regular full-time personnel on an agency payroll at the beginning of each fiscal year (1 October). By employing intermittents for work of thirty-three to thirty-nine hours per week after the beginning of

75

the year and "attriting" them (or dropping them from the official payrolls) before a personnel count was made, agencies until 1978 had been able to show literal compliance with limitations.

In an executive memorandum in September 1977 President Carter encouraged more part-time employment among federal employees. (He had already defined alternative work schedules for women in the federal workforce as a distinct feminist issue during the presidential campaign of 1976. In a speech before the National Women's Political Caucus in October 1976, he promised, if he were elected president, to expand alternative work schedules in the federal workforce (among other things) as a means to improve the political and economic status of women in the United States.) This and the passage of the part-time employment law improved both the quality and conditions of part-time federal work. Agencies now were mandated to seek out and provide part-time employment options, while those currently employed in or applying for part-time work were entitled to full or pro-rated fringe benefits. (Part-time employment counts only as a pro-rata percentage of full-time in-grade employment for promotion considerations.) In annual personnel development programs submitted to the OPM by regulation, agencies must include specific goals and timetables for establishing part-time positions through grades GS 15. In essence the status of part-time employment for federal employees has been upraised and removed from the twilight zone of temporary clericals hired periodically during the year as a form of scab labor to meet peak agency workloads and still comply formally with absolute personnel ceilings.

The law clearly specified the work groups to be served by part-time employment and the benefits to be gained. Part-time employment would increase the availability of jobs and thus reduce unemployment (particularly among racial minorities by implication), and it would increase the opportunities of individuals with training and experience to keep their administrative skills current. It would also increase government efficiency and employee productivity because there would be fewer turnovers and less absenteeism, and work-hours would correspond more accurately to the actual times required to complete assignments. And it would serve to better employ those whose productive potential had gone underutilized in the past because of their inability to work a standard workweek— for example, older employees desiring a phased retirement, the handicapped, students needing to finance their education or gain vocational training, and "parents" (not specifying men or women) needing to balance their family responsibilities with supplementary income.

In contrast to the flexitime and compressed schedules law, the part-time employment law was generally considered very "political" by those involved in its passage and implementation: the federal government had now come to support a *qualitative* revision of conventional work modes within its own workforce in which working less than forty hours no longer required employees to sacrifice fringe benefits nor forced them into low-paid and low-status vocations. Observers have consistently stressed the broader implications of the law. If successful with federal employees, the law could be a precedent for similar reforms throughout the economy. The clear intent of the law was to expand part-time options for middle- and upper-level professional employees without de jure or de facto harm to their professional status for later career advancement in the federal workforce.

To convince agency heads to recruit part-time personnel and to counter their resistance and the even greater initial resistance of the OMB, the law provided for a phased-in change in the calculation of personnel ceilings. The OMB had always set personnel ceilings in terms of absolute numbers of official employees, whether or not they worked a full forty-hour week. During the fiscal years 1978-79 and 1979-80, in an experimental format termed "full-time equivalency," five agencies were allowed an absolute number of full-time positions rather than an absolute number of personnel for their ceilings. Thus they could hire as many employees as desired within their allotment of full-time positions. Anticipating that the substitution of full-time equivalencies for absolute numbers of employees would prove successful, the law stipulated, and the OMB later condoned, the adoption of full-time equivalencies for all federal agencies beginning with the 1981 fiscal year.

The success of the program established by the permanent part-time employment law can be judged by statistics compiled by the OPM for the twenty-five largest federal agencies in a June 1980 semiannual report on part-time employment submitted to the Senate Committee on Government Affairs (see Tables 1 and 2). In eleven months in 1979, part-timers increased by an average of 8 percent, per agency; eleven agencies averaged increases over 20 percent. It

77

Table 1

PART-TIME CAREER EMPLOYMENT IN FEDERAL AGENCIES IN 1979

Agency	As of 31 December 1979		Change in Part-Timers, 31 January-31 December 1979	Women[c]	Men[c]	Minority[c]	Handi-capped[c]	Under 23 Years[c]	Over 55 Years[c]
	Number	Percent							
	(1)	(2)	(3)	(4)	(5)	(6)	(7)	(8)	(9)
Agriculture[a]	5,090	4.2%	+6%	69.5%	30.5%	11.7%	4.5%	13.9%	6.9%
AID[a]	248	4.1	+20	—	—	—	—	—	—
Air Force[a]	1,224	0.5	+1[b]	62.0	38.0	21.5	5.5	12.8	6.4
Army[a]	1,864	0.6	+15	61.4	38.6	29.6	5.3	10.5	7.9
Commerce[a]	4,105	9.7	+219	68.2	31.8	17.2	5.5	8.1	5.4
Defense (other)[a]	136	0.2	+24	78.4	20.7	17.7	5.5	12.1	3.4
EEOC[a]	1	0.0	-66	100.0	0	0	0	0	0
Energy[a]	486	2.3	+60	83.9	16.1	14.2	7.8	17.1	8.8
EPA[a]	761	5.5	+82	79.0	21.0	28.1	3.0	15.5	3.8
GSA[a]	871	2.3	+121	63.7	35.9	34.4	5.0	11.9	7.5
HEW[a]	8,044	4.9	5	88.1	11.9	24.0	4.2	14.3	5.6

78

Table 1 (cont.)

Agency	(1)	(2)	(3)	(4)	(5)	(6)	(7)	(8)	(9)
HUD[a]	131	0.7%	5%	83.7%	15.4%	21.2%	6.4%	4.9%	8.9%
ICA[a]	39	0.4	-13	86.5	13.5	19.4	0	10.8	29.7
Interior[a]	4,727	5.9	+2	61.6	37.0	18.0	6.0	10.6	6.3
Justice[a]	372	0.6	+4	31.7	68.3	34.2	1.9	18.2	4.5
Labor[a]	543	2.3	+108	84.9	14.7	25.0	3.3	16.4	8.6
NASA[a]	122	0.5	+22	86.5	13.5	21.9	4.9	24.0	3.1
Navy	1,744	0.6	+3	65.8	34.2	30.2	4.6	7.6	7.5
NLRB	24	0.8	+60	95.0	5.0	25.0	0	15.0	0
NRC	38	1.2	-12	98.0	2.0	10.2	8.0	28.6	6.1
OOT	601	0.8	+21	81.9	18.9	18.0	3.1	10.0	14.7
OPM[a]	703	8.6	+13	83.4	16.6	29.1	4.1	19.0	5.7
State	139	0.6	+153	90.0	10.0	36.8	2.8	12.3	10.3
Treasury[a]	2,551	2.1	-33	80.6	19.4	20.8	4.8	12.8	9.8
VA[a]	14,374	6.2	-1	42.1	57.2	21.0	6.7	5.1	9.0
Overall Full-Time Federal Workforce:				37.6%	62.1%	22.1%	7.6%	7.9%	14.6%

Source: Arch S. Ramsay, Associate Director for Staffing Services, Office of Personnel Management, "Statement before the Subcommittee on Civil Service and General Services of the Committee on Governmental Affairs, United States Senate," 10 June 1980, p. 7; columns 1 and 3: SF-113; columns 4-9: Central Personnel Data File.

[a] Official part-time program established pursuant to Part-Time Career Employment Act of 1978.

[b] Based on April 1979-April 1980 data.

[c] As of 31 July 1979.

is important to note that the increases occurred while personnel ceilings were still being calculated according to absolute numbers of employees (except for the five agencies discussed above) and during a time of hiring freezes. In testimony before the Committee on Government Affairs in June 1980, Arch Ramsay of the OPM anticipated that the number of part-timers would increase once ceilings were calculated according to full-time equivalency; an additional stimulus would come from a two-year experiment granting direct authority to selected agencies (without OPM oversight) to identify, seek out, and hire individuals in local labor pools potentially inclined towards part-time employment but unaware of the option.[36] This direct authority would supposedly raise the priority of part-time employment in the annual program development plans and allocations of many federal agencies. According to one OPM official, it would benefit part-time employment because part-time had tended to get "lost in the bureaucratic shuffle" relative to the other program development changes required of all agency heads under the comprehensive Civil Service Reform Act of 1978.

More significant than the increases in part-time employment have been the qualitative changes in it by the end of 1979—evident both in the diverse work groups in the approximately 50,000 federal part-timers to whom it has appealed and in their reasons for selecting it. For example, in eleven of the agencies listed in Table 1, at least 20 percent of the male employees opted for permanent part-time work. Minorities, the handicapped, and employees over fifty-five on phased retirement have been well represented among those selecting it. As seen in Table 2, the largest increases in part-time work occurred among middle- and upper-level professional-technical personnel (GS 7-9 and 10-12). Surveys of the part-time labor force conducted in individual federal agencies (like OPM) have revealed that childbearing has prompted only 29 percent of employees to transfer to part-time, while others have cited a desire to continue their education for career advancement (26 percent) or to have more time for other interests (31 percent).[37] The impact of the program on changing sex roles was reported in the *Washington Post*: men as well as women in the upper grade levels had taken advantage of the part-time option to spend more time with their families or for other noncareer activities.[38]

In his Senate testimony, Ramsay discussed the benefits of the program specifically for female personnel in the Departments of

Table 2

FEDERAL PART-TIME PERMANENT EMPLOYMENT:
TRENDS BY EMPLOYEE GRADE, 31 JULY 1978-31 JULY 1979[a]

Employee Grades	Salary[b]	Part-Time Employees		
		1978	1979	Change
GS 1-3	$ 7,210-11,634	7,169	8,846	+23%
GS 4-6	10,049-16,293	12,889	15,710	+21%
GS 7-9	13,925-22,147	3,112	4,121	+32%
GS 10-12	18,760-32,110	1,884	2,548	+35%
GS 13-15	29,375-50,112	738	890	+21%

Sources: Ramsay, p. 8, and Central Personnel Data File.

[a]Does not include Postal Service employees.

[b]Full-time annual ranges as of October 1979.

Commerce and Labor. In the past many female field interviewers in both departments had been hired as "intermittents" without fringe benefits—even though many had worked in the same positions for fifteen to twenty years. With the formalization of part-time employment, these women would receive fringe benefits, and they would be elevated to a career status equivalent to that of employees in identical grades and with similar responsibilities in their departments.[39]

The relatively easy passage of the part-time law and its successful implementation to date can in part be credited to the careful projection of the reform by advocates in the House and Senate hearings on the proposal in 1977 and 1978 as well as behind the scenes. On the one hand, they did not completely downplay the appeal of the reform to the public conscience as a means of reducing sex discrimination, or deny that the part-time program would have advantages specifically for women. Federally Employed Women (FEW), an organization formed to advocate improved work opportunities for women in the federal workforce, in particular was closely involved behind the scenes in moving the part-time bill through Congress, and it has provided substantial technical expertise to Congressional and OPM staff in formulating specific personnel regulations for the final law.*

On the other hand (as we noted above), advocates structured the reform less as a feminist issue than as an incremental change beneficial to employers, employees, government, and many groups in society. (In the final draft of the law women are not even singled out as one of the specific groups allegedly benefiting from permanent part-time employment.) The strategy was similar to that used for alternative work schedules—i.e., mobilize the widest support and minimize political opposition, especially the anti-feminist sentiments among the emerging New Right. Perhaps not inadvertently the bill's Congressional status as a "sleeper" (in the words of one Congressional staffer)—i.e., a bill having low political visibility and little controversy surrounding it—was positively affected by the higher priority and visibility of the Civil Service Reform Act, which was also being considered and passed by Congress in 1978. This act, emphasizing improved efficiency in the federal workforce, established a more favorable political climate for the consideration of the part-time bill in that light. An official from Colorado commented during the House hearings: "I'm really glad to hear all the other testimony because before today I've heard mainly that this is a woman's issue. As I get more and more into it, I see and feel very strongly it should not be only a woman's issue."[40]

Indeed a major theme in the House and Senate hearings for justifying both the flexitime/compressed time and part-time bills was their alleged contribution to increased economic output and worker productivity, which had already been demonstrated with alternative work schedules in both the public and private sectors. Witnesses testified that bank officials in Massachusetts, state social workers in Wisconsin, employees in regional social security offices, and supervisors as well as assembly-line workers in industrial enterprises all produced more or performed more effectively when given the option of adjusting their work schedules or transferring to part-time shifts. They also testified that with alternative work schedules tardiness and absenteeism had been reduced and employee morale

---

*Lynn Revo Cohen, FEW's principal lobbyist, is a long-time specialist on part-time employment; prior to her association with FEW, she headed a part-time careers project in Women's Lobby, a national women's political interest group.

increased. The testimony and writings of numerous corporate executives, city and state planners, and academic management specialists lent further credence to the proposition that permanent part-time employment would be a mainstream and conventional change.[41]

As a precedent to legitimate the incremental nature of the reforms, Representative Gladys Spellman (D-Maryland) presented her flexitime-compressed time bill before the House Post Office and Civil Service Subcommittee and persuasively defended it by referring to the success of a similar program that she had instituted for county employees while a county legislator in Maryland. Neither she nor Representative Patricia Schroeder (D-Colorado), chair of the subcommittee and perhaps the leading feminist policy advocate in Congress, overemphasized the feminist aspects of either bill or pointed out that they were strongly backed by the Women's Congressional Caucus in the House of Representatives. In the OPM in 1977, Barbara Fiss, an administrative program analyst, won unanimous support for the bills among otherwise skeptical officials by emphasizing the widespread use of work reforms in the private sector and their proven managerial efficiencies from her personal knowledge. In the White House, Beth Abramowitz of the Domestic Policy Council was instrumental in getting President Carter to follow through on his 1976 campaign promise. In addition, she acted as a conduit to bring together Congressional staff, specialists in OPM, and OMB officials, who, while opposed to the provision in the part-time bill for personnel ceilings to be based on full-time positions, nevertheless were politically neutralized not to oppose the bill publicly. An earlier version of the part-time bill had passed the Senate in 1976 but had languished and died in the House, in great part because of the rigid adherence of OMB officials to absolute personnel ceilings.

In addition to increased output and productivity, reduced transportation costs and increased accessibility of government agencies to the public were included among the major broad-based benefits which would be derived from the bills. With employees on flexitime and compressed work schedules, federal offices allegedly could remain open outside of the normal eight-hour and five-day schedules, during which many in the private sector work and cannot take time off to go to government agencies. Furthermore, regional officials in the western time zones could call Washington officials and find some still at work past the normal closing time for the eastern time zone.

Prior to and during the hearings, Congressional and executive staff specialists mobilized interest in the bills among a wide array of interest groups for the handicapped and older Americans to demonstrate that the legislation had appeal for other than just women. Indeed the House Select Committee on Aging and the Senate Sub-committee on Aging (of the Labor and Human Resources Committee) had long sponsored legislation to expand part-time employment opportunities for middle-aged and older Americans and had developed a strong policy commitment to it. Older American interest groups like the Gray Panthers and the National Association of Retired Federal Employees not only testified in favor of the bills during the hearings, but also used their political ties to help build a broad coalition for the part-time legislation. Moreover, it was far from accidental that the first non-Congressional witness during the House hearings would be Bronfenbrenner, who stressed the importance of alternative work schedules as a means of reducing family stress and improving family stability and the quality of childrearing. Defining alternative work schedules as a pro-family and pro-child issue deflects criticism of the reform as an attempt to weaken traditional family structure by increasing the number of mothers who work.

Representatives Stephen Solarz (D-New York) and Yvonne Burke (D-California) introduced alternative bills to the initial House bills which could have flagged open political opposition as "radical" feminist reforms. The Solarz bill obligated most federal agencies to adopt flexitime and compressed work schedules, and the Burke bill, cosponsored by forty-five other members of the House, required that an absolute and increasing percentage of positions in each GS grade be set aside for part-time employment over the next five years; the intention was to have 10 percent of federal employees on part-time within that period.

The Solarz bill (based on provisions of model alternative work schedule bills drafted by women's interest groups) was criticized in the House hearings by Civil Service Commission officials who objected to losing control over agencies. The Burke bill was criticized by male union leaders, who feared that the "set-aside" provision would discriminate against regular full-time personnel in grade advancement, and by Civil Service officials who claimed that it would be impractical and politically difficult to enforce such a pro-vision. They pointed out that a similar provision had been set up in

Massachusetts but had not ever been met. Several officials feared that minimum quotas of part-timers would create widespread resentment among agency heads against the very principle of part-time employment. In contrast to the civil service commission of Massachusetts, which is smaller and has been less administratively aggressive, OPM has a large administrative staff which would be both honor-bound and more capable of compelling literal compliance by agencies to any "set-aside" provisions Congressionally authorized. With the passage of the Civil Service Reform Act, agencies would be overburdened with paperwork, and these quotas would further aggravate their personnel problems; for their administrative survival, agency heads might unite in opposition to any part-time programs. OMB was at best lukewarm to the principle of part-time in 1978; the opposition of a number of agency heads would have sounded the death knell of any part-time bill.

The concerns of OPM officials may not have been unfounded. Even though both the Solarz and Burke bills were rejected during the mark-up session of the full Post Office and Civil Service Committee of the House, 84 members in the House still voted against the final quite moderate version of the part-time bill when it came to a vote, and 141 members voted against the flexitime/compressed time bill, which failed to receive the necessary two thirds majority under suspension of the House rules and was approved only on a second vote.

Despite a semblance of wide support for the final bills, those directly involved in their passage were aware that feminist advocacy groups were the prime movers. As one policy participant observed:

Although there was testimony and lobbying from a wide spectrum of considerations, interests, and groups, the major support and staying power of support—indeed, the people who really drafted the legislation—were members of various women's groups in and out of government; and it was they who essentially got the legislation through. The others were merely window dressing to broaden the political appeal of the legislation and legitimate it.[42]

Following a pattern evident in other Congressional legislation for women successfully passed in very recent years, the successful passage of these two bills also testified to the ability of a loose network of feminists in and out of government to focus public consideration on the incremental, broad-based, and nonfeminist advantages of reforms intended primarily for working women.[43] However, the linkage of alternative work schedules with broader issues was not just a political strategy to gain passage of the bills; it also reflects a fundamental underlying change in the American women's movement, as well as a shift in the general political climate toward increased support for women's issues from other groups and interests in society.[44]

In the early 1970s the leadership in the women's movement had a narrow base—professional, middle-class, and college educated. They supported exclusively "feminist" issues which often found them at odds with other groups—e.g., trade unions, civil rights organizations, and the liberal wing of the Democratic Party—with which they should have found common ground. The opposition of the national AFL-CIO leadership to the Equal Rights Amendment (ERA) when it was proposed in 1972-73 symbolized the extent of mutual distrust; union leaders perceived that the orientation and priorities of women's groups threatened working-class Americans in general and working-class women in particular.

Perhaps a turning point in the distrust came with the formation in 1974 of the Coalition of Labor Union Women (CLUW)—women trade-union activists and officials concerned with the marginal role of women in the trade-union movement, the insensitivity of a male-dominant union leadership to the problems of working women, and the narrow base and concerns of women's groups at that time. By the end of the 1970s CLUW had raised feminist concerns to a much higher priority within the trade-union movement and had become an institutionalized force in trade unions akin to the union subgroups like A. Phillip Randolph branches, which represent black trade unionists. Its growing impact could be seen on several levels: the increasing number of women trained and recruited from local CLUW chapters for local, state, and regional union work; the endorsement by the AFL-CIO of women's concerns like the ERA and comparable pay for work of comparable value to raise wages in female-dominant vocations; and the election in 1980 of the first woman to the national executive council of the AFL-CIO—Joyce Miller, President of CLUW and Vice-President of the Amalgamated Clothing and Textile Workers.[45]

As a result of changes in the women's movement (reflected, among other factors, in the growing impact of CLUW in trade unions), there has been a building of political bridges among groups and a broadening of the so-called "women's political network" nationally. Women in different organizations and social classes have begun informally to work together for common goals based on an implicit awareness that they have all suffered as women from various forms of discrimination. Women's groups and trade unions have jointly sponsored and lobbied for reforms in the national health insurance program and for changes in social security and pension coverage for homemakers. Women's groups have allied with civil rights and poverty organizations in such groups as the Ad-Hoc CETA Coalition to support increased federal spending for CETA programs.[46]* Black feminists like Eleanor Holmes Norton, prominent in the Carter administration as chair of the Equal Employment Opportunity Commission and a visible spokesperson for the problems of both black and women's groups, personified the growing union between women's groups and a broader liberal constituency for their concerns.

By the latter 1970s, the women's movement had also matured politically. Groups like the National Organization for Women (NOW), while not abandoning a basic commitment to their female constituency, began to reach out to noncareer women as well as to other groups. In 1975 Betty Friedan warned that the problems of American women could not be solved by women alone and that women must forge coalitions with other groups on the basis of common suffering from the same systemic inequities; NOW responded by redefining its political strategy and positions on issues in such a way as to appear less exclusive and threatening to other interests and groups in their own priorities.[47] It redefined what had been exclusively "feminist" issues as human issues which affected men as well as women and working women as well as homemakers. In turn, the growing political influence of women's groups and issues nationally seemed evident in the extent to which the liberal-labor coalition embraced them by the latter 1970s as a natural part of its membership and action agenda for reform. A contributing factor in the

*Among the groups in the CETA coalition by 1980 were the Urban League, the National Urban Coalition, the Women's Work Force, the League of Women Voters, the American Federation of State, County, and Municipal Employees (AFSCME), the National Congress for Community Economic Development, and the Community Legal Services of Philadelphia.

new alliance between the liberal-labor coalition and women's groups was a common threat posed by the New Right, whose growing political influence could be attributed in part to the fears it aroused in depicting the changing role of women and to its organization of opposition to issues like the ERA and abortion rights. A cross-cutting if informal alliance of women's and liberal-labor groups seemed to share a common perspective on problems and reforms, even though the relevance of individual reforms and their priority still varied for the different groups and their particular constituencies. The Democratic Party Convention in 1980 adopted a platform supporting federal Medicaid funding for abortions and prohibiting campaign funds to any Democratic candidate opposing the ERA— and what had been women's issues at the beginning of the 1970s had thus apparently become an integral part of the mainstream liberal orientation in American politics by the end of the decade.

As women's groups reformulated their strategy, they began to forge broader support for alternative work schedules among groups attracted to the reforms for their own reasons. These reasons have expanded the scope of affected interests linked to the work reforms, which if they had remained perceived just as a women's issue would probably never have generated the necessary visibility and legitimacy for American decision-makers. The 1978 federal laws and increasing sentiment in favor of alternative work schedules in some state governments and the private sector can only be explained by the linkage of the issue with these other affected interests and concerns. Three of the most fundamental concerns to which alternative work schedules have been linked are unemployment, equality, and the quality of American lifestyles and the workplace. Let us consider these in some detail.

UNEMPLOYMENT AND EQUALITY AS DETERMINANTS OF POLICY

As indicated in Chapter 2, policy support for reduced work shifts in the USSR has come from (among others) economists and officials who have begun to question a dogmatic commitment to full employment and who are concerned with the low labor productivity, slow growth, and irrational underutilization of the labor force to which this commitment has contributed. The problem of an overabundance of unskilled workers dragging down the Soviet economy has become more serious as efforts have increased to introduce new technology and rebalance the mix of automation with fewer and more highly skilled workers to stimulate long-term growth. By advocating a reduction of work-hours for women, they seem to have found an issue through which they can publicly air their concerns about the negative effects of overemployment on the economy — the major problem of all Eastern European systems. Pronatalists have joined these advocates for their own reasons, as they too would like to reduce the labor force attachment and hours worked by Slavic and Baltic women to encourage higher birthrates among them. Selective unemployment of a predominantly unskilled and politically passive female labor force is one way to interpret the broad support and implications of reduced work shifts in the Soviet policy context.

In contrast, in the United States growing support for alternative work modes has emanated from liberal economists and policy advocates primarily concerned with the inability of the American economy to lower unemployment rates below 7 percent even in good times. Among these have been Fred Best (policy analyst with the National Commission on Employment Policy and the Economic Development Department of California); Barry Stern (policy analyst in the Office of the Assistant Secretary for Education); Isabel Sawhill; Representative Schroeder; Eleanor Holmes Norton; Sar Levitan (director of the Center for Policy Studies at George Washington University and a principle architect of the Great Society programs during the 1960s); Gene Livingston (Chief Deputy Director of the Employment Development Department of California); California Senators James Mills (president pro tempore) and William Greene (chair of the Industrial Relations Committee); and many trade union officials, particularly in AFSCME. These economists and policy advocates agree that the declines in economic growth and the failures of federal employment programs to alleviate unemployment since the early 1970s can be traced to underlying changes in the American economy and a general reluctance of government decision-makers to recognize these changes in drafting new programs. Conventional economic programs in the last two decades have been frustrated by four major phenomena: inflationary pressures, an unprecedented growth in the civilian labor force, a value reassessment of whether unlimited economic growth should be the highest priority of economic policy, and a technological revolution with a concomitant expansion in the average education of the labor force.

First, because of the worldwide inflation since the early 1970s (attributable in part to numerous increases in the price of oil), governmental pump-priming to stimulate a demand for new jobs has only fueled already high inflationary rates to dangerous double-digit figures, while increases in prices and employer costs have led to recessionary downturns and a slower increase in new jobs than anticipated or economically justified by governmental expenditures in new job program monies. Conventional Keynesian premises about the ability of government to maintain an optimal balance among expenditures, inflation, and real growth have seemed to lose their relevance. In the last few years the interpretations of liberal and conservative economists have crisscrossed and overlapped as they have groped for new models and concepts (like "stagflation") to account for an economy experiencing both rising prices and declining growth rates.[48] Furthermore, by the end of the decade candidates for public office had become very sensitive to charges of fueling inflation through excess federal outlays to stimulate the demand for new jobs. Thus even if traditional economic measures to reduce unemployment still worked (which they no longer seemed able to do under a complexity of inflationary forces internal and external to the American economy), a national political will to address the problem of unemployment was seriously lacking.

Second, as a proportion of the adult population (which of course has also grown in absolute terms), the labor force has increased from 58.1 percent in 1960 to 61.6 percent in 1975; economists expect that it will grow to at least 63.2 percent by 1985.[49] Much of this growth can be attributed to the changing values and rising expectations for meaningful employment of women and racial minorities, both of whom in the past would either not have entered the labor force or would have been excluded because of sex and racial discrimination. This added supply of job claimants explains the seeming paradox that thirteen million new nonagricultural jobs were created from 1973 through 1979 while total unemployment rates in the 1970s continued to rise and reached what appeared to be a floor of 6-7 percent. The simple reason is that with women and racial minorities, more people are actively seeking work. In addition, as a result of a Congressional law in 1978, the retirement age for most workers was extended to seventy, so older workers are remaining in their positions longer, and thus fewer positions are opening up to workers just entering the labor force. Like a rat on a revolving wheel running just to stay in place, the American economy would have to create at least twenty-one million more jobs in 1990 than existed in 1975 to reduce unemployment to what was previously considered a full-employment rate of 4 percent.[50]

Third, contributing to the problems of endemic inflation and an increase in job claimants has been a questioning of the "more is better" philosophy. With the emergence of environmental consciousness, plants and industries that impair health and pollute the environment no longer are automatically welcomed as godsends to offer jobs and increase economic growth.[51] Moreover, growing numbers of Americans recognize that there are real limitations to growth because of the energy crisis. Given that energy reserves are dwindling worldwide, industries which might increase jobs in the short run are not necessarily promoted if they would wastefully expend or demand new energy resources to operate.

State governments have begun to examine the possible advantages of flexitime in terms of gasoline savings during peak commute times. In 1980 the National Governors' Association and the Intergovernmental Personnel Administration funded a study of energy savings from flexitime through the National Council for Alternative Work Patterns, and a study in Denver has examined the gasoline savings from compressed work schedules for city employees. The concern with energy usage has been prompted not just by the reality of dwindling resources, but also by a realization that rising energy costs have forced a reduction in the number of jobs available and will continue to do so in the long run. As a larger segment of the public has become aware of tradeoffs between the values of economic growth and those of environmental safety, health, and energy depletion, now more often than two decades ago in the United States, questions such as the following have been raised: What must be sacrificed to create further economic growth and more jobs? Is the sacrifice worth the short- and long-run costs to future generations? Given the costly and limited energy resources, can economic growth produce more jobs?

Fourth, as a result of the technological revolution—computers, robots on assembly lines, semi-conductors, and electronic word processors—labor intensity in many plants and offices has declined. To remain productive and competitive in world markets, American industries will probably increase their investments in new technologies, which may lower the rate of growth in new jobs during the 1980s and 1990s. Moreover, some skeptics predict that the new technology will further dehumanize the work environment and alienate employees from their work.

The problems connected with automation have been exacerbated by the educational overqualification of recent entrants into the labor market.[52] By 1980, 66 percent of all Americans 25 and older had a minimum of a high school degree and 55 percent of federal employees had at least some college education; 20 percent of all American workers are expected to have a four-year college degree by 1985.[53] While the number of professional-technical jobs has continued to increase over recent years, it has failed to keep pace with the supply of professional-technical graduates entering the labor force. As a result, the disparity has increased between the number of skilled jobs available and the number of workers with higher education. At the same time, however, a general college background inadequately prepares students for the specific kinds of new vocations opening up in a technologically revolutionary economy, and they will be forced to accept jobs at lower salaries and skill levels than their actual vocational aptitudes and education would warrant. As previously noted, by 1979 the number of women enrolled in colleges had surpassed the number of men, and in the 1970s the average educational attainment of black workers increased from two years of high school to at least one year of college. (By 1980, the census disclosed that 51 percent of all blacks had at minimum a high school degree.) With their education advancing and their career aspirations growing, women and racial minorities will add to the cumulative sense of frustration felt by the "new breed" of workers (to use a term posited by Daniel Yankelovich) who have come to expect a higher quality of work life with real opportunities for advancement, self-fulfillment, and personal growth.[54] Surveys by Yankelovich have revealed that one half of college graduates feel unfulfilled and underutilized in their jobs compared to one third of non-graduates.[55]

The cumulative effect of these long-term changes on traditional macroeconomic growth policies has been such that they no longer can or will work in reducing unemployment. New ways must be devised to spread a diminishing number of jobs among a larger, more educated and more demanding labor force. Microeconomic changes in the number of hours worked have been gaining increasing support among economists and policy advocates. Evidence of their ability to marshal support has been particularly evident in California. In November 1977 a one-day hearing was held in the California Senate Select Committee on Investment Priorities and Objectives on alternative work modes as a means to reduce state unemployment rates. Not only did the hearing reflect California's path-breaking role in devising such programs, but it also assumed the appearance of a national policy forum as officials from the federal government and other states testified that the California experiments had relevance for national problems of work and unemployment.

Several witnesses at the hearing discussed an innovative program instituted in Santa Clara and San Mateo counties.[56] As a consequence of the national recession of 1975-76 and severe budget deficits, county supervisors had been forced to propose massive layoffs in county health and welfare departments. Rather than accept the layoffs, the local public service unions and the county governments negotiated a program termed Voluntary Reduced Hours. Every six months employees would be given the option of participating in the program by accepting a reduction in their annual salaries between 2.5 and 20 percent; in turn, they would receive a commensurate number of unpaid vacation days. These vacation days would be covered by full health and social security benefits and would be added to the cumulative days of employment in paid status (although they would be calculated at a lower hourly rate). In essence the employees would exchange some earnings for additional leisure time. As a result of the program, the counties were able to retain a regular complement of professional and technical employees, and no full layoffs were necessary.

Although the program was originally intended as an improvisation to save jobs during the recession, 18 percent of the employees eligible for the program in Santa Clara county have continued to enroll in some form of it, and a "voluntary reduced hours" provision has become a standard feature of labor contracts for county public service employees. Participation remains voluntary, and employees have the option of changing their reduced time percentage or dropping out from the program every six months. Conversely, departmental supervisors retain the right of refusing participation to particular employees; some have refused fearing that if a part-time staff met the service performance of a full-time workforce, county governments would have justification to reduce their annual salary budgets and staffs in the future. The program has had mixed success and employees have expressed qualified enthusiasm, but local trade-union officials have been actively involved and have been able to negotiate fair terms and protection for their members against arbitrary abuses of the program (such as work speedups). From testimony at the 1977 hearing, it seems to have succeeded as a short-term measure to weather budget deficits by retaining a current workforce and service performance. If continued (even on a more limited scale), the program could provide the basis for hiring additional employees and increasing services without significant increases in salary budgets.

Similar reduced time or work-sharing programs have been adopted nationwide—at Pacific Telephone and Telegraph, the California Department of Motor Vehicles, the *Washington Star*, Hewlett Packard, Pan American Airlines, the Western Electric Company, and the state of Wisconsin. In all of them the first priority has been the provision of employment for regular employees and a voluntary and selective adjustment in the terms of employment to retain as many workers as possible in sectors threatened with increasing costs or declining demand.[57]

The various programs have resulted in numerous projected benefits. First, employees have not been laid off; in consequence they have not had to depend on unemployment or welfare payments, and they and their families have been spared the intangible psychological damage of job uncertainty. Moreover, given the voluntary nature of such programs, a reduction in income has not seemed oppressive, and given the increasing trend toward families with two wage-earners, the reduction of one income has not caused the hardships it might have caused two decades ago. Second, employers have been able to maintain profitability margins sufficient to keep their companies operating with a normal complement of employees. The possible disadvantages of an aggregate reduction in work-hours and the added costs of contributing to health and social security benefits for part-timers have been more than offset by a reduction in termination costs for training new employees or rehiring old ones and by increases in labor productivity and the quality of work from employees on reduced work schedules. Third, unemployment levels have been somewhat stabilized without unnecessary and inflationary government outlays for unemployment insurance, welfare benefits, and public service jobs. Economists have conservatively estimated that if 20 percent of the national labor force accepted an average 10 percent reduction in current earnings in exchange for vacation time and if only 50 percent of that time were used to hire the unemployed, approximately one million new full-time jobs would be created. As one observer noted, such a microeconomic adjustment for California alone would lead to approximately 100,000 new jobs without necessitating any inflationary expenditures to generate those new jobs by the state or federal governments.[58]

None of these projected benefits have as yet been overwhelmingly convincing to either employers or employees. Employers still profit more by laying off employees than retaining them on reduced time or work-sharing arrangements. For laid-off workers employers do not have to pay social security, health, or unemployment insurance contributions, which may cost as much as one third of gross salary outlays. Moreover, two part-time workers would cost employers more in terms of unemployment insurance than one full-time worker because salary ceiling levels determine how much employers must contribute for each employee. For example, for a ceiling of $20,000, employers would be taxed on about $6,000-$7,000 per employee; thus two part-timers earning $10,000 each would cost twice as much as one full-time employee earning $20,000. Like employers, employees have been reluctant to accept alternative work schedules. With spiraling inflation, many—even those in two wage-earner families—cannot afford to exchange even a small portion of their forty-hour wages for additional vacation time.

Partly to counter the disincentives against work-sharing and encourage employers to try it rather than lay off workers, California— again in the vanguard—in July 1978 instituted "Short-Time Unemployment Compensation" (STC) as a supplement to its standard unemployment insurance compensation program. Following the basic outline set down by Gene Livingston,[59] the STC (known also as "Shared Work Unemployment Benefits") provided unemployment insurance for employees who were working less than five days a week. It was implemented in November 1978 on a three-year trial basis, and a review of its effects was scheduled for 1981.

Legislative momentum for some type of STC preceded the passage in November 1978 of Proposition 13, which significantly reduced local revenues through across-the-board decreases in property tax rates.[60] Members of the Senate Committee on Industrial Relations had consulted with government administrators in Western European nations with lengthy experience in work-sharing programs before developing draft bills on STC. The anticipated approval of Proposition 13 created a sense of urgency among committee members and chair William Greene, prime sponsor of the legislation. Although it was feared that primarily public-sector jobs would be cut after Proposition 13 passed, the final STC law included both private- and public-sector employees. Indeed by June 1980, only 8 of 840 firms adopting work-sharing STC for their employees were in the public sector; typically the private-sector firms were in manufacturing and employed fewer than 50 workers.[61]

Under the work-sharing STC plan, when an employer out of economic necessity must lay off part of his workforce, he can apply to the Economic Development Department for a work-sharing plan by which all employees are retained but their total weekly hours are reduced by an amount equivalent to the aggregate number of hours of those who otherwise would have been laid off.[62] In turn, the state agrees to compensate these employees with unemployment benefits for the hours they no longer work. For example, if a firm opts for STC work-sharing instead of laying off 20 percent of its workforce, the employees will work and receive wages for four days and receive from the state 20 percent of their normal unemployment benefits for the fifth day (usually amounting to one half or less of their daily salary). However, the STC program carries restrictions: reduced work time must be at least 10 percent for firms to qualify for the program, and STC benefits apply for a maximum of 20 weeks. By June 1980 the program covered only 37,475 employees; the vast majority of unemployed (430,000) fell under the provisions of regular unemployment insurance benefits requiring almost a complete dismissal from their jobs to be eligible for benefits.

California has been the only state so far to adopt a work-sharing STC plan. In the other states, according to a federal-state formula, weekly benefits from partial unemployment cannot exceed the difference between those benefits and an employee's salary. Thus employees essentially must be unemployed almost four days a week to qualify for benefits without exceeding the ceiling allowed. In consequence, neither employers nor employees have very much incentive to devise work-sharing plans. Wages from two or three days of work per week would make the employees completely ineligible for any unemployment insurance payments, which essentially penalize employees even for marginal labor-force attachment.

Advocates of the California STC plan have pointed to its financial merits as well. The unemployment compensation paid out to participants is more than recouped by their contributions to the Social Security and Unemployment Insurance Trust Funds. Furthermore, both the state and federal governments have benefited because wages are taxable while public assistance payments are not. According to Livingston, the most important benefit of the program has been that it has saved jobs, many of which would perhaps have been lost permanently and resulted in higher unemployment rates for the state in 1979 and 1980.[63]

The promise of the California work-sharing STC in spreading available work around and holding down unemployment rates has attracted interest and support at the national decision-making level. In Congress the most outspoken advocate of STC has been Patricia Schroeder, who introduced a bill in June 1980 mandating the Secretary of Labor to use $10 million over three years to draft model legislation patterned after California's in other states, make grants and provide technical assistance to states voluntarily adopting trial programs, and conduct controlled demonstration projects evaluating the effectiveness of STC in various locales. Schroeder's bill languished in the House Ways and Means Committee and failed to be voted upon by the full House in 1980. A major problem of the bill appeared to be its unfortunate timing (at least as evidenced by the formal testimony during the hearing on it on 26 June 1980).[64] It was considered along with two other more conventional unemployment compensation bills which would have had more immediate and visible effects by extending unemployment benefits by 1980 for areas experiencing long-term high unemployment. (Unemployment figures for May 1980 had shown significant increases as a result of massive layoffs in the automobile industry and other manufacturing sectors during a recession early in the year.) In addition, STC was criticized as a somewhat premature policy for the federal government; the California program had yet to be proven effective, pending the completion of a study by the California Employment Development Department and the U.S. Department of Labor.

Schroeder's bill focuses on the need for the federal government to be a pacesetter in reducing unemployment rates and altering the typical pattern in which layoffs are borne by a "relative few to pay for the cost of a recession."[65] Eleanor Holmes Norton, the long-time enthusiastic advocate of work-sharing, remarked the following when Schroeder's bill was introduced:

> It is a good idea because for the first time since the New Deal it gives us some flexibility in dealing with hard-core unemployment that we as a nation have been very unsuccessful in dealing with . . . . Because of economic circumstances, work-sharing is a concept whose time has arrived nationally. You have to remember that in Europe and Japan work-sharing is wholesale. We are a country that has tolerated large-scale unemployment, where our allies have not. I think that there will be less opposition to work-sharing because California has already begun to show that work-sharing works.[66]

The relative success to date of alternative work schedule programs can be attributed as much to the general recognition that unemployment is a persistent national dilemma as to the persuasive arguments of advocates. Not only would lowered unemployment rates represent broadly based benefits nationwide, but also if they were lowered by means of alternative work schedules, no one would have to bear any direct costs. Thus work-sharing can be logically defended in the political arena as one pragmatic solution to unemployment.

The pragmatic spirit and mix of broadly perceived benefits with few direct costs to any groups or individuals do not color another affected interest and concern to which alternative work schedules have been closely linked during recent years in the American policy context—namely, systemic job discrimination, especially against racial minorities, and the polarizing conflict over attempts to alleviate racial job discrimination through special hiring and promotion privileges for these minorities. The 1960s in the United States were characterized by the passage of civil rights legislation in 1964, 1965, and 1968, the establishment of specific federal agencies to implement that legislation, and a clear-cut philosophical division between liberals and conservatives over the merits of civil rights. In the 1970s controversial federal regulations—under the rubric of "affirmative action"—attempted to implement that legislation. Special efforts would now be made to increase the share of minority job hirings and university placements. Public and private employers would be monitored to ensure their compliance with federal guidelines; those unwilling to meet these guidelines would be subject to various sanctions, ranging from a loss of federal monies and contracts to civil damages and criminal fines. In essence affirmative action means an attempt must be made by employers, prompted by government, to level up racial minorities to a starting point in the American economy from which they can then factually compete on a par with whites in the society. As noted, under Title VII of the Civil Rights Act of 1964, women were deemed a discriminated group under affirmative action, although (as we noted in our earlier discussion of the U.S. Labor Department) federal agencies have been less diligent in pushing affirmative action programs for women than for racial minorities.[67]

The federal commitment to affirmative action sparked growing controversy and public opposition, particularly by the latter 1970s. Many white workers felt unfair reverse discrimination was being perpetrated against them by the federal government in collusion with racial minorities. Their sense of resentment was heightened during the recession of 1979-80, when many in the manufacturing industries were laid off while the government at least formally continued to endorse affirmative action programs in hiring for racial minorities and women. In the 1980 Republican Party platform there was a conspicuous absence of endorsement for affirmative action, and the support for Ronald Reagan from ultra-conservative groups totally opposed to special preferences for racial minorities indicated the extent to which it had become politically profitable to question the very premises of programs designed to aid disadvantaged groups. There were also crucial desertions from the ranks of liberal academicians and groups which had been strong advocates of civil rights during the 1960s. Termed "neo-conservatives" and closely associated with journals like *Commentary* and *Public Interest*, these erstwhile liberal academics (like Nathan Glazer) denounced the government's efforts as "affirmative discrimination" and rejected what they argued were the institutionalization of arbitrary racial and sex quotas which violated the true spirit of equal opportunity underlying liberal traditions of American culture. Advocacy groups of American Jews, many of whom had been in the forefront of civil rights supporters during the 1960s but who had suffered from the imposition of affirmative action quotas, filed *amicus curiae* briefs in support of litigants challenging the constitutionality of affirmative action programs and guidelines. Indeed court cases involving university admissions and workplace hirings and promotions bitterly divided liberals among themselves.

The malaise and divisions among liberal groups committed to egalitarian ideals were aggravated by the moral issues involved. On the one hand, in terms of substantive equality it seemed clear that because of historical patterns of discrimination and their racial caste status at the bottom of the socioeconomic ladder in American society, racial minorities could never achieve equality of opportunity without special compensations. Even critics of affirmative action programs have been unable to propose any objective measures of success in eliminating racial discrimination other than the numbers of minorities who have been admitted to universities or hired in work settings subsequent to the adoption of timetables or quotas.[68] On the other hand, in terms of procedural equality, a mainstay of the American liberal tradition, it would seem that decisions on job hirings, promotions, and layoffs should be based solely on a neutral principle of seniority, long fought for and won as a basic right of social justice for all American workers over the last four decades. That right is particularly important for white blue-collar males, who have experienced inequality of opportunity not because of race or sex but because of the rigid class divisions in American society.[69]

Even were the political differences over affirmative action not reflective of fundamentally irreconcilable views of social justice between advocates of substantive equality and procedural equality, efforts to enforce affirmative action programs in the 1970s were continuously stymied because of the general economic slowdown. Providing equality of opportunity with federal legislation seemed a heady possibility in the 1960s, when the economy was booming, stimulated by federal spending during the Vietnam War and unemployment below 4 percent; but it seemed less likely with the recessions of 1974-75 and 1979-80, a stagnant economy, and unemployment figures which did not fall below 7 percent. Even socially conscious employers found themselves unable to meet affirmative action guidelines because few new positions in their firms were becoming available. As Eleanor Holmes Norton pointed out, the 1979-80 recession was particularly devastating to racial minorities and women; they had only begun to gain a "toe-hold" in previously all-white male vocations during the 1970s, but now they were the first to be laid off because of low seniority, and they were "back on the streets."[70] Furthermore, they were caught in a vicious cycle: hired because of affirmative action, they were laid off because of low seniority, which they could not accumulate because they were the first to be laid off during economic downturns.

Against this background of controversy surrounding affirmative action and the inability of the economy to generate enough new jobs to make affirmative action possible, many policy-makers have seen an advantage in expanding alternative part-time employment options such as California's STC. First, such options would avoid the major political and economic obstacles associated with affirmative action. The total number of jobs would be expanded without taking away jobs from white males, and claims of reverse discrimination—and the racial animosities connected to those claims—would not be raised. In addition, the total number of jobs would be expanded without increasing inflation through federal expenditures for jobs programs. Some economists project that the absolute number of jobs would increase as a result of work-sharing and part-time modes because the labor productivity and output of more efficient part-timers would increase real gross national product and hence a demand for workers. White males would not be competing against women and racial minorities, and a surplus of demand for workers would make the goals of affirmative action realizable.

Because work-sharing would increase the number of positions available, employers could better meet affirmative action guidelines. Indeed one of the arguments in favor of the 1978 federal part-time law was that it would allow agencies to meet their own affirmative action guidelines, with more available slots at higher grades to be filled by women and racial minorities; by 1979 OPM officials were encouraging federal agency heads to design part-time hiring goals as part of their affirmative action plans.[71] In the private sector, according to one analyst, "The corporations of course are very aware of equal opportunity requirements, and they look upon part-time and work-sharing as one means to bring more women into higher-level management positions in their corporations."[72]

101

Second, an expansion of work-sharing and part-time modes would more likely achieve employment equality for women and racial minorities without being reversed by what political sociologists might term the reactionary "political temper of the times"— which is reflected in growing attacks on blacks in American cities during 1980, a seeming resurgence of the Ku Klux Klan, a greater tolerance for pseudo-racist views in public debates, and the landslide victory of Ronald Reagan and defeat of several liberal senators in the November 1980 elections. With the threat that the Reagan administration and a conservative Congress may remove the ability of federal agencies to enforce affirmative action programs, both women's and black civil rights groups may place a greater emphasis on work-sharing and part-time modes to allow women and racial minorities at least to hold onto or to enter positions no longer set aside for them in certain proportions under affirmative action.

To date few black civil rights leaders other than Norton have consistently endorsed alternative work schedules as a means to counter racial injustices in the labor market, but the current political situation may persuade them of the necessity for compomises in their long-term commitment to full-time jobs. Signs of change in political sentiment were already evident prior to the 1980 elections. For example, Senator Greene of California, the principal sponsor of STC, represents the predominantly black district of Watts in Los Angeles. In addition, during the 1980 hearings on Representative Schroeder's bill, strong endorsements for work-sharing came from the National Urban League, Benjamin Hooks (Executive Director of the NAACP), Richard Hatcher, (black mayor of Gary, Indiana), and Jesse Jackson (President of the Chicago-based Operation PUSH).[73] A lack of such endorsements during previous Congressional hearings in 1977 and 1978 had seemed by default to define alternative work modes as simply a "women's issue."

The Reagan administration, not wishing to leave festering massive unemployment in the inner cities and sensitive to charges of indifference toward minority problems, had indicated by 1981 that it was interested in rethinking conventional notions of work in order to reduce minority unemployment rates. Among administration proposals has been a special minimum wage for youths (lower than the national minimum wage for adults) in order to provide greater incentives for employers to hire unemployed inner-city teenagers. Moreover, the administration may encourage an expansion of work-sharing through legislation such as the Schroeder bill. Administration advisers may judge that employers would be more willing to hire four youths for what otherwise would be three job openings if there were a special youth wage, if youths could be hired for fewer than forty hours per week, and if their salaries were supplemented by unemployment benefits through some form of STC.

It seems apparent from testimony during the House hearings on Schroeder's bill that work-sharing STC would be a program which would meet the ideological litmus test of conservatism by letting the private sector resolve social problems free of any governmental dictate. Greene has attributed the swift passage of the STC in California in great part to the bipartisan support it received from liberals, conservatives, businessmen, and even tax-cutting Proposition 13 organizations;[74] companies like Motorola have endorsed the Schroeder bill not only as a pragmatic measure to save jobs, but also because it leaves initiative and control in resolving unemployment in the private sector.[75] Even the American Chamber of Commerce, while considering federal sponsorship of work-sharing "premature," did not oppose the concept outright during testimony it submitted on the Schroeder bill.[76] And it is interesting to speculate that since President Reagan and his highest White House advisers come from California, they are at least likely to be familiar with the work-sharing STC reform instituted in their native state since 1978.

The political attractiveness of work-sharing STC for the Reagan administration is still conjectural. Yet it may be that Schroeder was encouraged enough by political signals from the Reagan staff to reintroduce her bill in April 1981, at least with the expectation that if the bill passed Congress, it would not be vetoed by Reagan. In May 1981 Secretary of Labor Raymond Donovan indicated further administration interest in alternative work schedules by proposing to end a long-standing Labor Department ban on industrial work completed at home and open job opportunities in cottage industries — not dissimilar from the "homework" option in the Soviet Union.[77] As in the Soviet Union, the political climate in the United States may lead the national leadership to expand alternative work schedules, but for reasons very different from those advanced by supporters in the Soviet academic-research community (as noted in Chapter 2) or by American interest groups committed to greater equality for women and racial minorities.

SOCIOCULTURAL DETERMINANTS OF POLICY

Significant as the problems of unemployment and racial discrimination are in American politics, the chronically unemployed in the United States still constitute an unorganized, divided, and politically marginal group unthreatening to decision-makers,[78] and racial discrimination in employment remains a highly contentious issue not totally accepted or understood by a majority of white Americans. Very few public or private decision-makers in the 1970s were so bold as to endorse alternative work schedules solely or even primarily to reduce unemployment or to equalize job opportunities for racially discriminated groups. On the contrary, it appears that concerns with unemployment or discrimination have been offered by advocates of alternative work schedules chiefly to broaden the base of appeal for work reforms, not as their primary reasons for supporting the reforms. Confronted with major problems, decision-makers will tend to rationalize reforms which they can defend in their own self-interest, which seem to represent safe, limited departures from the status quo, and which already seem to have gained acceptance in the predispositions and attitudes of a majority of the public. Because alternative work schedules now fit these criteria, they appear to be realistic and practical reforms. Their "practicality" stems from major sociocultural changes during recent years and the attempts of decision-makers to cope with these changes.

The current prominence of the alternative work schedules issue can only be understood against a background of long-term changes within the labor force. An indisputable sign of a major shift in the labor force has been a growing concern by management, trade-union officials, and political leaders over phenomena that became known through the pop sociology of the 1970s as "blue-collar blues" or the "Lordstown syndrome."[79] Specifically the phenomena referred to emerging discontent and dissatisfaction among a new generation of industrial workers, who were less inclined to accept the dictates of the Protestant work ethic and more reluctant to defer to traditional authority relations in the workplace. This new generation was the product of the "baby boom" from 1946 through 1965. By 1985 the baby-boom generation is expected to make up one third of the population in the United States.[80] Demographers and sociologists would dispute whether those in the baby-boom generation represent a distinctive phenomenon in American society—i.e., whether their anti-establishment attitudes and values will carry throughout their adult lives and fundamentally alter society—or whether their attitudes reflect a transitory stage in socialization typical of rebellious and undisciplined youth throughout history. Nevertheless, their very numbers and their entry into the labor market during the 1960s and 1970s (when anti-war sentiments and the drug culture legitimated a questioning of authority) have so reshaped conventional worker attitudes that national surveys have identified the emergence of a prevalent "new breed" among American workers.[81] In contrast to past generations, members of this "new breed" were much younger and more highly educated on average, more anti-establishment and questioning of social-class identities, and less willing to accept that regimentation and monotony in assembly–line work were unchangeable conditions. They did not have memories of working–class solidarity and of struggles to gain union recognition in the 1930s; they expected wages and pension benefits as a birthright and were less willing to believe that alienation on the job was the necessary price of job security.

As Kanter and Stern have concluded, the "new breed" expects to be treated with respect and dignity by employers, feels both the right and necessity to participate in managerial decisions affecting its work environment, and wants a higher quality of work–life in which jobs offer opportunities for personal growth, a feeling of progress, and career mobility.[82]* As opportunity and power were generally not available under conventional work settings, the new generation exhibited dissatisfaction and rebellious attitudes toward both employers and union leadership through increased rates of absenteeism and tardiness, high rates of turnover, general indifference to jobs and unions, and falling rates of labor productivity.

*Kanter has argued that a general absence of opportunity and power in the jobs filled by many women has been the major structural reason inhibiting women psychologically and behaviorally from achieving greater equality in the labor force (Rosabeth Moss Kanter, "The Impact of Organizational Structure: Models and Methods for Change," in Ratner, ed., pp. 311-27).

These phenomena first gained notoriety at the Lordstown, Ohio, Chevrolet plant in the early 1970s: rebellion among younger workers spilled over into systematic and deliberate sabotage of assembled automobiles and wildcat strikes against newly automated assembly-line procedures, which workers considered a further management speed-up to squeeze additional profit at the expense of the workers' self-worth and creative control of the work environment.

More skeptical sociologists question the contentions of (for example) Yankelovich and Kanter and Stern that there has been a fundamental generational shift in values among American workers.[83] Their skepticism seems not totally unfounded, for such contentions are often based on closed-ended and vaguely worded survey questions whose responses can be interpreted in different ways and tend to exaggerate aggregate changes over time. Furthermore, even if the survey measures are valid, worker alienation at a sociopsychological level of analysis may be more directly dependent on such factors as fluctuations in personal life cycles, as workers individually experience different aspirations and seek different rewards at changing stages in their lives.

Despite the skepticism of some sociologists, more corporations and trade unions perceived that a generational shift had become widespread in the 1970s, and they structured a policy context in which workplace reforms became a major priority. Corporations like General Motors suddenly became aware of a need to rethink conventional procedures of management and organization which had not been challenged since the introduction of standardized assembly-line procedures ("Taylorism") by Henry Ford in the 1920s. There was a growing corporate awareness that autocratic approaches would no longer prove effective but could prove counterproductive to worker enthusiasm and motivation. Plant organization would have to be adapted to the emerging concerns and demands of younger workers; greater emphasis would have to be placed on worker-management communication in devising more human work environments.[84]

General Motors (GM), the largest American corporation, has been a bellwether in industry. Its commitment to a new management style has evolved into the corporation's so-called Quality of Work Life (QWL) approach in the 1970s. Under QWL, GM managers have been instructed to devise more flexible work patterns and participatory forums in concert with plant workers and local officers of the United Automobile Workers (UAW). New work patterns would eliminate some of the more monotonous and emotionally stultifying aspects of the work environment, while the forums would give workers some direct participation in shaping the work environment and in making planning decisions. The normal adversarial relationship between union and management has not been eliminated, but the intent is to seek common grounds of understanding and concern between workers and management and to resolve commonly recognized problems jointly.

The commitment of GM to worker participation through QWL has not been motivated solely by concerns over worker rebellion or growing management-labor tensions. It has been prompted as much by a concern that labor productivity in GM specifically and in the United States in general was declining relative to that in other industrialized nations like Japan and West Germany.[85] GM executives had become aware through their international affiliates that in these other countries since 1945 workers had often directly participated with management in designing work environments and arriving at plantwide decisions; both Japanese and German workers were made to feel that they had an important stake in the final products manufactured in their plants, and worker alienation had been somewhat alleviated by making workers feel they were part of a team effort.

GM division managers are somewhat autonomous in formulating personnel policy, so innovations in worker participation vary from plant to plant. However, by 1980, in 80 of the 150 plants in the United States QWL committees had been formed. Made up of workers delegated by UAW locals and management representatives, the committees meet periodically and propose specific changes. In addition, approximately 400 GM staff specialists in QWL help to devise programs for the problems of concern to the committees.*

In some plants QWL committees have discussed and implemented proposals intended to reduce widespread absenteeism or drug abuse; in others they have helped initiate teamwork approaches in which

*The very origins of most QWL committees reflect an innovation in union-management collaboration. When a particular GM plant indicates it is having severe problems in the work environment and would like to form a QWL committee, a QWL specialist in the UAW and one from GM will visit the plant, address the workers and management, and work out particular plant problems with them.

employees decide on and share responsibility for certain operations rather than awaiting orders from a supervisor in the hierarchical chain of command. New GM plants—particularly in the southern United States—have been designed with a view to employee morale and teamwork approaches. Potential employees have been carefully screened for a psychological aptitude to work cooperatively rather than in the traditional assembly-line method. In some of the southern plants employees are given responsibility as a team to complete all phases of assembly on an industrial component rather than perform only one operation on an assembly line. One outgrowth of QWL has been annual surveys of white-collar GM employees regarding the work environment; the surveys have provided direct employee feedback on specific issues for QWL committees.

Within GM top officials began to place increased importance on QWL managerial abilities in considering lower-level executives for promotion. Through annual QWL conferences, retraining sessions for middle-level executives in QWL approaches, and a clear mandate from the international offices in Detroit, executives were cued that their advancement up the corporate ladder would presume their demonstrated commitment to QWL management methods. One executive summed it up as follows: "QWL in the 80s must be so accepted as management philosophy that people who can't accept it really can't be part of GM's top management groups."[86] Another executive expressed the same sentiment:

It's fair to say that after a decade of emphasizing QWL managerial approaches that nobody is going to be promoted within GM to a divisional general manager unless that person has a proven track record in QWL style of management . . . . For every manager in GM still unwilling to change and still inclined to be an autocrat in treating workers and organizing production, there are now fifteen who because of their exposure to QWL know there are better ways expected by GM to use our workforce.[87]

GM's growing concern with work environment issues and the cooperative spirit between GM and the UAW are not isolated phenomena in the American private sector, nor is it likely that they represent passing fads. In the early 1970s, following alarms about declining worker morale and labor productivity, Congress established an independent National Center for Labor Productivity and the

Quality of Work Life (later renamed the American Center for the Quality of Work Life) in Washington, D.C. to monitor and encourage labor-management reforms in the private sector. As more companies took an interest in the issues of work environment, worker morale, and labor productivity in the decade, a source guide was compiled describing the experiments of private firms, ranging from quality-of-work-life and work-team principles to worker takeover and management of the workplace; it listed twenty-five centers in the United States engaged solely in doing research and aiding unions, employers, and employees in devising work environment reforms.[88] Adversity appeared to be the major factor inducing workers and management to cooperate in adopting work reforms. By 1981, in an effort to avoid plant closings and job losses, a modified work-team principle termed "quality circles" was being implemented from steel plants in Weirton, West Virginia, to toolmaking firms in Mt. Pleasant, Iowa. In quality circles workers meet with management representatives on a monthly basis and on company time to discuss production problems, recommend solutions, and provide an arena for workers to affect plant production decisions.[89]

In June 1979 the Communications Workers of America (CWA) took an unprecedented step in American trade-union history: they mounted a national demonstration against the dehumanizing job pressures resulting from increased automation and computerization in their workplaces.[90] Entitled "Job Pressures Days," the demonstration included informational picketing of the American Telephone and Telegraph Company (AT&T), the major employer of the 625,000 CWA members. The protesters objected to the heightened monotony associated with increased automation, while CWA President Glen Watts urged AT&T to allow more direct employee participation in workplace decisions and to expand the opportunities for alternative work schedules.

The concern with alternative work schedules represents a consistent evolution in the priorities and concerns of the CWA. A somewhat untypical union with a larger than normal proportion of white-collar members, the CWA reflects an emerging trend not only of expanding unionization among public-sector white-collar workers, but also of changing collective bargaining concerns for all unions. In essence, the CWA and other public-sector unions representing white-collar workers have pushed for a more meaningful voice in decision-making for their membership and a less rigidly hierarchical work setting, which is still typical in plants with blue-collar workers and is accepted as the norm by the unions representing them.[91] The CWA has been a prime mover behind the National Council for Alternative Work Patterns (NCAWP) since 1976, and CWA members have been board members of the NCAWP.*

Changing concerns in the union movement can be observed at several levels. For one thing, the rebellious mood of rank-and-file members has been directed not just against employers but also against the union leadership, who is older, conservative, and male-dominant, and seems out of step with the concerns of the younger members. For another, in the last twenty-five years there have been continuous declines both absolutely and proportionally in the number of unionized workers. Total union membership in the United States had fallen from 34 percent in 1955 to 22 percent by the end of 1979, and membership in the AFL-CIO, from 16 million (21 percent of the work force) to 13.6 million (13.1 percent). Declining numbers have paralleled the decreasing economic and political influence of the union movement: from 1977 through 1980 it was unable to wrest any meaningful union legislation out of a Democratically controlled Congress and Democratic presidency; there is a greater tendency among even liberal legislators to vote against union issues; and (with some recent exceptions among newly opened industrial plants in the south) union organizing efforts have fallen, unions have lost half of all representational elections, and an increasing number of decertification elections has removed unions from industrial plants. Perhaps the most significant change confronting unions is the large increase of women in the workforce. (In addition, there has been an increasing number of new jobs in the clerical, retail, hospital, and food service sectors, which are dominated by women.) Women have traditionally been reluctant or difficult to organize into unions. While 20 percent of male workers in the United States belong to unions, only 15 percent of women do, even though the proportion of women in trade unions has increased from 23.9 to 28.1 percent since 1970, somewhat parallel to their increasing number in the workforce.[92]

*Indeed the national headquarters of the CWA and the NCAWP occupy offices on different floors of the same office building in Washington, D.C.

Union leaders have drawn the logical conclusion that the viability of the trade union movement will depend in the 1980s and 1990s on its ability to motivate women into joining unions. In part, the leaders can rationalize the low percentage of unionized women as a result of circumstances beyond their control. For one thing, 80 percent of working women are concentrated in four female-dominant sectors (clerical, sales, low-skilled factory work, and service) which have been the most difficult for unions to organize; for another, many women hold a traditional female attitude that their job will be only temporary and will not require membership in a union to protect wages and job security. Yet union leaders have begun to appreciate that the lack of pro-union sentiments among working women can be directly attributed to the low percentage of women they see in union leadership positions and the low priority unions have placed on issues of immediate concern to women—e.g., childcare, occupational safety and health, and alternative work schedules. The leaders' awareness has been spurred in part by the CLUW. For example, a 1980 CLUW study found that of 397 executive board members on 15 national unions and 2 employee associations, only 46 (12 percent) were women— and even this was an inflated figure because of the inclusion of 12 women on the board of the American Nurses' Association (with a total female membership of 97 percent) and 8 women on the board of the American Federation of Teachers (with a total female membership of 60 percent).

In all fairness (as one officer of CLUW remarked), it is somewhat unfair "just to play the numbers game" in counting women in top union positions as an indication of their limited role.[93] Times have changed more than mere numbers would indicate. Since the early 1970s there have been significant increases in the number of women elected shop stewards, local presidents, and state or regional officials. By the mid-1980s these women will have risen to central staff positions and will constitute a significant leadership reserve from which more women will be elected onto the executive boards of their unions and even to the major office of union president. Symbolic of the increased sensitivity toward making women visible in top positions, the hard and fast rule that only presidents of affiliated unions can serve on the national executive council of the AFL-CIO was broken with the appointment in 1980 of Joyce Miller, the first female member, who is only Vice-President of the Amalgamated Clothing and Textile Workers.

With more women actively involved in unions, the cause and effect relationship between a predominantly male union leadership and a lack of union interest in women's issues has begun to wane. Like corporations dealing with a different kind of blue-collar worker in the 1970s, unions are dealing with a different membership, and their self-interest in survival will make it imperative for them to concentrate on these issues. One female union activist summarized the impact of women on future union agenda as follows:

> If you look at the increase in union membership over the last few years, you'll note that the majority of it has been female . . . and looking at the change in the number of women working, you realize that you have a great opportunity there of organizing . . . . If some people in the national union leadership begin to support our concerns with certain issues only because it's profitable or advisable from an organizational perspective, we have no real problem with that . . . . I think there are certain issues of greater concern to women, . . . and women have brought them to the forefront . . . . Thus they are aware of the traditional bread and butter concerns, but also aware of more immediate needs and have encouraged greater union support for these "women's concerns". . . . Alternative work schedules . . . has been a particular plea of our younger trade-union women because of the household. We are supporting this problem for family reasons and thus increasing the range of support which may already exist for other reasons at the local level. Women have instigated and developed new concerns for work-related and work-environment issues, which affect both men and women union members. Five years down the road you're going to see a package in conventional collective bargaining that embraces very special concerns, not the least of which will be occupational safety and health and alternative work schedules.[94]

While changing attitudes among blue-collar workers and substantial increases in the numbers of working women have done much to increase interest in alternative work schedules in the United States, these have not been major factors in the Soviet Union. However, a third change in the United States—the aging of the population—has parallels in the Soviet Union. The increased number and importance of older citizens have generated greater political support for alternative work schedules in both countries. As we noted in Chapter 2, the continued involvement of older workers in the labor force past their usual retirement age has become a major commitment of Soviet labor policy. They are particularly needed to fill service-sector jobs in cities in the European regions which are experiencing serious labor shortages as the leadership attempts to increase the availability of consumer services.

In the United States a major economic crisis—the financial bankruptcy threatening the social security system—has linked the concept of alternative work schedules with workers who would normally retire at the age of sixty-five. A larger proportion of the population is now living longer and receiving retirement benefits. By 1977 there were an estimated twenty-two million Americans past the age of sixty-five; preliminary statistics from the 1980 decennial census showed that the ratio of wage-earners contributing to social security to individuals drawing benefits had declined from 35:1 in 1945 to 6:1 in 1980.[95] Not only were fewer wage-earners supporting more retirees, but Congress, concerned with the economic plight of retirees on fixed incomes, passed amendments to the Social Security Act in 1978 providing beneficiaries with annual cost-of-living increases pegged to the Consumer Price Index. In addition to the increases in longevity, strains on the social security system come from the spiraling rates of inflation (which drove up the costs of Medicare health benefits for retirees) and unemployment (which reduced the numbers contributing into the system).

Government analysts predict an even greater financial strain on the social security system in the near future in connection with the eighty million Americans born during the baby boom of 1946-65.[96] The oldest age cohorts in the baby-boom generation had entered the labor force in 1980 and begun to contribute into the social security system; indeed it is anticipated that the baby-boom generation will be the major population group in the labor force to keep the system minimally solvent. However, a problem will arise when the baby-boom workers begin to retire and draw benefits in the second and third decades of the twenty-first century. Given a longer average life expectancy and declining birthrates in the generations succeeding them, it is projected that the baby-boom generation will constitute 27-30 percent of the entire population. In 1980 it was expected that by 2025 the ratio of wage-earners to recipients of benefits would be 4:1, and that the former would have to contribute twice as much from their salaries into the social security system as they did in 1980.[97] Because such a ratio is likely to bankrupt the system before 2025, a two-year study by a Presidential Commission on Pension Policy recommended that the social security retirement age for those born in 1946 and later be raised from sixty-five to seventy by 2010.[98]

Some analysts concede that nothing less than an entire reform of the social security system would be sufficient to make it financially solvent. Yet comprehensive reforms confront immense political obstacles. As a temporary stopgap to stem the collapse of the system, among the amendments in 1978 to the Social Security Act Congress mandated automatic increases in salary deductions for the social security system. (The proposed increases were so politically unpopular that the Democratically controlled Congress extended the original starting date to 1 January 1981—i.e., after the elections of November 1980.) Yet even this stopgap measure threatened to accelerate the already spiraling double-digit inflation and affect the proposed income tax reduction of 10 percent for 1981.

Proposals to reduce benefits for those currently on social security or those about to retire have been strongly resisted. The depth of resistance became evident in 1979, when a carefully planted political leak to the press proved sufficient to prevent the publication of recommendations by a presidential task force on social security to reduce cost-of-living allowances for beneficiaries and partially tax social security benefits. In the late 1970s as well, as a result of opposition by federal employee unions, a proposal that federal employees be included in the social security system was roundly rejected. (Federal employees have their own pension fund.) Failing to recognize the general resistance to a reduction of benefits, President Reagan suffered his first major political defeat in May 1981. He proposed a short-term package of reforms to save the social security system which included reductions in the cost-of-living increases for retirees and reduced benefits for those retiring at age sixty-two. By a vote of ninety-six to nothing, the Senate rejected the proposal and passed a resolution committing itself to oppose any reforms that would involve a reduction of benefits for retirees.

In addition to the strong resistance against reduced benefits, a comprehensive reform of the social security system would be a complex procedure. As one Congressional staffer pointed out, such a reform would have to go through no less than sixteen committees of Congress before it could be voted on by the full House and Senate. Gaining consensus from these diverse committees could take several years and several sessions of Congress. Even were a comprehensive reform introduced in 1982, final legislation might not pass both houses until the mid-1990s. Moreover, provisions could not be suddenly altered without allowing current participants sufficient time to rearrange their retirement goals. Thus a need to phase in major changes in social security over at least ten or fifteen years has been almost universally accepted by those involved in drafting reforms.[99]

As a consequence of the controversy and uncertainty surrounding reforms in social security, increasing numbers of policymakers and advisers have begun to consider the benefits of various forms of permanent part-time employment for those past the formal retirement age. Two obvious advantages would be increased revenues for the social security system (part-time workers would contribute to it) and reduced expenditures in retirement benefits (part-time workers would not be drawing full benefits). The report by the Presidential Commission on Pension Policy noted these advantages and indicated specific short-term federal actions which could expand alternative work patterns (both part-time and flexitime for those desiring full-time jobs): demonstration programs with alternative work patterns for older workers in federal employment programs such as CETA; extension of part-time work options for older workers in the federal civil service, following the 1978 Congressional guidelines for permanent part-time and flexitime work; and job retraining and redesign for older workers in the private sector through federal tax incentives and/or specific federal contract requirements for their hiring by private contractors.[100]

Alternative work schedules for older workers seem to have support across the political spectrum. In 1978 Congressional legislation raising the retirement age to seventy for most public- and private-sector employees, abolishing mandatory retirement for federal employees, and specifying older federal employees as a group to benefit from the federal permanent part-time employment act passed by large majorities. Throughout the 1980 election campaign conservative Republicans and liberal Democrats supported the principle that Americans be allowed to work at least part-time past the age of sixty-five.* The change in administrations did not reverse this emerging consensus in favor of phased retirement. Among his proposed social security reforms in May 1981, President Reagan had included a provision which would raise the ceiling on permitted earnings for retirees past sixty-five without reducing their social security benefits. In essence retirees would have a financial incentive to work at least part-time while drawing full social security benefits. The only serious opposition to this proposal stemmed from the fact that it did not provide for a phase-in period before the measure would take effect and that it involved sharp reductions in benefits for those desiring early retirement at sixty-two. However, the principle of phased retirement has become almost universally accepted as a positive change and a necessity.

It may be that demographic changes have made alternative work schedules a necessity, but support for them among Americans whatever their age or sex may reflect underlying cultural changes as well. For example, acceptance has diminished for a conventional capitalist worldview which long assumed that "normal" lives follow a prescribed linear pattern of schooling, productive work over a forty-year lifespan, and societal rewards for that work with paid retirement at sixty-five. The stereotypical ideal of the average American male in this worldview is well known: he graduates from high school or college in his late teens or early twenties, marries and begins his family in his mid-twenties, works steadily (advancing in authority and gaining in salary), raises a family in his thirties and forties (with his wife working intermittently to supplement family expenses but primarily staying home to raise the children), and happily retires at sixty-five and moves to Florida or Arizona to play golf and live off his pension. The central logic of this ideal has always been the unquestioned sequence of life stages programmed as "normal" and "desirable" and the primary value assigned to work in defining

---

*A classic liberal-conservative Senatorial campaign waged in Iowa that year serves as an example. The liberal incumbent, John Culver, and his conservative opponent, Charles Grassley, agreed on little during their pre-election debates except that older Americans should be encouraged to work past retirement through future amendments to the social security system. The winner, Grassley (who had previously served on the House Select Committee on Aging), was appointed to the Senate Select Committee on Aging in 1981. After Florida and Arizona, Iowa has the highest per capita population over sixty-five in the United States.

self-worth in American society. (Those even vaguely familiar with the last half century of events in the Soviet Union can no doubt recognize parallels in its culture and in government policies designed to instill a similar sense of self-discipline and voluntary adherence to a rigid life pattern centered around work, deferred gratification, and eventual rewards at retirement.)

Particular to the United States in the 1970s has been the very clear waning of the Protestant work ethic from the culture and a greater questioning by Americans over the last two decades about the quality of their lives, which have been dominated by a prescribed life pattern, and the alleged importance of work as the sole validation of self-worth. The stereotypical ideal seems to have lost both its relevance and its attractiveness. Its relevance has been shattered in several ways: women now remain in the labor force full-time throughout their marriages; there have been major transformations in conventional American family life (e.g., an increasing divorce rate); many men and women in mid-life are concerned with closing options and wish to start fresh through new jobs or formal education; and the inflationary economy and threatened cutbacks in social security benefits have so reduced savings and income from pensions that few can afford to retire to Florida or Arizona (assuming many men have not died from the emotional and physical damages incurred from a total forty-year absorption in their jobs). Its attractiveness has begun to ring hollow: men are becoming more involved in their families and childrearing and see in them emotional sources of self-fulfillment while deemphasizing the overriding importance of work; the "California lifestyle," celebrating immediate gratification and leisure, became a life pattern preferred by younger adults; and older Americans began to express a desire for options in addition to full retirement, questioning the life sequences in which a forced retirement seemed "nothing but a short parole whose nature is determined by the previous 30 or 40 years before retirement."[101]

The most immediate change in values appears to be against the seemingly lock-stepped nature of so many lives and the necessity of working full-time for a set period of years. As we have noted, California has been in the forefront in new popular attitudes and governmental policies challenging the conventional precepts. It is important to point out that the personal motivation for many of those participating in its work-sharing experiments of the mid-1970s

117

has been a desire to have more freedom and control of their lives. Consistent evidence from survey data and local work experiments indicates that growing numbers of Americans no longer automatically accept the necessity or desirability of working full-time in a lengthy prescribed period.[102]

The prevailing attitude among Americans seems to be that work should be combined and alternated with other things like family, education, and leisure. The particular mix of time expended on work relative to other activities will depend on what sociologists have characterized as the "family life cycle":[103] greater options for part-time work in the early periods of childbearing and childrearing for both parents, full-time jobs for both parents once their children enter school, work sabbaticals or work-sharing modes for adults in their mid-forties who wish to enter new careers or pick up their education, and gradual phased retirement with part-time work for older individuals wishing to continue working through their early seventies. Alternative work schedules appear for many to be a more flexible format in which time invested in work and in other interests can be individually tailored and better matched to their growing desires for control over their lives. Alternative work schedules constitute one of the benefits which Kanter and Stern contend more Americans have come to expect as their right from their jobs beyond mere direct income.[104]

Whatever their age, sex, race, or educational level, increasing numbers of Americans seem to share a disquiet about the set terms of their lives and their work in conventional American culture. Perhaps no other factor politically explains the growing support for alternative work schedules among the public and decision-makers than the ability of its advocates to point out the cultural shift in society and to project that the reforms are relevant for this shift and could potentially be supported by almost everyone, and perhaps it most clearly distinguishes the policy context and significance of alternative work schedules in the United States from those in the Soviet Union. Whereas in the former alternative work schedules have been closely identified with the cultural shift away from assembly-line monotony and toward a more humane workplace and lifestyle, in the latter they have been linked with government policies to emphasize "American-style" assembly-line efficiency and labor productivity. While Americans are retreating from a set lifestyle through alternative work schedules, Soviet advocates hope to reinstill it through heightened work discipline and efficiency from reduced work shifts. At worst, Soviet advocates have failed to dispel the impression of many opponents that work reforms have been motivated as well by a desire to turn back the clock for Soviet women and reinforce the more traditional cultural norms in which women's primary role will again be that of mother and homemaker.

ECONOMIC AND POLITICAL CONSTRAINTS

The issue of alternative work schedules even in the United States, however, has been far from noncontroversial and far from gaining unanimous support. Indeed the reasons for opposition to reduced work shifts in the United States bear striking similarities to reasons in the Soviet Union. In both nations opponents perceive the reforms not as essentially administrative innovations but as radical departures from the status quo, threatening both their position and self-interest.

As we observed in Chapter 2, opposition to reduced work shifts in the Soviet Union has tended to form among those who would be most affected by them: professional and skilled women, government and academic policy advisers who have foreseen grave economic setbacks from reduced shifts, sociologists who reject the simplistic pronatalist orientation linked to reduced work shifts, and industrial managers, whose material and administrative self-interest would be directly impaired. As in the Soviet Union, the opponents of the reforms in the United States are those who are convinced that the immediate short-term changes from the reforms would seriously harm their position and authority. They reject alternative work schedules as the misguided utopianism of radical reformers on the political left or the Machiavellian schemes of political opponents disguised as benign social change. They are suspicious of the negative unintended consequences from the reforms and unwilling to institute changes different from those attempted in the past.

In contrast to the Soviet Union, conflict over alternative work schedules in the United States has been quite open, and we can isolate the major opponents to the reforms as well as the reasons for their opposition. The least political opposition has arisen against flexible work schedules and a moderate amount against compressed work schedules, while the greatest resistance has arisen against the various work-sharing and permanent part-time reforms.[105]

The limited controversy connected with flexible work schedules can be explained by two factors: they involve minimum changes in the traditional work mode (workers still work eight hours daily and five days a week), and there is no overt identification in these reforms with particularly disadvantaged social groups (like women). All workers have been equally included under flexible work schedules adopted during the 1970s.

Where resistance to flexible work schedules has arisen, it has reflected traditional labor-management conflicts and nagging suspicions on both parts that the other side will gain an unfair advantage from the reforms. First, older union leaders particularly suspect that any change enthusiastically embraced by management must ipso facto be contrary to the interests of unions and workers. For them flexible work schedules constitute only a new subtle "gimmick" devised by management to extract increased profits at the expense of workers through speed-ups at the workplace. Their suspicions linger despite the persistent arguments by reform advocates that flexible work schedules humanize the workplace and reduce worker anxiety and exhaustion. Indeed their suspicions are heightened by the fact that advocates have persuaded management—through numerous time-budget studies and via professional consultants—that the reforms raise per capita labor productivity and the cost-efficient utilization of a firm's workforce. Some union leaders feel that only the narrow self-interests of management are served by flexible work schedules, which increase worker output without requiring management to pay commensurate wage increases for the workers' increased labor productivity.

Second, a more general fear of union leaders has been that flexible work schedules would undercut the influence of unions by projecting the unfounded image that management is benign and concerned with the interests and needs of the workforce. Even the most liberal union leaders have voiced doubts about reforms premised on the so-called new cooperative spirit between workers and management. They suspect that the package of reforms represents nothing other than a sham foisted by management on the workforce as a more subtle anti-union tactic of the 1970s.[106] By creating a false impression of management's solicitous concern for the well-being of workers, flexible work schedules—like other quality-of-work-life and corporate democracy reforms—will undermine the ability of unions to organize workers. Younger workers particularly, whose rebellion against the traditional workplace has forced management initiatives in such areas as flexible work schedules, will be more easily seduced into believing that they can trust management to look out for their interests without formal union representation. It has not escaped the attention and worry of (for example) the UAW that GM has tended to introduce its QWL reforms in newly built plants in the south, which has traditionally been less open to union organizing efforts.

Third, union leaders have consistently pointed to aspects of the reforms which would weaken the leverage of unions in collective bargaining and whittle away hard-fought gains. For example, many union-represented workers have the right to take time away from work for personal emergencies (like doctors' appointments) and count it against their cumulative paid sick-leave time. Union leaders fear that under flexible work schedules mangement would insist that workers make up their time away from work by working outside the core periods. They anticipate a similar loss in bargaining leverage over wages if workers concede their right to premium pay rates for evening work. In addition, they suspect that flexible work schedules will allow more workers to engage in "moonlighting" (that is, take second jobs in their off-time) and thus undermine the wage leverage of regular full-time workers in these "moonlighted" sectors.

Finally, it appears that older union leaders fear reforms such as flexible work schedules because of an inherent political threat to them. Most of them have risen to the top of their union hierarchies through a skillful advocacy of conventional bread-and-butter issues like wages and benefits. The shift in union priorities to a new agenda of problems related to the workplace may have left some of them uncomfortable and unable to offer a commitment convincing to their rank-and-file membership. It may be that the priorities of all unions by the mid-1980s will focus on occupational safety, health, and alternative work schedules, but until now it has essentially been the younger unionists who have pushed these issues—often despite a lack of enthusiasm or even outright opposition from their national leadership.* (The CWA has been one of the few unions in which the national leadership has led rather than followed the rank-and-file on such issues.) The generation gap in union leadership has meant that issues of the work environment have pitted a younger leadership against an older leadership, who may (rightly) perceive that the younger leaders are capitalizing on these issues to embarrass the older leaders and generate political opposition to them.

If lack of trust in management is a major factor behind union resistance to flexible work schedules, a lack of trust in workers accounts as well for the reluctance of managers to institute the reforms. The reforms presume a fundamentally different managerial attitude of trust toward employees: employers must have confidence that their workforce will not cheat in calculating the hours worked each day. Because of the new presumption of trust and cooperation, it has been somewhat difficult for employers to insist on the retention of punch-clocks or other supervisory tools. However, many managers still fear that employees would violate the trust by not putting in their prescribed eight hours when given some freedom in setting their hours.

In essence, well before the introduction of flexible work schedules, there must be a psychological climate of trust between employers and employees. Lacking that, workers may cheat on their hours if they are not supervised, or management may overreact and anticipate cheating. In either situation, management will perceive the reform as a dismal failure. Enough allegations of "failure" have occurred that employers considering flexible work schedules have disregarded statistical evidence that flexible work schedules contribute to significant reductions in employee absenteeism and tardiness and increased labor productivity. One policy analyst has concluded

*For example, pressure from their locals forced the national leadership of the National Federation of Federal Employees (NFFE) and the American Federation of Government Employees (AFGE) (the major unions representing federal employees) to support the 1978 flexitime/compressed time and part-time bills. The locals had backed experiments with flexitime and part-time since the early 1970s—most often without the formal approval of their national leadership and often at the initiative of women in the locals. Originally, the national leadership intended to testify against the flexitime/compressed time and part-time bills in 1976, but locals of the AFGE in the Social Security Administration mounted a successful campaign at their national convention for resolutions supporting both bills.

that the lack of managerial trust explains a continuing opposition to the reforms by many firms: "Companies already forward looking and anxious to maintain communications are more likely willing to experiment with flexitime . . . . It is usually companies afraid of losing control over their own employees who have been reluctant to introduce flexitime; there is a lack of trust and fear that workers will somehow cheat."[107]

Even employers who trust their employees have been reluctant to institute flexible work schedules because of the increased administrative responsibility. The regimented nature of an eight-hour work shift guarantees predictability and structure. Declining employee morale and labor productivity may be the by-products of this predictability and structure, but the employers' responsibility has been limited to following set procedures and expecting a compliant workforce to be on the job during set hours. Advocates of flexible work schedules point to another negative by-product of regular shifts: a conditioned decline in the capability of employers to administer their workforce. Regular shifts have minimized the need for employers to carefully set down and allocate tasks and goals for their workforce; rather than effectively utilize their workforce, it has been much easier for them simply to command. Flexible work schedules require new patterns of administration and a more involved and capable management. Employers and supervisors must be more flexible in orchestrating their workforce; they must predetermine employee tasks and harmonize the workflow because employees under flexible schedules arrive and leave at different times of the day.

Employers have anticipated these additional burdens and have resisted flexible work schedules as an unnecessary complication of their managerial role—and weak and noninnovative managers have been most likely to resist changes in the traditional work modes.[108] Such resistance to flexible schedules, however, is not uniquely American or even capitalist. As we noted in Chapter 2, a major reason for the opposition of Soviet industrial managers to reduced work shifts has been their fear that greater demands would be placed on them to utilize their workforce effectively and innovatively. Soviet managers are notorious as autocratic overseers who administer the workforce through set rules and standardized shifts. They are trained and recruited in a hierarchical command system and conditioned to run their enterprises like military garrisons at constant war with the barrage of quotas emanating from Gosplan and the central ministries. Such a managerial corps may compound the problems of flexible work schedules in the Soviet Union.

Compressed work schedules have been a more controversial issue than flexible work schedules—especially for union officials. For them the same concerns about management exploitation of workers and an undermining of union influence seem magnified in connection with this type of reform because it requires a more radical break from tradition. Two types of compressed schedules are currently in use: weekly and biweekly. In the former, employees bank forty hours by working four days a week and ten hours a day; in the latter, they bank eighty hours over a two-week period by working perhaps fifty hours the first week and only thirty hours the second week. In either alternative union officials have objected to the requirement that employees waive their right to premium pay, overtime pay, and overtime provisions when working in excess of eight hours daily or forty hours weekly. Overtime pay and provisions were established under the Fair Labor Standards Act in 1935; union officials reason that employees are setting a dangerous precedent by waiving these protections for what may be highly questionable improvements in their work conditions. At one extreme, officials suspect that management has instigated compressed work schedules, calculating that profits would increase if overtime and premium rates did not have to be paid. Moreover, officials have not been impressed by the widespread and successful adoption of compressed schedules in Western Europe, where (advocates point out) workers have not been exploited by the reform. They counter that premium and overtime pay and provisions have never been strictly enforced in Western Europe or carefully monitored by unions.[109] As in the case with flexitime, older union officials may be out of touch with rank-and-file sentiments on compressed schedules, and younger workers and women may be more willing to yield premium and overtime protections for three-day weekends.

Union sensitivity about premium and overtime provisions became particularly evident during the Congressional hearings on the flexitime/compressed time bill in 1977 and 1978. The president of the American Federation of Government Employees (AFGE) submitted testimony opposing compressed time alternatives for federal employees on the grounds that these were an unwarranted infringement of their premium and overtime protections;[110] a representative of the National Federation of Federal Employees (NFFE) offered a vague and lukewarm endorsement of the reform— but only if the final bill had specific stipulations protecting the rights of employees not wishing to be included and guaranteeing union participation in drafting a changeover in any agency.[111] As we discussed above (pp. 84-85), union resistance was sufficient to defeat overwhelmingly and very early the Solarz version of the bill. Not only was the flexitime/compressed time law passed just as a three-year experiment, but also detailed qualifications limit the circumstances in which federal employees can waive their premium and overtime protections.

Public-sector employees are extremely reluctant to support compressed work schedules because these employees have an image problem. In recent years the public, imbued with a "Proposition 13" mentality, has widely viewed them as lazy and wasteful of taxpayer money. Such a public may find it difficult to accept that public-sector employees could work for only four days and receive a three-day weekend, "coddled" at the expense of the taxpayer.* As the concept of compressed work schedules becomes more widely accepted, some of this public resistance should fade. However, the image of public-sector employees is currently at a low point, and their unions have been reluctant to pursue the issue for fear that it could fuel the strongest public prejudices.

In contrast to union leaders, managers in general have perceived that compressed work schedules could be beneficial to them. Problems with workers cheating on their time would be minimal because under compressed work schedules all employees would work the same set hours. Furthermore, savings in energy usage, more effective plant utilization, and reduced labor costs for overtime appear to be irrefutable. However, managers have been concerned that the waiving of premium and overtime provisions could embitter management-union

---

*The political scope of this problem was discussed during the 1978 Senate hearings. Congressmen supportive of compressed work schedules—such as Senator Thomas Eagleton, who presided over the hearings—confront an immense political obstacle of justifying their support to their constituents, as well as to their political opponents. (See *Flexitime and Part-time Legislation, 1978,* pp. 41-42 and 56-57.)

relations. It is not surprising that managers have been hesitant to push an issue about which top union officials have not been very enthusiastic and which could restir management-union conflict. Where union locals have initiated a movement toward compressed work schedules, managers have been willing to follow—but cautiously, in order not to give the appearance of violating an implicit accord with union officialdom. To some extent managers fear that they would "lose control" of workers under compressed work schedules. Many managers continue to work an eight-hour shift, so workers under compressed schedules would be unsupervised two hours a day. As we have noted, many managers must overcome a psychological distrust of their workers before they can institute alternative work schedule reforms.

If unions and management can maintain enough trust to experiment further with these reforms, and if communications between them remain open in such nonpartisan forums as the National Council for Alternative Work Patterns and research centers promoting work environment changes in the United States, their reservations about flexible and compressed time schedules should eventually prove unfounded. Then both sides should be willing to expand these alternative work options in the 1980s and 1990s.

Unions at least in principle have accepted the justifications offered for flexible and compressed time schedules, and they have gone along (despite suspicions) with individual flexible and compressed time experiments strongly endorsed by workers and union locals. However, with the notable exceptions of top officials in the CWA and AFSCME, most national union officials—including those of the AFL-CIO—adamantly reject the need or even the philosophical rationale for work-sharing or permanent part-time options. The AFL-CIO opposed even the compromise part-time bill in 1978; the presidents of the AFGE and the NFFE objected to proposed reductions in full-time positions.[112] Indeed it would be fair to state that the issue of work-sharing and permanent part-time employment most clearly symbolizes the generational gulf between an older male union officialdom and a changing labor force.

In essence, union officialdom still instinctively fails to comprehend the changing demographic and cultural realities of an American labor force and economy over the last two decades; their vision of employment and economic issues seems rooted in the classic liberal-conservative divisions of the early 1960s. They continue to interpret policies premised on a predominantly white male labor force, families with only one wage-earner, and workers primarily concerned with full-time jobs and higher wages. They reject work-sharing and permanent part-time employment as they rejected un-skilled "scab" labor and temporary jobs, which (they claim) manage-ment and conservative politicians foisted upon the labor force to exploit the white male working class, increase profits, and exacerbate self-defeating competition among workers for an artificially limited number of new jobs. Thus far they have been deaf to the claims of reform advocates that work-sharing and permanent part-time options would eliminate occupational segregation and increase vocational opportunities for women and racial minorities, adjust to the growing reality of two wage-earner families, and respond directly to the fact that workers seem less concerned with full-time jobs and more with increased leisure time.

In economic policy union officials remain uncompromisingly wed to the New Deal precept of pump-priming by the federal gov-ernment to stimulate growth and to the notion of federal jobs programs, whereas work-sharing and permanent part-time options are premised on the inapplicability of New Deal precepts for the contemporary economy or political situation. Pump-priming or federal outlays for jobs programs cannot be economically justi-fied with the current high level of inflation; moreover, with the resurgence of the conservative right, national consensus and sup-port for federal jobs programs have essentially been eliminated—as is clear from a watered-down version of the Humphrey-Hawkins Full-Employment Act passed in 1978. Union officials still assume that systemic change with an expanding economy will over the long run solve the problems of occupational segregation and low wages confronting women and racial minorities; proponents of work-sharing and part-time employment argue that systemic change through economic growth is a necessary but not sufficient solution to these problems. They feel that systemic change without structural alterations will leave the disadvantaged work groups as far behind in wage levels and vocational opportunities as they would be in a slow-growth economy.

Indicative of union resistance has been the opposition of the AFL-CIO to the work-sharing and STC reforms instituted in California.[113]

It argues that if such reforms were adopted nationally, they would neither reduce unemployment nor increase job opportunities for women and racial minorities, and it offers several reasons to support its claims.

First, such reforms would contribute to unemployment because it is easier for employers to shift their employees to part-time work than to lay them off. Under regular unemployment insurance, employers bear a heavy financial burden for full layoffs; they are taxed for unemployment insurance according to their "experience rating" (a measure of their absolute layoffs in the recent past). Work-sharing and STC reforms would allow them to avoid financial penalties for de facto layoffs and would legitimate their cost-cutting measures. As a result, the costs for failing to provide full employment, which should be borne by society as a whole through regular unemployment insurance—and which should galvanize that society through its political representatives to legislate federal jobs programs—would be passed onto isolated employees who have been forced to accept arbitrary reductions in their incomes through work-sharing. Generally the AFL-CIO views such reforms as seductive political ploys (promoted by otherwise well-meaning liberal reformers) which undermine the nationwide political commitment to full employment and federal jobs programs—which are the only genuine long-term solutions to unemployment.

Second, the AFL-CIO questions whether even in the short run such reforms would spread the available amount of work around. Advocates of the California reforms assume—incorrectly—that employers will benignly institute work-sharing to protect the jobs of women and racial minorities, but the AFL-CIO claims that they will act in their immediate self-interest. It contends that employers can lay off women and racial minorities with low seniority at the beginning of a recession and then institute work-sharing for the remaining employees at no cost to themselves. From a union perspective, only employers would profit from such reforms: they would not have to pay higher taxes for unemployment insurance or fringe benefits for employees on part-time shifts; the higher labor productivity of part-time employees would justify raising output norms for full-time employees; and more employees competing for the same number of jobs would increase the leverage of employers in collective bargaining. AFL-CIO officials are not convinced that union locals and workers themselves have been the most enthusiastic proponents of work-sharing and part-time reforms; in addition, they note that 90 percent of the work-sharing programs in California have been formed in nonunion firms, even though California is one of the most highly unionized states in the United States.*

For most national union officials, the only variation of a reduced work shift that would not arouse suspicions would be an across-the-board reduction of the normal workweek from forty to thirty-seven hours, with the retention of the salaries and benefits from the forty-hour week. The UAW broached this type of reduction during collective bargaining in the mid-1970s, but it was seemingly an opening bargaining chip which was forgotten once serious negotiations over salaries and benefits commenced. Since declining increases in labor productivity are a major concern in the United States, however, such a proposal is not likely to receive much consideration by federal officials, Congress, or private employers. Yet we should recall that a few Soviet advocates of reduced work shifts have interpreted the reform to justify a reduction of work hours without a reduction in salaries for women in physically arduous occupations with high turnover rates.

In a major sense the work-sharing and part-time employment reforms are vulnerable to greater opposition from the public than are compressed work schedules. In the public sector these reforms would increase the absolute number of employees, even though the payrolls and equivalent full-time positions would remain the same. As we have noted, the issue of allegedly padded payrolls of public bureaucracies has aroused intense political furor during recent years. Both Carter in 1976 and Reagan in 1980 successfully campaigned against a wasteful federal bureaucracy, and numerous referenda cutting state budgets were passed by wide voter margins from 1978 through 1980. Reducing the absolute size of the public-sector workforce at the federal and state levels has become unquestionably identified in the public mind with greater government efficiency, and a number of politicians have successfully played on public resentment against padded government payrolls to win political office.

*In part union claims center on a problem of semantics. As of May 1980 only 11 percent of California firms on work-sharing were unionized, although 25.5 percent of the workers in these firms were union members. (See the testimony by Fred Best in *Unemployment Compensation Bills [1980]*, p. 74).

Indeed the OMB's opposition to the federal part-time bill and the establishment of full-time equivalency ceilings for federal agencies in 1976-78 stemmed from the fear of a negative public reaction. Published federal employee figures reflecting a change to part-time shifts would probably show an absolute increase in the federal work-force on full-time equivalency, even though agency payroll budgets and the equivalent number of hourly federal positions might not increase. The OMB fear finally surfaced during the Senate hearings on the part-time bill in 1978, as Senator Eagleton and several other Congressional and OPM witnesses tried to devise counterarguments to a political storm which would be inevitable if increases in the federal workforce resulted from the enactment of the part-time bill.[114] At best, they anticipated the extreme political difficulty in attempting to convince both the public and opportunistic office-seekers that more federal employees under full-time equivalency ceilings would not mean an increase in the size of the federal workforce. However, even members of Congressional appropriations committees were unlikely converts, for most of them were used to making budget decisions based on regular forty-hour employees. If they would fail to appreciate that two federal employees sharing one forty-hour position would not increase the number of agency employees, an already skeptical public and opportunistic office-seekers would hardly be any more sophisticated in comprehending the lacunae of full-time equivalency ceilings.

Decision-makers who defend the part-time reforms have an added problem. To convince employers to institute work-sharing and STC reforms rather than lay off workers, and at the same time not to deprive part-time employees of full social security and health benefits, additional state or federal funds would have to be provided over the next few years. As we have noted, employers have not rushed to emulate the California example of work-sharing and STC because of financial disincentives. California has removed some of these disincentives to institute work-sharing, but Congress would have to pass a special program in order to stimulate similar reforms in the other states.

Unfortunately the social security and unemployment insurance trust funds are already running serious deficits because of the recessionary economy and high unemployment rates, and (as discussed above) the social security system confronts unique long-term financial stresses stemming from the aging of the population. Representative Schroeder and other advocates of the California-type reforms contend that over the long run the federal government would not be paying out more for unemployment under STC because payments for regular unemployment insurance would decline with fewer layoffs and employees who would otherwise be laid off would be paying into the fund for the days they would be working. However, the failure of the Schroeder bill in 1980 to even come to a vote in the House foreshadows difficulties for similar legislation. Federal deficits are growing rapidly, and the first priority of both the Congress and President is to reduce the size of the federal budget. In addition, any attempts to amend the social security system to maintain benefit levels for employees on permanent part-time employment at their full-time salary levels will likely stall in Congress. Not to penalize employers in paying full health benefits for their part-timers would require the enactment of a federally financed comprehensive health-care program for all Americans. With a currently conservative Congress and administration, the chances of passage for such a program are more remote than they were in the 1970s.

Even if political obstacles at the federal level to work-sharing and part-time employment were overcome, employers in the private sector could still be unconvinced that the reforms would offer benefits to them. As we have noted, like industrial managers in the Soviet Union, they have been extremely suspicious that reduced work shifts under any label would seriously impair the operations of their firms. There would be additional employer costs in training new part-time employees; there would be major concerns over whether skilled workers and lower-level supervisory personnel could adequately carry out their responsibilities on part-time; and most employers (in the United States as well as in the Soviet Union) retain a deeply held prejudice that true professionalism means a willingness to commit at least forty hours of one's week to one's job. Moreover, as with compressed work schedules, managers have been reluctant to push work-sharing and part-time reforms in order not to aggravate union-management relations. They fear—quite rightly—that if they advocated the reforms too forcefully, it would arouse even greater opposition from most current national union officials. (Some of these concerns have not yet surfaced in the Soviet Union because Soviet advocates of reduced work shifts have been somewhat evasive over whether skilled and professional women would be included under the reform.)

In summary, because of converging economic, social, and cultural determinants and changes in the United States, alternative work schedules will become an even more salient issue in the 1980s and 1990s. Before the reforms gain wider acceptance, however, advocates will have to overcome deep-rooted fears, prejudices, and uncertainties of unions, management, and a public culturally conditioned to more traditional work modes. The Protestant work ethic and forty-hour week are as much cultural phenomena as they are economic foundations. To challenge them is to open to debate stabilizing forces in American society, and it is to politicize the reforms and generate opposition from those whose immediate self-interests might be threatened.

In the United States no less than in the Soviet Union, the issue of alternative work schedules is not one whose supporters and opponents can be easily grouped into the traditional categories of liberal and conservative in the political system. The issue has become symbolic of fundamental shifts and emerging policy orientations which render traditional political groupings of supporters and opponents somewhat obsolete and meaningless. Those advocating the reforms in both systems tend to be more future-oriented and more confident that only such new kinds of reforms can resolve the basic economic and social problems of their nations. Opponents remain viscerally tied to a past image of their societies and remain committed to a narrow range of limited and predictable reforms which they have applied to socioeconomic problems in the past.

Chapter Four

CONCLUSION: WOMEN, WORK, AND POLITICS
IN THE USSR AND UNITED STATES

On the international level, the most recent period of Soviet-American relations has been typified by increasing tension, conflict, bitter recriminations, and polarization. In the early 1970s a spirit of detente seemed to usher in conciliation and restraint between the two nations and led to arms agreements and scientific and cultural exchanges, but the end of the decade witnessed the invasion of Afghanistan by the Soviet Union, the shelving of a signed but unratified SALT-II arms-control treaty by the United States Senate, a U.S. grain embargo and boycott of the Olympic games in Moscow in 1980, and American suspension of industrial orders and scientific-cultural exchanges to the Soviet Union.

Historians would probably contend that the two nations bear equal blame for the worsening relations, and even the atmosphere of cordiality during the height of detente in the early 1970s never covered over the quite disparate ideological world views and political priorities which each nation brought to its interpretation of Soviet-American detente. In the United States the Vietnam War marked the collapse of bipartisanship in foreign policy among those who constitute the informed attentive public for foreign-policy issues.[1] False expectations that detente would lead to long-term liberal changes within the USSR and a mellowing of the Soviet leadership were bound to have been disappointed by Soviet behavior, and those disappointed expectations inevitably led to intense political divisions in the Democratic and Republican Parties over proper Soviet-American relations and a general waning of public support for the policies of the early 1970s. By the time of the 1980 elections, there was widespread acceptance within leadership circles and the attentive public of the United States that the Soviet Union was involved in a military buildup and expansionist thrust in its foreign policy, and a

133

concomitant belief that such actions necessitated vast increases in spending for American conventional and nuclear arms. With the election of Reagan it became fashionable once more to refer to the Soviet Union as a totalitarian state ruled by ideological zealots who will lie and scheme their way to world conquest.

In the Soviet Union, though the leadership is less accountable to shifting public sentiments in its conduct of foreign policy, disillusionment over detente also seemed inevitable. Since the Jackson-Vanik amendments of 1974 linking Soviet-American trade to concessions by the Soviet leadership in its Jewish emigration policy, the immediate economic and technological gains from detente probably seemed for anti-detente elements in the top Soviet leadership far short of what its supporters within the party Politburo (like Brezhnev) had promised.[2] With the Camp David accords shutting out the USSR from the Middle East and the Egyptian-Israeli settlement, and with harsh American criticism of Soviet-Cuban involvement in Africa, all Soviet leaders may have come to believe that detente had failed to gain the USSR the respect and status it merited as a global equal of the United States and a superpower. If the American leaders contended Soviet meddling in Africa violated the spirit of detente, Soviet leaders may have come to believe that the United States was not only treating the Soviet Union as a second-rate nation, but also was actively conspiring to organize an anti-Soviet alliance of China and Japan against rightful Soviet world interests.[3]

Worsening external relations between the two nations precluded a recognition of common interests, although ironically leaders in both nations throughout the 1970s slowly came to recognize very similar economic and social problems. In attempts to alleviate their somewhat parallel problems, the leaders of both nations on their own have moved toward a common awareness of the strategic role women play in their labor forces. With that awareness has evolved a common willingness at least to experiment in changing the traditional terms of work to make them more compatible with the special needs and demands of working women. In both nations the emerging policy consensus supportive of alternative work schedules represents part of a broader underlying shift in policy perspectives and priorities away from those which have guided decisions in the past. From a global perspective, the appearance of alternative work schedules as a major policy issue in both the Soviet Union and the United States as a response to similar socioeconomic problems highlights the reality of an internationalization of issues and policy-formation, cutting across national-cultural boundaries and defining priorities and approaches along a common realm of universally shared experiences. As we stated in Chapter 1, our central theoretical concern has been whether the important political differences between the Soviet Union and the United States have affected their policy responses despite similar types of reforms being instituted to cope with similar kinds of problems. Let us assess our findings.

For the leadership of the Soviet Union, part-time work symbolizes a determination to place greater emphasis on labor force effectiveness rather than on the total number of workers in devising future long-term economic policies. It reflects a sobering realization among more Soviet economic decision-makers that the Stalinist approach to economic growth by mobilizing all potential labor reserves no longer will work. An ever-expanding labor force has not contributed to real economic growth, but rather has constrained the effective absorption of new technology and automation into the production process. Over recent decades the Soviet economy has become so dependent on its women workers that their continued underutilization threatens permanent economic stagnancy. If more women were assigned reduced work shifts, the absolute number of unskilled workers for whom jobs must be made in the present Soviet economy and who drag down labor productivity could be significantly decreased, or women could use the additional free time to upgrade their skills to become more productive workers in a technologically expanding Soviet economy. At one extreme, advocates of female reduced work shifts in the USSR have implied abandoning the dogmatic commitment to full-time employment for all Soviet adults as the assumedly unquestionable achievement and advantage of Soviet socialism over Western capitalism. At the opposite extreme, support for female reduced work shifts has merged with the position of pronatalist Soviet policy advisers, who perceive the reform as a further means to stem declining birthrates in the key Slavic and Baltic ethnic nationalities over the next two decades. For both sides, however, changing the terms of work for women has become an urgent necessity to alleviate long-term economic and social problems in the nation.

For the leadership of the United States, alternative work schedules symbolize an underlying policy shift to redress the problems of sexual and racial discrimination in the workplace, prompted not just by moral anguish over inequalities in society, but by economic considerations as well. Even conservative decision-makers unmoved by the plight of women and racial minorities have come to appreciate that an underutilization of both groups crowding into the job market in ever increasing numbers contributes to low growth rates and declining labor productivity retarding the American economy. With limited growth and increasing energy costs threatening to reduce the number of new jobs created over the next two decades, it may be that the only solution for keeping unemployment below 7-10 percent will be to spread the existing jobs around through work-sharing or permanent part-time options. At one extreme, support for alternative work schedules has developed as a reaction against the premises and utility of conventional liberal-labor approaches dating from the New Deal to resolve the unprecedented problems of unemployment and inequality in American society during the last two decades of the twentieth century. At another extreme, alternative work schedules reflect a profound sociocultural transformation in the United States— one in which worker dissatisfaction, increased leisure time, an aging population, and changing sex roles have made the reforms both more practical and widely desired.

If alternative work schedules symbolize a policy shift in both nations, the nature of the policy debate over the reforms mirrors the wide gap in values and approaches to problems of working women inherent to the two different political systems.

In the USSR numerous studies and surveys published over the last two decades by identifiable policy specialists on women's issues in Soviet institutes have documented the realities of sex discrimination and inequality still prevalent in Soviet society.[4] Yet the recommendations forthcoming from these studies have seemed immeasurably less than called for by the depth of the problems revealed and analyzed. From the Procrustean bed of Marxism-Leninism, policy specialists still must structure their analyses and recommendations around dogma asserting that private property and capitalism alone cause sex discrimination and that the absence of both under socialism logically precludes any objective roots for systemic discrimination in the USSR. Ideologically no debate can proceed from the premise that the system itself has tolerated or contributed to inequality or discrimination. Thus the policy specialists are seriously limited in the scope or logic of alternatives which they can offer to remedy what are inherently systemic problems of sex discrimination outlined in their published studies. Only in articles evaluating the suppressed status of women in Western capitalism have these Soviet policy specialists been able indirectly to raise questions about similar systemic problems in their own country.

Nothing less has been evident in the controlled policy debate surrounding part-time work for women in the Soviet Union. Only in criticizing the phenomenon of temporary female workers in the West have policy specialists been able to intrude caveats about an expansion of part-time work for women in the USSR. As a consequence, advocates have portrayed the reform as no more than a segmental change; they have been unable to raise in debate or even speculate about the broader ramifications of the reform upon Soviet politics, culture, and society. Such a comprehensive focus on part-time work as a policy issue would violate a basic canon of Soviet political life, for the Soviet political system, society, and culture cannot be even implicitly challenged as necessitating any fundamental changes. The system is not flawed, but only suffers "shortcomings."

In contrast to advocates in the United States, no one in the USSR has or could argue that part-time work would be desirable as a cultural change to eliminate the irrational value placed on work and the lock-stepped nature of Soviet adult lives absorbed in their jobs. The California leisure-time cultural phenomenon is anathema to the Marxist-Leninist culture, which is based on the unquestioned virtues of selfless dedication and internalized discipline on the job of citizens committed to building the material-technical base of communism. In contrast to the United States, no one in the USSR has or could argue that part-time work is necessary to stem declining labor morale and widespread worker alienation. Although isolated problems in the labor force are now more openly admitted in the Soviet press, ideologically Soviet workers cannot suffer a sense of alienation and are both more enthusiastic and productive than their exploited counterparts in Western capitalism.

The only problem areas with which part-time work has been linked in the Soviet policy debate are those uncensored "shortcomings" legitimated for open discussion by the Soviet leadership: inefficiencies in the centralized command economy, inequitable family and childrearing responsibilities between husbands and wives, the declining quality of childcare by women overburdened by their dual work and family roles, and declining birthrates among Slavic and Baltic women. None of these problems—particularly when considered in isolation—necessarily implies that the Soviet political economy itself is fundamentally flawed or requires systematic change. The "shortcomings" are those terms of debate safely monitored and depoliticized within predictable and isolated boundaries. However, were part-time work linked with a need for fundamental cultural change or presented as a means to reduce widespread worker disaffection and alienation, it would legitimate open and mass political challenges to a system which has tolerated or perpetuated such flaws. Were advocates to urge a rational-comprehensive consideration of the reform to include its ramifications on the overall role and status of women, it would necessitate a debate over sex discrimination in Soviet society, and such debate could undermine the legitimacy of the system.

Contrary to the intentions of Soviet leaders, debate over part-time work may contribute to a rational-comprehensive approach on women's issues and to the emergence of a feminist orientation and mass political challenge. Indeed the need for such an approach in five-year plans was explicitly raised in the 1978 EKO and Central Trade Union Council conference. In addition, the Soviet leadership over the last decade has encouraged some greater policy input for women in decision-making institutions. For example, in 1976 special parliamentary commissions to review legislation affecting women were established in the national Supreme Soviet and all republic soviets; local "women's councils" have been activated and given greater visibility in residential units and industrial enterprises; and the number of women recruited as Party members and Party-state local officials has increased significantly since 1971. Unofficially it appears that an independent feminist orientation has surfaced even within the dissident movement of the country. Frustrated by official tolerance for systemic inequalities and abuses of women in Soviet society, some female dissidents in 1979 began to publish a *samizdat* journal in Leningrad entitled *Women and Russia*.[5] While four leaders of the dissidents were exiled from the Soviet Union, the interest they stirred among Soviet women may reflect a potential mass feminist consciousness which could eventually spill over into official policy outlets of the special women's parliamentary commissions, the "women's councils," the increasing number of female Party members and Party-state local officials, and the policy advisers on women's issues in government-academic institutes.

At times in the last decade the consideration of part-time work as a segmental change seems to have gone beyond the acceptable terms of public debate. Critics of the reform have not been reluctant to question the discriminatory impact of the reform on working women. By raising concerns that established Soviet policy can be discriminatory against women, the critics have implicitly legitimated discussion over other facets of Soviet policy which may also discriminate against women. Indeed even the supposedly apolitical and cowed women in the Soviet labor force since 1971 have made an independent and conscious political choice in an authoritarian system by their very act of omission—namely, by not opting in very large numbers or with very much enthusiasm for part-time shifts.

Quite different have been the terms of debate and the policy orientation surrounding alternative work schedules as an issue in the more open and politically democratic United States. The issue very clearly has been spontaneously advanced from below by those groups and individuals who do not make up the American political establishment. Their point of departure in defending the reforms has always been the need both to improve opportunities for disadvantaged groups in American society and to instill more humane values in American capitalism. Uppermost in their concerns have been the systemic problems of sexual and racial discrimination, intolerably high unemployment rates (particularly affecting disadvantaged groups), the dehumanizing work environment, and a culture destructive of human growth and overly obsessed with materialism and work as primary values. From the perspective of reform advocates, these problems are both real and could be partly alleviated by changing the traditional forty-hour work week, which limits job opportunities for women and racial minorities, artificially inflates unemployment levels, constrains the freedom of workers to shape their work environments, and deprives all Americans emotionally by forcing them into arbitrary life-stages. In the United States alternative work schedules represent a distinctly feminist approach and priority, advanced by women's interest groups most alarmed about systemic sex discrimination. In the USSR the status of women

139

and the impact of reduced work shifts on them have never been more than secondary value concerns. Soviet advocates have been primarily concerned about the growth of the economy or the size of the future population over the next two decades.

If politics would be defined as a conflict over fundamental values in a nation, there has been a "politics of alternative work schedules" only in the United States. Even in pushing federal reforms in 1978, American advocates have never shied away from open debate and consideration of the broader value changes likely to result from full-scale adoption of workplace reforms in American life. In the USSR, fundamental values underpinning the economy, culture, and society cannot be subjects of political debate. The controlled and depoliticized nature of debate over part-time work reflects this inability in the Soviet Union to question the broader value implications of reforms. In the United States, alternative work schedules are widely recognized as a fundamental political change, and the ability of advocates to convince decision-makers and the American public of the need for that change will ultimately determine the extent to which the reforms are adopted. In the USSR, reduced work shifts will only gain the support of Soviet decision-makers to the extent that advocates convince them that the reform will not threaten status quo values and does not portend fundamental change.

In the United States, alternative work schedules have been openly defined as a civil rights issue for women and racial minorities, whose real life opportunities might be enhanced by altering traditional work modes. In the USSR, they cannot be a civil rights issue in an authoritarian system which does not uphold, let alone encourage, civil rights as a basic political value. As Barbara Jancar and Gail Lapidus have concluded from their studies of women in the Soviet Union, the authoritarian nature of Soviet communism inherently constricts any changes directed toward greater equality for women.[6] Our cross-national policy study confirms their conclusions. Even the exactly same issue of alternative work schedules has a policy significance less beneficial for women in the Soviet Union than in the United States, where independent feminist groups can form coalitions and advance changes congruent with their defined goals of greater sexual equality.

In spite of the inherent political differences in the Soviet Union and the United States, the two nations seem destined to accept both the necessity and practicality of expanding alternative work schedules for their labor forces. In the USSR, the impetus for reduced work shifts arises from the extreme economic and social problems confronting the leadership, a continuing need for more skilled workers and technology in the production process, an inability to absorb large numbers of full-time unskilled workers, and the political threat posed by unskilled workers laid off through automation. Administrative reforms to generate greater efficiency and higher labor productivity must be priorities throughout the 1980s, particularly if the Party leadership remains reluctant to institute fundamental changes in the overly centralized and inefficient command economy. The political climate to push such reforms may have improved with Brezhnev's death in November 1982 and may continue to improve with the imminent passing by the mid-1980s of the entire older generation at the center of Soviet political life with which Brezhnev was closely associated since the end of World War II. Already the early indirect signs from speeches and actions taken by Yuri Andropov, Brezhnev's immediate nominal successor, intimate a new leadership consensus evolving first around a rejection of Brezhnev's past limited and timid experimentation in economic policy and second around the need for bold full-scale reforms to restir growth by disciplining Soviet workers and otherwise compelling them to exert greater efforts. Reforms already in place but never implemented much beyond the experimental stages during the Brezhnev era—like reduced work shifts—are likely to be seized upon under this emerging new consensus if they promise greater discipline and efficiency of the Soviet labor force.

In this context, as we observed in Chapter 2, among the arguments raised in support of part-time work by Soviet advocates have been the higher productivity and efficiency of female part-timers, who produce more per hour with less energy, machinery, and material costs per worker than do regular full-time workers. Moreover, the implication among some Soviet advocates in the 1970s was that the higher output norms achieved by female part-timers could then be set as the baseline for all regular Soviet workers in the same jobs. Thus for those Soviet neo-Stalinists outraged by the decline of worker discipline under Brezhnev and for those reformers exasperated by the waste and inefficiency of the Soviet command economy, a common political ground for compromise by the mid-1980s may be such reforms as part-time employment for more Soviet workers, particularly women. For neo-Stalinists, part-time work would be a way to discipline the Soviet workers by forcing them to work harder and produce more if they are to earn baseline salaries which would be set at higher output norms; for reformers, part-time work would be a way to reduce irrational central controls and induce greater market mechanisms in the economy by forcing industrial managers to use their wage funds and allotted workers more efficiently.

In the United States, even with the apparent political swing to the right with the 1980 election, the impetus for alternative work schedules also seems irreversible. With national unemployment reaching 10.8 percent by the end of 1982 and projected budget deficits threatening to exceed $200 billion by the end of 1983, the Reagan administration may be more willing to experiment with various work-sharing policies and unemployment insurance measures to increase the number of jobs rather than finance costly and, for the Reagan administration, ideologically unacceptable federal jobs programs. In turn, as a result of the electoral debacle suffered by American liberals in 1980, even old-line New Deal liberals in American unions may be more willing to accept alternative work schedules. Unemployment and discrimination will remain priority concerns of the liberals, but isolated from power at the national center in Washington, they may find themselves compelled to support new remedies which do not necessitate massive federal expenditures for jobs programs or controversial affirmative action initiatives by federal bureaucracies.

In this context, a new breed of younger liberals within the Democratic Party, like Senators Paul Sarbanes and Paul Tsongas, by 1982 challenged their fellow Democrats to develop new approaches to problems like unemployment and discrimination no longer reducible to New Deal or Great Society solutions in the more complicated economic times of the 1980s and with a changing American electorate who in 1980 voted into office Ronald Reagan and a number of conservative senators pledged to reducing the size of the federal government. Work-sharing and short-time compensation experiments, dismissed as political sell-outs by old-line New Dealers in the 1970s, may seem to have greater merit for both New Deal and new breed liberals redefining their objectives and political resources in the 1980s, particularly if a coalition supporting these reforms can be formed pragmatically with conservative leaders in the White House and Congress. The common political ground for compromise between

142

liberals and conservatives would be their awareness that such reforms could increase economic growth and the number of new jobs available to women and racial minorities. Even the fragmentation of political power in the United States, criticized as a barrier to meaningful policy responses on the national level to women's issues, could prove a substantial virtue in generating political support for these reforms in the 1980s. Alternative work schedules established for the federal workforce in 1978 and the various experiments with work-sharing in California illustrate the advantage of a fragmented political system in which the effectiveness of such reforms can be proven and precedents set short of any national policy commitment or response.

In sum, although the significance and meaning of alternative work schedules as an issue vary sharply in the Soviet Union and the United States, both nations will no doubt converge in the proportion of their labor forces shifted to alternative work schedules over the next two decades. Different reasons will prompt the leaderships to sponsor and endorse the changes, but in both nations the number of workers on alternative work schedules by the year 2000 may yet come to be understood as a subtle but important indicator of underlying political change in both nations.

ABBREVIATIONS USED IN REFERENCES

American Women Workers (1977) U.S., Congress, Joint Economic Committee, *American Women Workers in a Full Employment Economy, A Compendium of Papers*, submitted to the Subcommittee on Economic Growth and Stabilization, Joint Economic Committee, Congress, 95th Cong., 1st sess., 1977.

Coming Decade (1979) U.S., Congress, Senate, Committee on Labor and Human Resources, *The Coming Decade: American Women and Human Resources Policies and Programs, 1979, Hearings*, before the Committee on Labor and Human Resources, Senate, on Examination of Conditions and Opportunities Confronting American Women in Our Nation's Workplace, 96th Cong., 1st sess., 1979, Parts 1-2.

CDSP *Current Digest of the Soviet Press*; Columbus, Ohio.

EKO *Ekonomika i organizatsiia promyshlennogo proizvodstva* (Economics and organization of industrial production), Novosibirsk.

Flexitime and Part-time Legislation (1978) U.S., Congress, Senate, Committee on Governmental Affairs, *Flexitime and Part-time Legislation, Hearing*, before the Committee on Governmental Affairs, Senate, on S. 517, S. 518, H.R. 7814, and H.R. 10126, 95th Cong., 2nd sess., 1978.

Leisure-Sharing (1977) California, Legislature, *Leisure-Sharing Hearing*, before the Senate Select Committee on Investment Priorities and Objectives, California State Senate, 1977.

National Conference (1977) *National Conference on Alternative Work Schedules — Resource Packet*, sponsored by the National Council for Alternative Work Patterns, Chicago, Illinois, March 21-22, 1977.

144

Part-time Employment (1977)

U.S., Congress, Committee on Post Office and Civil Service, *Part-time Employment and Flexible Work Hours, Hearings*, before the Subcommittee on Employment Ethics and Utilization of the Committee on Post Office and Civil Service, House of Representatives, on H.R. 1627, H.R. 2732, and H.R. 2930, 95th Cong., 1st sess., 1977.

PKh

Planovoe khoziaistvo (Planned economy), Moscow.

RK&SM

Rabochii klass i sovremennyi mir (The working class and the contemporary world), Moscow.

SG&P

Sovetskoe gosudarstvo i pravo (Soviet state and law), Moscow.

SI

Sotsiologicheskie issledovaniia (Sociological research), Moscow.

Soviet Economy (1979)

U.S., Congress, Joint Economic Committee, *Soviet Economy in a Time of Change, A Compendium of Papers*, submitted to the Joint Economic Committee, Congress, 96th Cong., 1st sess., 1979, vols. 1-2.

ST

Sotsialisticheskii trud (Socialist labor), Moscow.

Unemployment Compensation Bills (1980)

U.S., Congress, Committee on Ways and Means, *Unemployment Compensation Bills, Hearing*, before the Subcommittee on Public Assistance and Unemployment Compensation of the Committee on Ways and Means, House of Representatives, on H.R. 6540, H.R. 6690, and H.R. 7529, 96th Cong., 2nd sess., 1980.

VE

Voprosy ekonomiki (Problems of economics), Moscow.

Work Force (1980)

The Changing Character of the Public Work Force, Proceedings of the Second Public Management Research Conference; cosponsored by the General Accounting Office, General Services Administration, Office of Management and

Budget, and Office of Personnel Management, Washington, D.C., November 17-18, 1980.

Working Women Speak (1979)   *Working Women Speak: Education, Training, Counseling— A Report on Six Regional Dialogues Sponsored by the National Commission on Working Women*, The National Advisory Council on Women's Educational Programs, Washington, D.C., 1979.

NOTES

Chapter 1

1. The following are among the most theoretically sophisticated and important contributions to comparative public policy over recent years: Arnold Heidenheimer, Hugh Heclo, and Carolyn Teich Adams, *Comparative Public Policy: The Politics of Social Choice in Europe and America* (New York: St. Martin's Press, 1975); Harold L. Wilensky, *The Welfare State and Equality: Structural and Ideological Roots of Public Expenditures* (Berkeley: University of California Press, 1975); Barbara Wolfe Jancar, *Women under Communism* (Baltimore: Johns Hopkins University Press, 1978); Gary P. Freeman, *Immigrant Labor and Racial Conflict in Industrial Societies: The French and British Experiences, 1945-1975* (Princeton: Princeton University Press, 1979); Howard M. Leichter, *A Comparative Approach to Policy Analysis: Health Care Policy in Four Nations* (New York: Cambridge University Press, 1979); Carolyn Teich Adams and Kathryn Teich Winston, *Mothers at Work: Public Policies in the United States, Sweden, and China* (New York: Longman, 1980); Valerie Bunce, *Do New Leaders Make a Difference? Executive Succession and Public Policy under Capitalism and Socialism* (Princeton: Princeton University Press, 1981).

2. *Equal Employment Policy for Women: Strategies for Implementation in the United States, Canada, and Western Europe*, ed. Ronnie Steinberg Ratner (Philadelphia: Temple University Press, 1980).

3. *Ibid.*, pp. 30-40, 144-46, 158, 422-24, and 427-28.

4. On the concept of policy "tendencies" of actors in the policymaking process and its advantage over the concept of "interest groups" in interpreting Soviet policy conflicts, see Franklyn Griffiths, "A Tendency Analysis of Soviet Policy-Making," in *Interest Groups in Soviet Politics*, ed. H. Gordon Skilling and Franklyn Griffiths (Princeton: Princeton University Press, 1971), pp. 335-78. On the application of policy tendencies to distinguish conflicting orientations in the Soviet policy debate over women's issues, see Gail Warshofsky Lapidus, *Women in Soviet Society: Equality, Development, and Social Change* (Berkeley: University of California Press, 1978), pp. 285-334.

5. As examples, see Adams and Winston, pp. 8-21, and Ronnie Steinberg Ratner, "The Policy and Problem: Overview of Seven Countries," and her summary chapter, both in Ratner, ed. This collective volume itself reflects the emergence of an international feminist policy tendency:

the case studies in the volume were originally prepared for an international conference on equal employment policy at Wellesley, Massachusetts, in 1978 which brought together over sixty-five policy specialists from twelve advanced industrialized nations.

6. Virginia H. Martin and Barbara Fiss, "Alternative Work Schedules: Definitions," in *National Conference (1977)*, pp. 4-6.

7. See *Leisure-Sharing (1977)*, pp. 10-12 and 67-68; Fred Best and James Mattesich, "Short-Time Compensation and Work Sharing: A New Alternative to Layoffs," in *Unemployment Compensation Bills (1980)*, pp. 93-131; and "Work Sharing: The MacNeil/Lehrer Report"; United States Corporation for Public Broadcasting, televised transcript, 6 June 1980.

8. Gunther Schmid, "Selective Employment Policy in West Germany: Some Evidence of Its Development and Impact" (Berlin: International Institute of Management, Discussion Paper Series, July 1978), p. 14; cited in Best and Mattesich, p. 123.

9. Steven Rattner, "Soaring Unemployment Rates Alarm Europe," *New York Times*, 26 October 1981, p. 6.

10. Fred Best, "Short-Time Compensation in California," in *Unemployment Compensation Bills (1980)*, pp. 80-86, and comments of Gene Livingston, Chief Deputy Director of the California Employment Development Department, in "Work Sharing: The MacNeil/Lehrer Report."

11. *Leisure-Sharing (1977)*, pp. 41-66.

12. John D. Owens, "Flexitime: Some Management and Labor Problems of the New Flexible Hour Scheduling Practices," *Industrial and Labor Relations Review* 30, 2 (January 1977): 152-61; and "Part-Time Employment: An International Survey" (Geneva: International Labor Office, 1973). (Both reprinted in *National Conference [1977]*, pp. 48-67.)

13. *Alternative Work Schedule Directory, 1st ed.* (Washington, D.C.: National Council for Alternative Work Patterns, 1978).

14. As examples of the international pooling of expertise and the role of multinational corporations, see Owens, and the testimony of Heinz Hengstler in *Part-time Employment (1977)*, pp. 79-84.

15. On the significant increases in labor-force participation by women since 1960, see Ratner, "The Policy and Problem," pp. 2-4, 13-14, and 16-17.

Chapter 2

1. A. Novitskii and M. Babkina, "Nepolnoe rabochee vremia i zaniatost' naseleniia," *VE*, no. 7 (July 1973): 133-34; E. V. Porokhniuk and M. S. Shepeleva, "O sovmeschenii proizvodstvennykh i semeinykh funktsii zhenshchin-rabotnits," *SI*, no. 4 (October-December 1975): 102; and

T. Skal'berg, E. Matirosian, and L. Kuleshova, "Rabota s nepolnym rabochim dnem—vazhnoe sredstvo privlecheniia trudovykh resursov," *ST*, no. 2 (February 1977): 106. Novitskii is an economist who is a long-time advocate of the part-time reform.

2. *Zakonodatel'stvo o pravakh zhenshchin v SSSR (Sbornik normativnikh aktov)* (Moscow: Iuridicheskaia Literatura, 1975), pp. 98-99.

3. On the limitation of the right to part-time work under Article 26 to specifically designated groups, see Skal'berg, Matirosian, and Kuleshova, p. 103. On the inclusion of part-time shifts under "privileges" allowed under Soviet labor law, see L. A. Okun'kov: "Okhrana truda zhenshchin v evropeiskikh sotsialisticheskikh stranakh," *SG&P*, no. 3 (March 1974): 96-101; "Organizatsiia oplaty truda rabochikh i sluzhashchikh v SSSR," *ibid.*, no. 7 (July 1978): 47-55; and "Otraslevye l'goty dlia rabochikh i sluzhashchikh v sovetskom zakonodatel'stve," *ibid.*, no. 8 (August 1979): 21-29.

4. S. E. Kotliar and S. Ia. Turchaninova, *Zaniatost' zhenshchin v proizvodstve (Statistiko-sotsiologicheskii ocherk)* (Moscow: Statistika, 1975), p. 98; E. B. Gruzdeva and E. S. Chertikhina, "Zhenshchiny v obshchestvennom proizvodstve razvitogo sotsializma," *RK&SM*, no. 6 (November-December 1975): 143.

5. L. Kuleshova and T. Skal'berg, "Rezhim nepolnogo rabochego vremeni (Na primere Estonskoi SSR)," *VE*, no. 6 (June 1979): 135-36.

6. A recent overview of the advantages of part-time work for women, students, invalids, and pensioners from the standpoint of both the Soviet economy and the particular work-related needs of these groups is presented in A. Novitskii, "Reservy trudovykh resursov: sotsial'no-ekonomicheskii aspekt," *Kommunist*, no. 2 (January 1980): 44-56.

7. *Ibid.*, pp. 49 and 51.

8. Kuleshova and Skal'berg, p. 135. On a flexitime experiment in Tallinn plants, see the discussion in "Eksperimental'naia stranitsa—nasha idea: skol'ziashchii grafik, pri kotorom kazhdyi sam sebe stanovitsia 'tabel'shchi-kom'," *Literaturnaia gazeta*, no. 1 (4 January 1978): 12.

9. Kuleshova and Skal'berg, p. 135; and Skal'berg, Matirosian, and Kuleshova, p. 107. Also see *Trud*, 8 January 1978, for a description of flexible work shifts in one Estonian plant which allow workers to alter their daily shifts from 4 to 10.5 hours (depending on their needs) while accumulating the weekly norm.

10. For a recent assessment of the homework option, see "Eksperimental'naia stranitsa: nadomnichestvo," *Literaturnaia gazeta*, no. 24 (19 December 1979): 10. For earlier discussions which grouped the homework option with part-time shifts for women and pensioners, see "Ratsional'no ispol'-zovat' trud nadomnits," *ST*, no. 1 (January 1974): 88-89; I. Bagrova, "Kak sovmestit' sovmestimoe?," *Nedelia*, no. 32 (3-14 August 1977):

11; and P. Demidov, "Tovarishch pensioner—razmyshlenniia po otvetam," *Izvestiia*, 14 September 1977, p. 2.

11. "Basic Guidelines for the Economic and Social Development of the USSR in 1981-85 and in the Period up to 1990," *Pravda* and *Izvestiia*, 5 March 1981 , pp. 1-7; translated in *CDSP* 33, 16 (20 May 1981): 22.

12. "On Measures to Increase State Assistance to Families with Children," *Pravda* and *Izvestiia*, 31 March 1981, p. 1; translated in *CDSP* 33, 13 (29 April 1981): 9-10.

13. E. Ye. Novikova, V. S. Iazykova, Z. Ia. Iankova, *Zhenshchina. Trud. Sem'ia. (Sotsiologicheskii ocherk)* (Moscow: Profizdat, 1978), pp. 83-84; A. E. Kotliar and S. Ia. Turchaninova, "Rezhim i usloviia truda—vo vse smeny," *EKO*, no. 3 (May-June 1978): 57-64; and L. Kuleshova, "Rezhim nepolnogo rabochego vremeni pri organizatsii truda zhenshchin," *PKh*, no. 12 (December 1978): 54.

14. Z. Ia. Iankova, "Razvitie lichnosti zhenshchiny v sovetskom obshchestve," *SI*, no. 4 (October-December 1975): 45-47; and E. Ye. Novikova and B. P. Kutyrev, "Kolichestvo i kachestvo truda—obsuzhdenie 'kruglogo stola'," *EKO*, no. 3 (May-June 1978): pp. 25-26. Some participants in the Novikova and Kutyrev study expressed fundamental disagreement with the concept of differential work norms for women; see p. 26.

15. Among those who have equated part-time shifts with extended maternity leaves, see A. Ia. Iankova and V. S. Iazykova, *XX vek i problemy sem'i (po itogam XII mezhdunarodnogo seminara po issledovaniiu sem'i)* (Moscow: Znanie, 1974), pp. 45-46, and A. E. Kotliar and A. Shlemin, "Problemy ratsional'noi zaniatosti zhenshchin," *ST*, no. 7 (July 1974): 116-17. Among those who contrast the advantages of part-time shifts to the career disadvantages of lengthy maternity leaves are N. M. Shishkan, *Trud zhenshchin v usloviiakh razvitogo sotsializma* (Kishinev: Shtiintsa, 1976), pp. 97-98 and 166-76, and Z. Gosha, "O sovmeshchenii zhenshchinoi funktsii materinstva s rabotoi v obshchestvennom khoziaistve," in *Sotsial'no-demograficheskie issledovaniia sem'i v respublikakh sovetskoi pribaltiki*, ed. P. Gulian et al. (Riga: Zinatne, 1980), pp. 22-23. On the nuances between maternity leaves and part-time shifts, see Gail Warshofsky Lapidus, *Women in Soviet Society: Equality, Development, and Social Change* (Berkeley: University of California Press, 1978), pp. 314-17 and 326-27.

16. Among Sonin's most recent articles, in which he has restated his support for such reforms and analyzed the problems of Soviet working women in the overall context of labor inefficiencies, are the following: "Problemy raspredeleniia i ispol'zovaniia trudovikh resursov," *ST*, no. 3 (March 1977): 94-103; "Sotsial'no-ekonomicheskie problemy zaniatosti zhenshchin," in *Izmenenie polozheniia zhenshchiny i sem'ia*, ed. A. G. Kharchev (Moscow: Nauka, 1977), pp. 22-31; and "Ravnyi prava, neravnye nagruzki," *EKO*, no. 3 (May-June 1978): 5-18. A number of Sonin's articles published

in limited-edition and specialized books and journals over the last few decades have been reissued in *Razvitie narodo-naseleniia (ekonomicheskii aspekt)* (Moscow: Statistika, 1980).

17. "Eksperimental'naia stranitsa: nadomnichestvo," *Literaturnaia gazeta*, no. 24 (19 December 1979), p. 10.

18. On the relationship between part-time shifts and the quality of parenting by working women, see V. S. Nemichenko and Iu. M. Lukashuk, "Prodolzhit' raboty-zhenshchina zdes', zhenshchina tam. . . ," *EKO*, no. 4 (July-August 1979): 118-19; "Skol'ko imet' detei," *Izvestiia*, 10 March 1979, p. 3; and "Second Child" and "Once again about a Second Child," *Komsomolskaia pravda*, 18 April 1979, p. 4, and 2 February 1980, p. 4; translated in *CDSP* 31, 20 (13 June 1979): 13, and 32, 6 (12 March 1980): 9 respectively.

19. *XXV S"ezd Kommunisticheskoi Partii Sovetskogo Soiuza: Stenograficheskii otchet* (Moscow: Politizdat, 1976), vol. 2, p. 286. The resolution was approved on 5 March 1976.

20. On the inclusion of the reduced work provision in Article 35, see Robert Sharlet, *The New Soviet Constitution of 1977—Analysis and Text* (Brunswick, Ohio: King's Court Communications, 1978), pp. 87-88. On the public debate over a need for Article 35 (equating equal rights of women with special privileges granted them by the state), see the letters to the editor in *Pravda*, 25 and 31 July 1977, and 3 and 12 September 1977.

21. *Trudovye resursy SSSR*, ed. L. A. Kostin (Moscow: Ekonomika, 1979), pp. 124, 145-49, 281, and 289.

22. Kotliar and Turchaninova, *Zaniatost' zhenshchin*, p. 102.

23. Kuleshova and Skal'berg, p. 134.

24. Kuleshova, p. 63.

25. On the decline in old-age pensions, see N. Ye. Rabkina and N. M. Rimashevskaia, "Distributive Relations and Social Development," *EKO*, no. 5 (September-October 1978): 16-32; translated in *CDSP* 30, 47 (20 December 1978): pp. 3-4; on pensioners in Estonian enterprises opting to work full-time shifts, see Kuleshova and Skal'berg, p. 136.

26. See Alastair McAuley, "Welfare and Social Security," in *The Soviet Worker: Illusions and Realities*, ed. Leonard Schapiro and Joseph Godson (London: Macmillan, 1981), pp. 214-17.

27. Kotliar and Turchaninova, *Zaniatost' zhenshchin*, p. 99; N. V. Panova, "Voprosy i byta zhenshchin," in *Problemy byta, braka i sem'i* (Vil'nius: Mintis, 1970), p. 90 (based on Panova's 1966-67 survey of Lithuanian women); V. D. Uzdenova, "Znachenie i puti sovershenstvovaniia ispol'zovaniia truda zhenshchin v usloviiakh razvitogo sotsializma"; dissertation abstract, Rostov State University, 1974, p. 15 (based on Uzdenova's survey of women in Rostov industrial enterprises); and T. A.

Mashika, *Sotsial'no-ekonomicheskie osobennosti truda zhenshchin pri sotsializme* (Kiev: Naukova Dumka, 1981), p. 150 (based on Mashika's survey of women in a Ukrainian factory).

28. Shishkan, pp. 171-75, and L. M. Kuleshova and T. I. Mamontova, "Zaniatost' zhenshchin na rezhimakh s nepolnym rabochim vremenem," *SI*, no. 2 (April-May 1979): 90-92.

29. *Ibid.*, p. 91, and Shishkan, p. 176.

30. *Ibid.*, pp. 171-76; Kuleshova and Mamontova, pp. 90-92. For similar findings on a linkage between insufficient or inadequate daycare facilities and a greater willingness of women to accept part-time shifts, see Panova, p. 91; Skal'berg, Matirosian, and Kuleshova, pp. 105 and 107; Mashika, p. 150; and N. I. Tatarinova, *Primenie truda zhenshchin v narodnom khoziaistve SSSR* (Moscow: Nauka, 1979), p. 110. Mashika and Tatarinova are the only ones who draw the logical conclusion that an adequate provision of daycare facilities would allow many women to work full-time.

31. Shishkan, pp. 173-74, and Panova, p. 91. Perhaps as a veiled comment on Soviet reality, in a study of women exploited on reduced work shifts in Western capitalism, a Soviet sociologist found that there is a relationship between low family income, expenses of childcare and consumer services, and the calculations inducing women to work part-time (L. P. Arskaia, "Zaniatost' s sokrashchennym rabochim dnem (eye rol' v evoliutsii tsikla trudovoi aktivnosti zhenskogo naseleniia)," *RK&SM*, no. 2 [March-April 1975]: 76-77).

32. Shishkan, pp. 173-74; and Novitskii and Babkina, p. 137. On the unwillingness of highly educated and well-off women in Western capitalism to accept part-time work, see Arskaia, p. 77.

33. Shishkan, p. 177; Kuleshova, p. 58; Porokhniuk and Shepeleva, pp. 103 and 107; Kotliar and Shlemin, pp. 116-17; Kotliar and Turchaninova, *Zaniatost' zhenshchin*, p. 100.

34. Benefits to professional women were the initial focus of discussion in "Second Child" and "Once again about a Second Child," *Komsomolskaia pravda*, 18 April 1979 and 2 February 1980.

35. Among those who have either criticized part-time shifts for women as discriminatory or alluded to others alleging such discrimination, see the following: V. Tkachenko in *Kommunist Belorussii*, no. 10 (October 1963): 58 (cited in Porokhniuk and Shepeleva, p. 106); Uzdenova, pp. 14-15; Kotliar and Turchaninova, *Zaniatost' zhenshchin*, p. 99; Kotliar and Shlemin, pp. 116-17; Tatarinova, p. 111; I. N. Kanaeva, "Perspektivy razvitiia sem'i i zhilishcha," in Kharchev, p. 153; L. P. Shakhot'ko, *Rozhdaemost' v Belorussii (sotisial'no-ekonomicheskie voprosy)* (Minsk: Nauka i Tekhnika, 1975), pp. 124-25; and Mashika, pp. 149-51.

36. The Soviet figure is cited in Iu. B. Riurikov, "Deti i obshchestvo (O nekotorykh aspektakh demograficheskoi politiki)," *Voprosy filosofii*,

no. 4 (April 1977): 118. In the United States preliminary figures from the 1980 census revealed that families headed by a single parent had dramatically increased from the 1970 figures of 12.3 percent to 19.1 percent, with an estimated 17 percent of all American families headed by single women. (See John Herbers, "Census Data Show Gains in Housing and in Education," *New York Times*, 20 April 1982, pp. 1 and 12).

37. Cited by Alexis Herman (director of the U.S. Labor Department's Women's Bureau, 1977-80, under the Carter administration) in *ibid.*, p. 275.

38. On the problems of child support, alimony, and income maintenance programs for single mothers in the USSR, see Peter H. Juvilier, "Women and Sex in Soviet Law," in *Women in Russia*, ed. Dorothy Atkinson, Alexander Dallin, and Gail Warshofsky Lapidus (Stanford: Stanford University Press, 1977), pp. 258-62, and Bernice Madison, "Social Services for Women: Problems and Priorities," in *ibid.*, pp. 314-15, 319-21, and 330-32.

39. On the complex policy context surrounding the 1974 reform, see Lapidus, *Women in Soviet Society*, pp. 304-7, and Alfred J. Di Maio, Jr., "The Soviet Union and Population: Theory, Problems, and Population Policy," *Comparative Political Studies* 13, 1 (April 1980): 124.

40. As an example of foot-dragging, see the complaints expressed by the chief official responsible for Lithuanian state subsidies about deliberate delays and resistance at the local level in "Zabota o materi-truzhenitse," *Sovetskaia Litva*, 8 March 1975, p. 2. Moreover, the complex rules and regulations governing eligibility may have allowed local officials wide discretion in implementing the reform, as evidenced in "Konsul'tatsii—posobiia na detei maloobespechennym sem'iam," *ST*, no. 10 (October 1977): pp. 149-52.

41. Piskunov and Steshenko first raised their criticism in *Demograficheskaia politika* (Moscow: Nauka, 1974). For a refutation, see Ye. L. Manevich: "Vosproizvodstvo naseleniia i ispol'zovanie trudovykh resursov," *VE*, no. 8 (August 1978): 41, and "Problemy vosproizvodstva naseleniia i trudovykh resursov SSSR," in Kostin, ed., pp. 126-27. Manevich is a Sector Head of the Institute of Economics in the Academy of Sciences.

42. McAuley, pp. 213-14.

43. Shishkan, p. 172.

44. N. F. Buriakova, "Zhenskii trud i problemy ego ispol'zovaniia v usloviiakh razvitogo sotsializma"; dissertation abstract, Kazakhstan State University, 1975, p. 25. As far as I have been able to ascertain, Buriakova is the only reform advocate who has linked part-time shifts for women with a policy of reducing work-hours for all Soviet workers, although Mashika, a critic of the current part-time reform, has argued for a change in which both men and women would have their shifts reduced (p. 151).

45. Porokhniuk and Shepeleva, p. 106.

46. *Ibid.*; Shishkan, pp. 168-71; Kotliar and Turchaninova, *Zaniatost' zhenshchin*, pp. 98-99; Kuleshova and Mamontova, p. 90; Mashika, p. 150.

47. Lapidus, *Women in Soviet Society*, pp. 325-29.

48. Uzdenova, p. 15.

49. Nancy S. Barrett, "Women in the Job Market: Unemployment and Work Schedules," in *The Subtle Revolution—Women at Work*, ed. Ralph E. Smith (Washington, D.C.: Urban Institute, 1979), pp. 66-69 and 80-88, and Herman, p. 277.

50. The 15 percent figure is cited by T. N. Cherkasov, "Obshchestvennye problemy zhenskogo truda v SSSR v usloviiakh razvitogo sotsializma," in *Vliianie nauchno-tekhnicheskogo progressa na izmenenie kharaktera zhenskogo truda v usloviiakh sotsialisticheskogo obshchestva (Tezusy dokladov Vsesoiuznoi naucho-prakticheskoi konferentsii)* (Ivanovo: All-Union Scientific-Research Institute of the Central Council of Trade Unions, 1975), p. 24 (cited hereafter as *Vliianie . . . konferentsii*). Only 1,250 copies of this volume were published and none were distributed overseas. More widely published and distributed articles have portrayed greater earning equality between men and women in Soviet families; for example, Iankova cites survey findings in which 79 percent of the women earned as much or more than their husbands (Z. Ia. Iankova, "Izmeneniia struktury sotsial'nykh rolei zhenshchiny v razvitom sotsialisticheskom obshchestve," in Kharchev, ed., p. 36).

51. As examples, contrast the negative evaluations of women in part-time jobs in Western nations with the positive evaluation of part-time shifts for Soviet women in Shishkan, pp. 29-30 and 166-76, and Z. M. Iuk, *Trud zhenshchiny i sem'ia* (Minsk: Belarus', 1975), pp. 20-21 and 121-24. Also see the noncommittal assessment of advantages and disadvantages of part-time work for women by the head of the Soviet Committee of Women, V. V. Nikolaeva-Tereshkova, *Zhenshchina i trud*; report presented at World Congress of Women, Helsinki, Finland, 14-18 June 1969 (Moscow: Komitet Sovetskikh Zhenshchin, 1969), p. 29.

52. Arskaia, pp. 70-82. A positive assessment of the part-time reform for the USSR was presented by Ye. B. Gruzdeva and E. S. Chertikhina, "Zhenshchiny v obshchestvennom sotsializme," *RK&SM*, no. 6 (November-December 1975): 143.

53. For example, see Skal'berg, Matirosian, and Kuleshova, p. 108.

54. Kotliar and Turchaninova, "Rezhim i usloviia truda," p. 64.

55. See references in footnotes 30-32 above.

56. On Soviet policy advisers who have linked part-time shifts or maternity leaves with cutting back expenditures for daycare facilities, see Lapidus, *Women in Soviet Society* pp. 308-9. Also see Tatarinova's criticism of Novitskii and Babkina (Tatarinova, pp. 110-11).

57. On a preference for maternity leaves over part-time shifts as pronatalist actions and a denial of discrimination against women, see V. A. Perevedentsev:

"Sem'ia: vchera, segodnia, zavtra . . . ," *Nash sovremennik*, no. 6 (June 1975): 129 and 131, and "Naselenie: prognoz i real'nost'," *ibid.*, no. 11 (November 1975): 130-31. On the association of part-time shifts with a gamut of pronatalist actions, see B. Ts. Urlanis, *Narodonaselenie: issledovaniia, publitsistika (sbornik statei)* (Moscow: Statistika, 1976), pp. 68 and 76-77. Among those associating part-time shifts with reforms to stimulate birthrates have been Shakhot'ko, pp. 124-25, and T. E. Chumakova, *Trud i byt zhenshchin (sotsial'no-pravovye aspekty)* (Minsk: Nauka i Tekhnika, 1978), pp. 119-20.

58. For earlier analyses of this policy position, see Lapidus, *Women in Soviet Society*, pp. 309-22, and Di Maio, pp. 125-27. Recent elaborations of this position include the following: T. V. Riabushkin, "Demograficheskaia politika i nauka," *SI*, no. 3 (July-September 1978): 46-55; L. E. Darskii, "Sotsial'no-demograficheskie issledovaniia problem rozhdaemosti," *SI*, no. 3 (July-September 1979): 10-19; A. A. Tkachenko, *Ekonomicheskie posledstviia sovremennykh demograficheskikh protsessov v SSSR* (Moscow: Statistika, 1978); T. N. Medvedeva, *Ekonomischeskie problemy rosta naseleniia i ispol'zovaniia trudovykh resursov v SSSR* (Moscow: Izdatel'stvo Moskovskogo Universiteta, 1978); T. V. Riabushkin and R. A. Galetskaia, *Dinamika i struktura naseleniia v sotsialisticheskom obshchestve* (Moscow: Statistika, 1979; and A. Ia. Kvasha, *Demograficheskaia politika v SSSR* (Moscow: Financy i Statistika, 1981).

59. *Ibid.* For distinctions between quantitative and qualitative measures of the "active" real labor reserve for Central Asian and European ethnic groups, see A. A. Tkachenko. On limitations to the "effective" utilization of labor reserves in Central Asia, see the frank appraisal in M. Orazgel'dyrev, "Podgotovka kadrov iz mestnogo naseleniia v respublikakh srednei azii," *VE*, no. 5 (May 1979): 84-91.

60. Manevich, "Problemy vosproizvodstva," pp. 124-26. For Manevich's views on the inefficient use of workers at the enterprise level, see "Vosproizvodstvo," pp. 38-48. On broader implications of the debate over differential population policy, see Murray Feshbach, "Prospects for Outmigration from Central Asia and Kazakhstan in the Next Decade," in *Soviet Economy (1979)*, pp. 656-709.

61. As examples, see Medvedeva, p. 147; Riabushkin and Galetskaia, pp. 209 and 219; and *Sotsiologiia i problemy sotsial'nogo razvitiia*, ed. T. V. Riabushkin et al. (Moscow: Nauka, 1978), pp. 354-55.

62. Kuleshova, pp. 54-63.

63. For example, see G. Sergeeva, "O professional'noi strukture rabotaiushchikh zhenshchin," *PKh*, no. 11 (November 1976): 37-46, and Z. Skarupo, "Sokrashchenie tekuchesti i uluchshenie ispol'zovaniia rabochei sily," *ibid.*, no. 6 (June 1977): 18-25.

64. See Kotliar and Turchaninova, *Zaniatost' zhenshchin*, pp. 91-93; Uzdenova, pp. 13-14; and A. K. Iurtsinia, "Razvitie lichnosti zhenshchiny pri sotsializme"; dissertation abstract, Latvian State University, 1973, p. 18.

65. Tatarinova, pp. 108-9, and Shishkan, p. 37. On the increased wage supplements for night-shift workers in certain Soviet industries, see *Vedemosti Verkhovnogo Soveta SSSR*, no. 44 (1976): 624.

66. Sonin, "Ravnyi prava," p. 11, and Shishkan, p. 116.

67. Nemichenko and Lukashuk, p. 123.

68. See Stanley H. Cohn, "Soviet Replacement Investment: A Rising Policy Imperative," in *Soviet Economy (1979)*, pp. 230-45.

69. "Demograficheskaia situatsiia i trudovye resursy SSSR," *VE*, no. 10 (October 1973): 158; "Guarding Women Workers' Health," *Izvestiia*, 24 May 1977, p. 5; translated in *CDSP* 29, 21 (22 June 1977): 11; and Christopher Davis and Murray Feshbach, *Rising Infant Mortality in the U.S.S.R. in the 1970s* (Washington, D.C.: International Population Reports, 1980), pp. 28-29.

70. S. P. Burenkov, "Rol' zdravookhraneniia v reshenii problem trudovykh resursov," in Kostin, ed., pp. 68-80; Ye. L. Manevich, "Defitsit i rezervy rabochei sily," *EKO*, no. 2 (March-April 1978): 83-84; and Kuleshova, pp. 59-60.

71. "Guarding Women Workers' Health," *Izvestiia*, 24 May 1977; E. Ch. Novikova, "Okhrana zdorov'e zhenshchin v SSSR," in *Vliianie . . . konferentsii*, pp. 10-11.

72. Davis and Feshbach. The authors consider poor hygienic standards in the society, unchecked environmental pollution, an inadequate health care system, and frequent abortions more significant factors than inadequate research.

73. That labor protection laws are sacrificed to expediency was noted by Z. A. Volkova, director of the laboratory for women's labor hygiene in the Institute for Labor Hygiene and Occupational Diseases of the Academy of Medicines (in Novikova and Kutyrev, p. 27). On the vagueness of laws prohibiting pregnant and breast-feeding women from working in harmful environments, see N. N. Sheptulina, "Konstitutsiia SSSR i razvitie zakonodatel'stva o trude zhenshchin," *SG&P*, no. 6 (June 1978): 29-30.

74. As examples, see Chumakova, pp. 40-52, 58-62, and 73-78, and V. N. Tolkunova, "Pravovoe regulirovanie zhenskogo truda v sotsialisticheskom obshchestve," in *Vliianie . . . konferentsii*, pp. 47-50.

75. Novikova and Kutyrev, pp. 22-23 and 27-28.

76. "Konsul'tatsii—novoe proiavlenie zaboty o zhenshchine-truzhenitse," *ST*, no. 2 (February 1979): 117-19.

77. Carolyn Teich Adams and Kathryn Teich Winston, *Mothers at Work: Public Policies in the United States, Sweden, and China* (New York: Longman, 1980), pp. 18-21, 104-5, 116-24, and 135-41. Also see Lapidus, *Women in Soviet Society*, pp. 322-34.

78. Major specialists and their original studies on working women published in the USSR over the last decade include the following: B. V. Mikhailiuk, *Ispol'zovanie zhenskogo truda v narodnom khoziaistve* (Moscow: Ekonomika, 1970); N. A. Sakharova, *Optimal'nye vozmozhnosti ispol'zovaniia zhenskogo truda v sfere obshchestvennogo proizvodstva* (Kiev: Vyshaia Shkola, 1973); Kotliar and Turchaninova, *Zaniatost' zhenshchin*; Iuk; Chumakova; Shishkan; and Tatarinova.

79. Novikova and Kutyrev, p. 29.

80. *Ibid.*, p. 19.

81. Orazgel'dyrev, p. 89, and A. A. Tkachenko, p. 51.

82. M. Ia. Sonin, "Izmeneniia professional'no-kvalifikatsionnoi struktury zhenskogo truda i sem'ia"; cited in Iankova and Iazykova, p. 14.

83. For the most recent Western studies from which these generalizations have been derived, see the following: Michael Paul Sacks, *Women's Work in Soviet Russia: Continuity in the Midst of Change* (New York: Praeger, 1976), pp. 69-99 and 141-65; Joel C. Moses, *The Politics of Female Labor in the Soviet Union* (Ithaca: Cornell University Center for International Studies, 1978), pp. 2-8, 11, and 14-17; Lapidus, *Women in Soviet Society*, pp. 161-97; Gail Lapidus, "The Female Industrial Labor Force: Dilemmas, Reassessments, and Options," in *Industrial Labor in the U.S.S.R.*, ed. Arcadius Kahan and Blair A. Ruble (New York: Pergamon Press, 1979), pp. 232-79; Michael Swafford, "Sex Differences in Soviet Earnings," *American Sociological Review* 43, 5 (October 1978): 657-73; and Robert C. Stuart, "Women in Soviet Rural Management," *Slavic Review* 38, 4 (December 1979): 603-13.

84. D. M. Karpukhin and A. B. Shteiner, "Zhenskii trud i trud zhenshchin," *EKO*, no. 3 (May-June 1978): 41-42; Kotliar and Turchaninova, *Zaniatost' zhenshchin*, pp. 59-62 and 72-74; and Gruzdeva and Chertikhina, pp. 138-39.

85. Ye. B. Gruzdeva, "Osobennosti obraza zhizni 'intelligentnykh rabochikh'," *RK&SM*, no. 2 (March-April 1975): 91-99; V. I. Lukina, "Kolichestvo detei v sem'e i sotsial'no-professional'nye peremshcheniia roditelei," *SI*, no. 4 (October-December 1979): 129-32; and Gosha, pp. 19-20.

86. Novikova and Kutyrev, pp. 23-24 and 26; Sonin, "Ravnyi prava," pp. 16-17; Karpukhin and Shteiner, p. 43; Mikhailiuk, pp. 113-14; Iurtsinia, p. 21; Moses, pp. 15-17 and 26-28.

87. A point raised (among other authors) by Sonin, "Ravnyi prava," p. 11.

88. Karpukhin and Shteiner, p. 43. Earlier findings on the low skill levels of women in the machine-building industry include Kotliar and Turchaninova, *Zaniatost' zhenshchin*, pp. 43-45, 67-69, and 83, and Uzdenova, p. 11.

89. Novikova and Kutyrev, p. 24.

90. Tatarinova, p. 46.

91. Karpukhin and Shteiner, p. 40; Tatarinova, pp. 18-19.

92. M. Fedorova, "Ispol'zovanie zhenskogo truda v sel'skom khoziaistve," *VE*, no. 12 (December 1975): p. 57; and Iurtsinia, p. 15.

93. Sonin: "Problemy raspredeleniia," p. 99, and "Ravnyi prava," p. 12.

94. Novikova and Kutyrev, pp. 21 and 25, and Nemchenko and Lukashuk, p. 122.

95. V. Moskovich, "Podgotovka rabochikh kadrov i potrebnosti proizvodstva," *VE*, no. 12 (December 1975): 46; and V. Moskovich and V. Anan'ev, "Professional'no-kvalifikatsionnaia struktura rabochikh," *ibid.*, no. 6 (June 1979): 57. Moskovich is a female economist and senior research associate in the Soviet Academy of Sciences Institute of Economics.

96. On the problems of an insufficient number of skilled personnel and generally poor vocational-technical training in the Soviet Union, see Moskovich, pp. 46-54, and Moskovich and Anan'ev, pp. 55-65.

97. Among those who conclude that Soviet women have lower rates of labor productivity and output than men are the following: Kotliar and Turchaninova, *Zaniatost' zhenshchin*, pp. 126 and 130-32; Uzdenova, pp. 11-12; and Sonin, "Problemy raspredeleniia," p. 99. Tatarinova emphasizes intervening factors and denounces (in what may be a veiled reference to "bourgeois" Soviet colleagues) "the bourgeois reactionaries in Western capitalist countries" who assert women workers are less effective than men (pp. 58-62).

98. *Ibid.*, p. 63, Karpukhin and Shteiner, pp. 42 and 44; and, for a similar turnover differential by sex in the Belorussian republic, V. D. Areshchenko et al., *Problemy stabilizatsii trudovykh kollektivov* (Minsk: Nauka i Tekhnika, 1982), p. 48. Yet Skarupo (among others) has found that women remain out of work for much longer periods between jobs than do men (p. 121).

99. Karpukhin and Shteiner, p. 43.

100. Shishkan, p. 114; and N. N. Rumiantsev, "Zolotye kadry," *EKO*, no. 3 (May-June 1978): 75.

101. *Ibid.*, p. 75.

102. B. V. Kutyrev, "Prestizh professii tekstil'shchitsy," *EKO*, no. 3 (May-June 1978): 65.

103. Karpukhin and Shteiner, pp. 43-44. In the study conducted by Skarupo 8.7 percent of women who left their jobs cited wages as the reason for leaving, compared to 24.9 percent of the men (pp. 119-20); in the study conducted by Areshchenko et al., 7.9 percent of the women cited wages, compared to 20.1 percent of the men (pp. 35-36).

104. David E. Powell, "Labor Turnover in the Soviet Union," *Slavic Review* 36, 2 (June 1977): 268-85; Walter D. Conner, "Workers, Politics, and Class Consciousness," in Kahan and Ruble, eds., pp. 323-27; Alex Pravda, "Spontaneous Workers' Activities in the Soviet Union," in *ibid.*, pp. 333-66; Jerry F. Hough, "Policy-Making and the Worker," in *ibid.*, pp. 367-96.

105. Rumiantsev, p. 75.

106. Tatarinova, pp. 58-61 and 111.

107. See the justifications for increased wage differentials and for formal vocational education in the following: Rabkina and Rimashevskaia, pp. 16-32; "How to Make Up for the Shortage of Workers: Not Just by Adding Manpower," *Sovetskaia Rossiia*, 22 July 1979, p. 2; translated in *CDSP* 31, 29 (15 August 1979): 2-3; Vasilii Parfenov, "Economic Survey: Pay People According to Their Work," *Pravda*, 7 April 1980, p. 2; translated in *CDSP* 32, 14 (7 May 1980): 19-20; V. Kostakov, "Questions of Theory: Labor Efficiency and Education," *Ekonomicheskaia gazeta*, no. 33 (August 1980): p. 10; translated in *CDSP* 32, 38 (22 October 1980): 15; and Hough.

108. A. G. Aganbegian, "Effectiveness of the Economic Mechanism: Where Can Reserves Be Found?," *Trud*, 19 January 1980, p. 2; translated in *CDSP* 32, 5 (5 March 1980): 11.

109. "Comrade L. I. Brezhnev's Speech at the Plenary Session of the CPSU Central Committee," *Pravda*, 28 November 1979, pp. 1-2; translated in *CDSP* 31, 41 (26 December 1979): 1-8.

110. "On the Further Strengthening of Labor Discipline and the Reduction of Personnel Turnover in the National Economy," *Pravda*, 12 January 1980, p. 1; translated in *CDSP* 32, 2 (13 February 1980): 14-15. The particular changes which were to follow from the resolution were discussed by N. A. Tikhonov (then First Deputy Prime Minister who became Prime Minister in October 1980), "Perveishaia zadacha organizatsii truda," *Kommunist*, no. 3 (February 1980): 3-14.

111. Sharlet, p. 89.

112. Kuleshova and Skal'berg, pp. 136-37.

113. On the extent of the hidden inflationary pressures, see Igor Birman, "The Financial Crisis in the USSR," *Soviet Studies* 32, 1 (January 1980): 84-105.

114. D. N. Karpukhin: "Trud—istochnik rosta obshchestvennogo bogatstva i blagosostoianiia," *VE*, no. 2 (February 1979): 94, and "Povyshenie effektivnosti ispol'zovaniia rabochei sily v promyshlennosti, stroitel'stve i na transporte," in Kostin, ed., pp. 159-62.

115. L. S. Degtiar': "Ob ispol'zovanii trudovykh resursov v stranakh-chlenakh SEV," *VE*, no. 1 (January 1974): 98-104, and *Problemy ratsional'noi zaniatosti pri sotsializme* (Moscow: Nauka, 1976), pp. 79-87 and 99-138.

116. Iuk, p. 123.

117. For an overview of the factors which have constrained economic reforms in the Soviet Union since 1965, see George R. Feiwel (with the assistance of Ida Feiwel), "Economic Performance and Reforms in the Soviet Union," in *Soviet Politics in the Brezhnev Era*, ed. Donald R. Kelley (New York: Praeger, 1980), pp. 70-103.

118. A. Miasnikov and A. Ananev, "By Skill, Not by Numbers," *Trud*, 17 July 1979, p. 2; translated in *CDSP* 31, 29 (15 August 1979): 4-5.

119. The experiment was the subject of a critical analysis in "Student Years: Maturing in Real Work," *Pravda*, 25 April 1981, p. 3; translated in *CDSP* 33, 37 (27 May 1981): 16-17.

120. Miasnikov and Ananev; and F. I. Gulitskii, *Sotsial'no-ekonomicheskie problemy trudovikh resursov Belorusskoi SSR* (Minsk: Nauka i Tekhnika, 1977), pp. 36-38.

121. These reasons have been either directly stated or implied by all part-time advocates. For example, see Kotliar and Turchaninova, *Zaniatost' zhenshchin*, pp. 103-4; Kuleshova and Mamontova, pp. 91-92; and Novitskii. Kuleshova's detailed defense of part-time shifts appeared directed to industrial managers and "the arguments of an economic nature . . . usually advanced against part-time work" (p. 55).

122. Among advocates of part-time shifts who have linked the reform with an expanded authority for placement bureaus have been Kotliar and Turchaninova, "Rezhim i usloviia truda," pp. 63-64; Kuleshova and Skal'berg, p. 134; and *Dvizhenie rabochei sily v krupnom gorode: problemy regulirovaniia*, ed. A. E. Kotliar (Moscow: Finansy i Statistika, 1982), pp. 187-89 and 199-210.

123. "On Improving Planning and Strengthening the Economic Mechanism's Influence in Enhancing Production Efficiency and Work Quality," *Pravda*, 29 July 1979, pp. 1-2; translated in *CDSP* 31, 30 (22 August 1979): 1-6 and 14.

124. Skal'berg, Matirosian, and Kuleshova, p. 109. To limit managerial discretion in turning down applicants for part-time shifts, these authors propose that local placement bureaus make independent determinations of what job vacancies would be suitably filled by part-timers, and if managers refuse to accept part-timers for these vacancies, they be accused of labor law violation (p. 108).

125. It is indicative that few Soviet citizens are even aware of the part-time option; see Shishkan, p. 167; Kuleshova and Mamontova, p. 91; and Novitskii, p. 54.

126. Fyodor Turovsky, "Society without a Present," in Schapiro and Godson, eds., pp. 179-80.

127. *Ibid.*

128. Among Western scholars who have emphasized the defining traits of the Brezhnev era, see the following: Gail Warshofsky Lapidus, "The Brezhnev Regime and Directed Change: Depoliticization as Political Strategy," in *The Twenty-Fifth Congress of the CPSU: Assessment and Context*, ed. Alexander Dallin (Stanford: Hoover Institution Press, 1977), pp. 26-39; Valerie Bunce and John M. Echols, III, "Soviet Politics in the Brezhnev Era: 'Pluralism' or 'Corporatism'?," in Kelley, ed., pp. 1-26; and Hough.

129. Sheptulina, pp. 30-31.

130. Novitskii, p. 54.

131. Kuleshova, p. 62.

132. On statistical projections, see *ibid.*, p. 58; on special treatment of part-timers in evaluating enterprise performance, see L. Rzhanitsyna, "Zabota o zhenshchine-truzhenitse i materi," *ST*, no. 2 (February 1980): 111-12.

133. Kotliar and Turchaninova, "Rezhim i usloviia truda," p. 63.

134. Gosha, pp. 15-23. Gosha is an economist affiliated with the Institute of Economics in the Latvian Academy of Sciences.

135. Bunce and Echols, and George W. Breslauer, "On the Adaptability of Soviet Welfare Authoritarianism," in *The Communist Party and Soviet Society*, ed. Karl Ryavec (Amherst: University of Massachusetts Press, 1978), pp. 3-25.

136. "The Report of the CPSU Central Committee to the Twenty-Sixth Congress of the CPSU and the Party's Immediate Tasks in the Fields of Domestic and Foreign Policy," *Pravda* and *Izvestiia*, 24 February 1981, p. 6; translated in *CDSP* 33, 9 (1 April 1981): 5-6.

137. *Ibid.*

138. *Ibid.*

139. "In the CPSU Central Committee and the USSR Council of Ministers—'On Measures to Increase State Assistance to Families with Children.," *Pravda* and *Izvestiia*, 31 March 1981, p. 1; translated in *CDSP* 33, 13 (29 April 1981): 9-10.

Chapter 3

1. A. E. Kotliar and S. Ia. Turchaninova, "Rezhim i usloviia truda—vo vse smeny," *EKO*, no. 3 (May-June 1978): 64.

2. On the limited impact of mass politics on women's issues and decision-making in the United States, see the conclusions of Carolyn Teich Adams and Kathryn Teich Winston, *Mothers at Work: Public Policies in the United States, Sweden, and China* (New York: Longman, 1980), pp. 152, 251-52, and 263-66. It appears that widespread debate over women's issues is detrimental to policy formation—as exemplified by the Equal Rights Amendment (ERA), which was passed by Congress in 1972 relatively easily and without controversy but was not ratified. On the problems in gaining successful ratification of the ERA with the politicization of the issue by opponents at the state level, see Janet K. Boles, *The Politics of the Equal Rights Amendment: Conflict and the Decision Process* (New York: Longman, 1979).

3. Carol S. Greenwald, "Part-time Work," in *American Women Workers (1977)*, p. 183. Greenwald is Commissioner of Banks in the Commonwealth of Massachusetts.

4. Nancy S. Barrett, "Women in the Job Market: Unemployment and Work Schedules," in *The Subtle Revolution—Women at Work*, ed. Ralph E. Smith (Washington, D.C.: Urban Institute, 1979), pp. 80-90.

5. On the problems resulting from full-time employment, see the testimony of Urie Bronfenbrenner in *Part-time Employment (1977)*, pp. 25-31, and that of Carol S. Greenwald in *Flexitime and Part-time Legislation (1978)*, pp. 38-53.

6. For example, see Richard J. Estes and Harold L. Wilensky, "Life Cycle Squeeze and the Morale Curve," *Social Problems* 25, 2 (February 1978): 277-92, and Harold L. Wilensky, "Family Life Cycle, Work, and the Quality of Life: Reflections on the Roots of Happiness, Despair, and Indifference in Modern Society," in *Working Life: A Social Science Contribution to Work Reform*, ed. Bertil Gardell and Gunn Johanssoon (London: John Wiley & Sons, 1981), pp. 235-65.

7. Ralph E. Smith, "The Movement of Women into the Labor Force," in Smith, ed, pp. 10 and 14.

8. *Ibid.*, pp. 1-13.

9. For an analysis of the causes and effects of increased female labor force participation, see Emma Rothschild, "Reagan and the Real America," *New York Review of Books* 28, 1 (5 February 1981): pp. 12-18.

10. Smith, "The Movement of Women," p. 19.

11. Isabel V. Sawhill in *Coming Decade (1979)*, pp. 548-49.

12. On the number of women enrolled full-time in American universities, see the Census Bureau's report summarized in *Des Moines Register*, 24 August 1980, p. 7A; on the proportions of women and men in vocational education, see *Working Women Speak (1979)*, pp. 3-4.

13. *Ibid.*, pp. 2-3.

14. Barrett, p. 50.

15. *Working Women Speak (1979)*, p. 4.

16. Willard Wirtz in *Coming Decade (1979)*, pp. 209-17. A summary of the survey was reprinted in *ibid.*, pp. 9-10, from *Business Week*, 5 February 1979.

17. Sawhill in *Coming Decade (1979)*, pp. 535-54, and in *American Women Workers (1977)*, pp. 40-57; Barbara B. Reagan in *ibid.*, pp. 90-102; Barrett, pp. 64-80; and Ralph E. Smith, "Women's Stake in a High-Growth Economy in the United States," in *Equal Employment Policy for Women: Strategies for Implementation in the United States, Canada, and Western Europe*, ed. Ronnie Steinberg Ratner (Philadelphia: Temple University Press, 1980), pp. 350-65.

18. *Ibid.*, pp. 358-62.

19. Lester C. Thurow, "Manpower Programs as Income Distribution," in *Employing the Unemployed*, ed. Eli Ginzberg (New York: Basic Books, 1980), pp. 99-109.

20. For specific changes governing women, see "New CETA Regulations: Some Improvements for Women," *Report of Women's Work Force* (Washington, D.C., Summer 1979).

21. Information in this and the following five paragraphs was derived from unattributed interviews conducted by the author with officials in the Department of Labor, Congressional staff, and women's advocacy groups in Washington, D.C. in March and April 1980 (cited hereafter as March-April 1980 interviews). For overviews of failures and problems in enforcing laws prohibiting sex discrimination, see Marcia Greenberger, "The Effectiveness of Federal Laws Prohibiting Sex Discrimination in the United States," in Ratner, ed., pp. 108-28; for a retrospective of CETA in light of Reagan's policies, see Ronald Smothers, "CETA Cutbacks Leaving Thousands Unemployed," *New York Times*, 11 April 1981, pp. 1 and 8.

22. "CETA Update: Women's Programs in Jeopardy," *Newsletter of Women's Work Force* (Washington, D.C.), 3 November 1979, pp. 1-2.

23. *Ibid.*

24. As an example, see Smothers, pp. 1 and 8.

25. Unless otherwise noted, the discussion in this and the following six paragraphs represents the author's composite from the following sources: Nona Glazer et al., "The Homemaker, the Family, and Employment," in *American Women Workers (1977)*, pp. 155-69; Greenwald, "Part-time Work," in *ibid.*, pp. 182-91; *Part-time Employment (1977)*; *Flexitime and Part-time Legislation (1978)*; *National Conference (1977)*; Barrett; Sandra L. Hofferth and Kristin A. Moore, "Women's Employment and Marriage," in Smith, ed., pp. 63-124; and unattributed March-April 1980 interviews.

26. On androgyny as a goal and its relationship to alternative work schedules, see Janet Zollinger Giele, *Women and the Future: Changing Sex Roles in America* (New York: Free Press, 1979), pp. 30, 108, 111-13, and 305-69.

27. Adams and Winston, pp. 28-30 and 225-27; and Rita Liljestrom, "Integration of Family Policy and Labor Market Policy in Sweden," in Ratner, ed., pp. 388-404.

28. The observations of this speaker were prompted by recent conversations she had had with a group of Swedish women on an official visit to the United States. On the obstacles in implementing androgynous policies in Sweden, see Liljestrom, pp. 392-403, and Eric Morgenthaler, "Sweden Offers Fathers Paid Paternity Leaves: About 10 Percent Take Them," *Wall Street Journal*, 30 January 1979, p. 1.

29. John D. Owens, "Flexitime: Some Management and Labor Problems of the New Flexible Hour Scheduling Practices," *Industrial and Labor Relations Review* 30, 2 (January 1977): 153-54.

30. See *Flexitime and Part-time Legislation (1978)*, p. 26.

31. On the 1978 survey, see *Alternative Work Schedule Directory: First Edition* (Washington, D.C.: National Council for Alternative Work Patterns, 1978), pp. 5-174; on the 1977 questionnaire, see Maureen McCarthy, "Report of a Survey of Alternative Work Schedules in State Governments," in *National Conference (1977)*, pp. 12-24.

32. On the path-breaking role of Wisconsin, Massachusetts, and California and causal factors associated with policy innovation at the state level, see Jack L. Walker, "The Diffusion of Innovation among the American States," *American Political Science Review* 63, 3 (September 1969): 880-99. In a sense the role of these states could be compared to that of Estonia in the Soviet Union: experimental breeding grounds for policy innovations like alternative work schedules, which are tested at the regional level before their wider dissemination at the national or Union-wide level.

33. For a complete list of affiliates of the National Council, see the appendix to *National Conference (1977)*, pp. 95-96. Indicative of its interest, McDonald's partially financed the 1978 survey of alternative work schedules for the *Alternative Work Schedule Directory*, to which a McDonald's official wrote the foreword.

34. Unless otherwise specified, the discussion on federal policy in the remainder of this section is based on the following: *Part-time Employment (1977)*; *Flexitime and Part-time Legislation (1978)*; "Memorandum to Heads of Departments and Agencies—Permanent Part-time Employment in Federal Agencies: September 1977-July 1978," United States Civil Service Commission, 28 December 1978; "The Part-time Career Employment Act of 1978: An Agency Guide on P.L. 95-437" (Washington, D.C.: Office of Personnel Management, 11 April 1979); "Rules and Regulations on Part-time Employment," *Federal Register* 44, 195 (5 October 1979): 57379-82; and unattributed March-April 1980 interviews.

35. Halcyone H. Bohen and Anamaria Viveros-Long, *Balancing Jobs and Family Life: Do Flexible Work Schedules Help?* (Philadelphia: Temple University Press, 1981), pp. 146-48 and 191-203. The survey was conducted in conjunction with the George Washington University Family Impact Seminar.

36. Arch S. Ramsay, Associate Director for Staffing Services, Office of Personnel Management: "Statement before the Subcommittee on Governmental Efficiency and the Subcommittee on Civil Service and General Services of the Committee on Governmental Affairs, United States Senate," 10 June 1980, pp. 5-6, and "Memorandum to Directors of Personnel on Experimental Part-time Direct Hire Program," 30 January 1980.

37. "A Survey of Permanent Part-time Employment in the Civil Service Commission Central Office 1978"; United States Civil Service Commission, April 1979.

38. Gail S. Rosenberg, "Careers: When Less Is More," *Washington Post*, 13 February 1980, p. B5.

39. Ramsay, "Statement before the Subcommittee," pp. 3-4.

40. *Part-time Employment (1977)*, p. 107.

41. See the testimony or written communications in the printed report of the 1977 House hearings, pp. 35-45, 79-84, 107-25, 135-37, 152-53, 180-82, 222-27, and 228-35, and those in the printed report of the 1978 Senate hearings, pp. 173-92, 193-216, 232-34, 242-48, 267-76, 292-93, and 387-452.

42. March-April 1980 interviews.

43. For an analysis of this strategy and case studies of recent Congressional actions on women's issues, see Joyce Gelb and Marian Lief Palley, "Women and Interest Group Politics: A Comparative Analysis of Federal Decision-Making," *Journal of Politics* 41, 2 (May 1979): 362-92. On the need for women activists to shape how policies are perceived and politically defended to defuse anti-feminist opposition and broaden the appeal of women's issues on economic and other grounds, see Ellen Boneparth, "Strategies for the Eighties," in *Women, Power and Policy*, ed. Ellen Boneparth (New York: Pergamon Press, 1982), pp. 303-11.

44. The analysis of changes in the women's movement in the paragraphs which follow is based in part on impressions from the March-April 1980 interviews.

45. For Joyce Miller's views of CLUW and its impact within the trade union movement, see A. H. Raskin, "Growing Acceptance for the Coalition of Union Women," *New York Times*, 19 October 1977, p. 55, and Philip Shabecoff, "Beyond the Women's Auxiliary," *ibid.*, 12 October 1980, p. 9E.

46. On the coalition's attempts to increase public-service employment spending and youth programs, see Geri Palast, "Memorandum to CETA Coalition, Friends of CETA and Other Interest Groups," Washington, D.C., 22 February 1980.

47. On Friedan's warning and the general shift among women's groups to a strategy of coalition, see Adams and Winston, pp. 134-35 and 265-66; see also the comments of NOW officials—e.g., Enid Nemy: "Women's Movement Sets Its Sights on the Future of the Family," *New York Times*, 20 November 1979, p. B 11, and "A NOW Convocation on 'New Leadership' Stresses Voluntarism," *ibid.*, 1 April 1981, p. 23.

48. For an illustration of how the interpretations of liberal and conservative economists have crisscrossed, see the discussion among Robert Lekachman, Herbert Stein, and Secretary of Labor Ray Marshall in "Is This the Road to Ruin? And Where's the Off-Ramp?," *New York Times*, 13 July 1980, p. E3.

49. See the testimony of Fred Best in *Leisure-Sharing (1977)*, p. 85.

50. *Ibid.*, p. 96.

51. For example, in 1977 there was a controversy in the California Senate over whether or not it was desirable for the Dow Chemical Company to open up new facilities in the state. On this controversy and a growing concern over the externalities which must be weighed relative to economic growth, see the comments of Senator James Mills in *Leisure-Sharing (1977)*, pp. 4-16.

52. On the impact of technology and education on the labor force, see the testimony of Barry Stern in *Leisure-Sharing (1977)*, pp. 98-111, and the analysis by Rosabeth Moss Kanter and Barry A. Stern, "Value Change and the Public Work Force: Labor Force Trends, the Salience of Opportunity and Power, and Implications for Public Sector Mangement," in *Work Force (1980)*, esp. pp. 69-73.

53. See *ibid.*, p. 69; Stern, p. 104; and John Herbers, "Census Data Show Gains in Housing and in Education," *New York Times*, 20 April 1982, pp. 1 and 12.

54. See Daniel Yankelovich, "The Meaning of Work," in *The Worker and the Job: Coping with Change* (Englewood Cliffs, N.J.: Prentice-Hall, 1974), pp. 19-48.

55. Daniel Yankelovich, "Work and the New Breed"; paper prepared for Work in America Institute Conference, Arden House, May 1978. (Both this paper and "The Meaning of Work" are discussed in Kanter and Stern, pp. 69 and 72.)

56. *Leisure-Sharing (1977)*, pp. 41-66.

57. *Ibid.*, pp. 112-41, 174-85, and Addendum—Edith F. Lynton, "Alternatives to Layoffs"; based on conferences held by New York City Commission on Human Rights, 3-4 April 1975, pp. 1-68.

58. *Ibid.*, pp. 92-93.

59. *Ibid.*, pp. 66-71.

60. On the origin and legislative history of short-term compensation in California, see Fred Best and James Mattesich, "Short-Time Compensation and Work Sharing: A New Alternative to Layoffs," in *Unemployment Compensation Bills (1980)*, pp. 95-98, and the testimony of Senator William Greene, in *ibid.*, pp. 68-73; also see the interview with Gene Livingston on "Work-Sharing: The MacNeil/Lehrer Report," United States Corporation for Public Broadcasting; televised transcript, 6 June 1980.

61. Best and Mattesich, pp. 98-106.

62. On general procedures and regulations, see *ibid.*

63. Livingston.

64. *Unemployment Compensation Bills (1980)*, pp. 19-40, 60, 68-76, 158-59, 164-65, 169, 196-210, and 222-24.

65. See interview with Eleanor Holmes Norton in "Work-Sharing: The Mac-Neil/Lehrer Report."

66. *Ibid.*

67. On negative assessments of various federal departments and agencies in implementing affirmative action programs for women, see the testimony and analyses in *Coming Decade (1979)* from Gloria Johnson (pp. 368-400), Bella Abzug (pp. 487-506), Isabel Sawhill (pp. 535-54), Mary Berry (pp. 720-43), and Women's Work Force (pp. 870-91).

68. Proponents of affirmative action have pointed out that opponents have no alternatives to the quota system; for example, see Ronnie Steinberg Ratner, "The Policy and Problem: Overview of Seven Countries," in Ratner, ed., pp. 41 and 51.

69. On the limited opportunities for social mobility from the lower social classes, see the detailed analysis in Richard de Lone and the Carnegie Council on Children, *Small Futures: Children, Inequality, and the Limits of Liberal Reform* (New York: Harcourt, Brace, Jovanovich, 1979).

70. Interview with Norton in "Work-Sharing: The MacNeil/Lehrer Report."

71. "The Part-time Career Employment Act of 1978: An Agency Guide on P.L. 95-437," p. 12.

72. March-April 1980 interviews.

73. *Unemployment Compensation Bills (1980)*, pp. 196-98, 230-34, 142-43.

74. *Ibid.*, pp. 69-70.

75. *Ibid.*, pp. 198-201.

76. *Ibid.*, pp. 187-88.

77. Philip Shabecoff, "Donovan Seeks to End Ban on Jobs at Home in Apparel Industries," *New York Times*, 2 May 1981, pp. 1 and 3. On a related trend of employees working at home, see Andrew Pollack, "Rising Trend of Computer Age: Employees Who Work at Home," *ibid.*, 12 March 1981, pp. 1 and 32.

78. See Kay Lehman Schlozman and Sidney Verba, *Injury to Insult: Unemployment, Class and Political Response* (Cambridge, Mass.: Harvard University Press, 1979).

79. Discussion and analysis of these phenomena became so commonplace that they could be considered part of the American conventional mass wisdom of the 1970s. For a government study that first recognized and examined the phenomena, see *Work in America: Report of the Special Task Force of the Secretary of Health, Education, and Welfare* (Cambridge, Mass.: MIT Press, 1973).

80. On changes resulting from the "baby-boom" generation, see Vincent Barabba (Director of the U.S. Bureau of the Census in the Carter administration),

"Demographic Change and the Public Work Force," in *Work Force (1980)*, pp. 29-40.

81. See Yankelovich, "The Meaning of Work," and "Work and the New Breed."

82. Kanter and Stern, pp. 66-77.

83. For example, see Wilensky, "Family Life Cycle," pp. 235-65.

84. The discussion which follows on employee problems and responses by General Motors is based for the most part on April 1980 interviews with General Motors and United Automobile Workers officials in Detroit, Michigan. (Cited hereafter as April 1980 interviews.)

85. See the comments of D. L. Landen, GM Director of Organizational Research and Development, in *Proceedings of the 1979 Executive Conference on Quality of Work Life* (Detroit, Mich.: General Motors, 1979), pp. 1-4.

86. *Ibid.*, p. 68.

87. April 1980 interviews.

88. Daniel Zwerdling, *Workplace Democracy: A Guide to Workplace Ownership, Participation and Self-Management in the United States and Europe* (New York: Harper & Row, 1980). A list of centers can be found on pp. 186-92.

89. See Agis Salpukas, "Quality Circles Aid Productivity," *New York Times*, 25 May 1981, pp. 17 and 19, and Richard Doak, "Management, Workers Talking in Circles," *Des Moines Register*, 31 May 1981, pp. 1F and 4F.

90. Helen Dewar, "Workers Protest Role as 'Robots,'" *ibid.*, 1 June 1979, pp. 1 and 8A.

91. Kanter and Stern, pp. 70-71.

92. Shabecoff, "Beyond the Women's Auxiliary." On the problems of low union membership and declining influence, see William Serrin, "Labor Faces Major Challenges as It Plans for Leadership Shift," *New York Times*, 15 November 1979, pp. 1 and A28, and Ann Crittenden, "Interest in Unionizing Increases Among Female Office Workers," *ibid.*, 9 July 1979, p. A14.

93. March-April 1980 interviews.

94. *Ibid.*

95. See "New Strategies for Education, Work, and Retirement in America" (Addendum to *Leisure-Sharing [1977]*), and comments of Vincent Barabba in David Yepsen, "GOP Governors Learn About Population," *Des Moines Register*, 18 November 1980, p. 4A.

96. On the long-term consequences of the baby boom, see Richard A. Easterlin, *Birth and Fortune: The Impact of Numbers on Personal Welfare* (New York: Basic Books, 1980); on problems for social security arising from it, see Warren Weaver, Jr., "Retiring at Age 65 is Receding Goal," *New York Times*, 9 March 1981, pp. 1 and 10.

97. Yepsen. The 4:1 ratio has proved to be overoptimistic: by March 1981 it was predicted that the ratio by 2020 would be closer to 3.5:1 (see Weaver).

98. "Study Reports of President's Commission on Pension Policy"; briefing to United States Congressional Staff, Washington, D.C., 27 March 1980, p. 5.

99. March-April 1980 interviews.

100. "Study Reports," p. 6.

101. "New Strategies for Education, Work, and Retirement in America," in *Leisure-Sharing (1977)*, p. 11.

102. *Ibid.*, pp. 30-31, 81-97, 112-40, 164-84, 199-206, 210-21; *Part-time Employment (1977)*, pp. 35-45 and 101-4; and *Flexitime and Part-time Legislation (1978)*, pp. 38-42 and 85-105.

103. For example, see Estes and Wilensky.

104. Kanter and Stern, p. 72.

105. Unless otherewise noted, the analysis of opposition to alternative work schedules in this section represents the author's distillation of the following sources: *American Women Workers (1977)*; *Leisure-Sharing (1977)*; *Part-time Employment (1977)*; *Flexitime and Part-time Legislation (1978)*; *Unemployment Compensation Bills (1980)*; *National Conference (1977)*; Smith, ed.; Zwerdling; "Work-Sharing: The MacNeil/Lehrer Report"; and March-April 1980 interviews.

106. As an example, see the comments of union officials in Zwerdling, pp. 167-82.

107. March-April 1980 interviews.

108. *Part-time Employment (1977)*, pp. 154-65.

109. *Ibid.*, pp. 176-77, and interview with Bert Seidman (Director of the AFL-CIO Social Security Department and a member of the National Commission on Unemployment Compensation) in "Work-Sharing: The MacNeil/Lehrer Report."

110. *Part-time Employment (1977)*, p. 171.

111. *Flexitime and Part-time Legislation (1978)*, p. 64.

112. *Ibid.*, pp. 61-65 and 217-26; *Part-time Employment (1977)*, pp. 60-68, 167, and 170-72.

113. Analysis of the AFL-CIO opposition to the California reforms has been based on the comments of Seidman in *Unemployment Compensation Bills (1980)*p. 169, and "Work-Sharing: The MacNeil/Lehrer Report." His comments coincide with the views expressed by union officials in the March-April 1980 interviews.

114. *Flexitime and Part-time Legislation (1978)*, pp. 9-11, 58-59 and 72-73.

Chapter 4

1. On the collapse of bipartisanship in American foreign policy, see Ole R. Holsti and James N. Rosenau, "Vietnam, Consensus, and the Belief Systems of American Leaders," *World Politics* 32, 1 (October 1979): 1-56.

2. On the disappointment over the limited gains from detente within the top Soviet leadership, see the analysis by a former Brezhnev adviser expelled to the West: Boris Rabbot, "A Letter to Brezhnev," *New York Times Magazine*, 6 November 1977, pp. 48ff.

3. On Soviet great-power aspirations seemingly rebuffed by the United States, see Vernon V. Aspaturian, "Soviet Global Power and the Correlation of Forces," *Problems of Communism* 29, 3 (May-June 1980): 1-24; Seweryn Bialer, *Stalin's Successors: Leadership, Stability, and Change in the Soviet Union* (New York: Cambridge University Press, 1980), pp. 236-39; and Jerry F. Hough, *Soviet Leadership in Transition* (Washington, D.C.: Brookings Institution, 1980), pp. 157-69.

4. See the references cited in note 78 of Chapter 2.

5. On the feminist movement among Soviet dissidents, see the interviews with the exiled leaders: Robin Morgan, "The First Feminist Exiles from the U.S.S.R.," *Ms.* 9, 5 (November 1980): 49ff. Selected translations from *Women and Russia* can be found in the monthly journal of Freedom House in New York City: *Freedom Appeals*, May-June 1980, pp. 3-12.

6. Barbara Wolfe Jancar, *Women under Communism* (Baltimore: Johns Hopkins University Press, 1978), pp. 206-13; Gail Warshofsky Lapidus, *Women in Soviet Society: Equality, Development, and Social Change* (Berkeley: University of California Press, 1978), pp. 335-46.

INDEX

Abortion rights, 88

Abramowitz, Beth, 83

Absenteeism, 26, 28, 38, 82, 105, 107, 122

Academy of Sciences (USSR), 14, 18, 21

"Active" real labor reserve, 24

Adams, Carolyn Teich, 2n

Ad-Hoc CETA Coalition, 87

Affirmative action, 57, 66, 68, 69, 98-104. *See also* Labor legislation in U.S.

"Affirmative discrimination," 99

AFL-CIO, 86, 110, 126, 127-29. *See also* Trade unions

AFSCME (American Federation of State, County, and Municipal Employees), 87, 89, 126. *See also* Trade unions

Aganbegian, A. G., 32, 32-33n, 62

Aged, The. *See* Older workers; Pensioners

Aid to Families with Dependent Children (AFDC), 18n

Alienation of workers, 92, 106, 107, 137. *See also* "New breed" workers

Alternative work schedules: broad appeal of, 88, 98, 104; and cultural changes, 109, 116-19; definition of, 3; and economic efficiency, 82-83, 101, 104; and equality, 135-36, 139-40, as incremental change, 72-74, 86; opposition to, 119-29, 131-32; policy context of in U.S., 54-57; policy context of in USSR, 10-22; as policy issue, 3, 6-9, 118-19, 134-35, 142-43; and sex roles, 70-72, 76, 84. *See also* Compressed time; Feminism; Flexitime; Older workers; Part-time employment; Quality of life; Unemployment, and efforts to reduce; Unemployment, as policy issue; Work-sharing

Amalgamated Clothing and Textile Workers, 111. *See also* Trade unions

American Center for the Quality of Work Life, 109

American Chamber of Commerce, 74, 103

American Federation of Government Employees (AFGE), 122n, 124, 126. *See also* Trade unions

American Federation of State, County, and Municipal Employees (AFSCME). *See* AFSCME

American Federation of Teachers, 111

American Nurses' Association, 111

American Telephone and Telegraph Company (AT&T), 109

Andropov, Yuri, 141

A. Phillip Randolph branches, 86

Apprenticeship programs (CETA), 65-66, 68

Article 40 (USSR Constitution, 1977), 41

Article 35 (USSR Constitution, 1977), 15

Article 26 (USSR labor code, 1971), 11, 16

Asian ethnic groups, 24, 25, 32. *See also* Pronatalism

AT&T. *See* American Telephone and Telegraph Company

Attitude changes of workers. *See* Alternative work schedules, and cultural changes; Labor force, changes in attitude of

Austria, 2

171

Automation. *See* Technological advance

Babkina, M., 22
"Baby boom" generation, 105, 113
Baltic ethnic groups, 15, 23-25 passim, 51, 89, 135, 138. *See also* Pronatalism
"Banking" of work time, 4, 13
Barrett, Nancy, 62
Basic Guidelines (USSR), 13, 52, 53
BAT. *See* Bureau of Apprenticeship and Training
Best, Fred, 89
Birthrate in USSR. *See* Pronatalism
Black workers. *See* Racial minorities
"Blue-collar blues," 104
Bohen, Halcyone, 74-75
Boldyrev, V. T., 23
Brezhnev, Leonid, 40, 47, 49, 52, 134, 141
Bronfenbrenner, Urie, 58-59, 60, 84
Bureau of Apprenticeship and Training (BAT), 66, 68
Bureaus of labor placement and information (USSR), 45
Burke, Yvonne (bill of), 84, 85

California: work experiments in, 73, 93-94, 117, 137; work-sharing program of, 4, 5, 129, 143. *See also* Short-Time Unemployment Compensation
"California lifestyle," 117
Canada, 2
Carter, Jimmy, 62, 66, 68-69, 76, 83, 129
Central Committee of CPSU. *See* Joint resolution (USSR)
Central Council of Trade Unions (USSR), 29, 31n
Central Labor Resources Research Institute (USSR), 47
CETA (Comprehensive Employment and Training Administration Act), 65-69, 87, 115

Chamber of Commerce. *See* American Chamber of Commerce
Child-support subsidy (USSR, 1974), 18-19
China, 2n
Civil Rights Act (1964), 99
Civil Service Commission, 84. *See also* Office of Personnel Management (OPM)
Civil Service Reform Act (1978), 78, 82, 85
Clerical sector, 110, 111
CLUW. *See* Coalition of Labor Union Women
Coalition of Labor Union Women (CLUW), 86-87, 111. *See also* Trade unions
Cohen, Lynn Revo, 82n
Comecon, 42
Commentary, 99
Commerce, Department of, 81
Committee on Government Affairs (U.S. Senate), 77, 78
Committee on Industrial Relations (California Senate), 96
Committee on Labor and Human Resources (U.S. Senate), 61, 84
Communications Workers of America (CWA), 73, 109-10, 122, 126. *See also* Trade unions
Community Legal Services (Philadelphia), 87
Comparable pay, 28n, 86. *See also* Equal pay; "Just pay"
Complex Long-Term Program of Developing the Population (USSR), 25n
Comprehensive Employment and Training Administration Act. *See* CETA
Compressed time: definition of, 3-4; and energy usage, 91; and federal employees, 55, 73-75; opposition to, 120, 124-26; in USSR, 12-13
Conner, Walter D., 35n
Constitution of 1977 (USSR), 15
Core time, 3. *See also* Flexitime

"Corporatism" in USSR. *See* Welfare policy (USSR)

Cottage-industry work, 13

Council of Ministers (USSR). *See* Joint resolution (USSR)

Cultural changes in U.S. *See* Alternative work schedules, and cultural changes

Culver, John, 116n

Darskii, L. E., 23, 24. *See also* "Qualitative" dimensions of labor reserves

Daycare facilities (USSR), 16, 22, 52-53

Democratic Party Convention (1980), 88

Demographic policy, differential (USSR), 24-25, 50. *See also* Pronatalism

Detente, 133-34

Differential population policy. *See* Demographic policy, differential (USSR)

"Difficult" work. *See* Hazardous work (USSR)

Discrimination. *See* Inequities, and discrimination

Divorce, 59, 117

DOL. *See* Labor, Department of

Domestic Policy Council, 83

Donovan, Raymond, 103

Eagleton, Thomas, 125n, 130

East Germany, 21

Economic growth: constraints on, 26, 36, 39; downturns in, 60-61; and proposals to increase, 39-42, 142-43; and stagnation, 40; and value reassessment, 89, 91. *See also* Recessions (U.S.); Technological advance

Education of workers, 59, 60-61, 92

EKO (Ekonomika i organizatsiia promyshlennogo proizvodstva), 31, 32-33n

Election (November 1980), 102

Employment and Training Administration (Department of Labor), 65

Employment Development Department (California), 97

Employment programs (U.S.). *See* CETA

Employment Project of the Iowa Commission on the Status of Women, 66

Energy crisis, 91

Equal Employment Opportunity Commission (U.S.), 29n, 87

Equality under socialism, 33, 49. *See also* Inequities

Equality vs. equity, 57, 100-4, 105n, 127, 136. *See also* Inequities

Equal pay, 27, 28n. *See also* Comparable pay; "Just pay"

Equal Rights Amendment (ERA), 86, 88

ERA. *See* Equal Rights Amendment

Estonia, 10, 11-12, 15-16, 47

Europe. *See* Western Europe

"Experience rating," 128

Fair Labor Standards Act (1935), 124

"Family life cycle," 58, 118

Family. *See* Alternative work schedules, and sex roles; Part-time employment, and sex roles; Pronatalism

Federal employees (U.S.), 73-78 passim, 83, 122n, 125, 130. *See also* Federal Employees Flexible and Compressed Work Schedules Act (1978); Federal Employees Part-time Career Employment Act (1978)

Federal Employees Flexible and Compressed Work Schedules Act (1978), 74-75, 83, 122n, 125

Federal Employees Part-time Career Employment Act (1978), 75-78, 81-83, 101, 122n

Federally Employed Women (FEW), 81-82

Feminism, 55, 56, 69-88, 138-39. *See also* Women's advocacy groups

FEW. *See* Federally Employed Women

Fiss, Barbara, 83

Flexible work hours. *See* Flexitime

Flexitime: definition of, 3; and energy usage, 91; and federal employees, 55, 74-75; and older workers, 115; opposition to, 120-23; success of, 73; in USSR, 12-13; for women, 7, 70, 75

Flexitour, 3

Ford, Henry, 106

France, 2, 5

Friedan, Betty, 87

Fringe benefits, 4-5, 20, 57, 76, 81, 113, 115, 131, 142. *See also* Social security system; Trade unions, and opposition to alternative work schedules

Full-employment policy, 56, 64

Full-time equivalency, 77, 130

Furloughs. *See* State furloughs

General Motors (GM), 106-8, 121

Generational shift. *See* Labor force, changes in attitudes of

Germany, Federal Republic of. *See* West Germany

Glazer, Nathan, 99

Gliding time, 3

GM. *See* General Motors

Gosha, Z., 48

GOSPLAN, 25-26

Grassley, Charles, 116n

Gray Panthers, 84

Greene, William, 89, 96, 102, 103

Growth. *See* Economic growth

Handicapped, The, 11, 12, 65, 76, 78, 84

Hatcher, Richard, 102

Hazardous work (USSR), 14, 27-28

Health benefits. *See* Fringe benefits

Hearings on labor legislation (U.S. House and Senate, 1977-78): and broad support for part-time legislation, 81-82, 84; and federal full-time equivalency, 130; and opposition to compressed time, 74, 124-25; and support for work-sharing, 102-3.

See also Federal Employees Flexible and Compressed Work Schedules Act (1978); Federal Employees Part-time Career Employment Act (1978)

Hewlett Packard, 94

"Homework," 13, 15, 103

Hooks, Benjamin, 102

House of Representatives. *See* Hearings on labor legislation (U.S. House and Senate, 1977-78); Post Office and Civil Service Subcommittee (U.S. House of Representatives); Select Committee on Aging (U.S. House of Representatives)

Humphrey-Hawkins Full-Employment Act (1978), 127

Hungary, 49

Inequities: and discrimination, 71, 98-101, 104, 136, 139; efforts to eliminate, 2, 56, 72, 135-36, 139-40; and government programs, 66, 68, 69; and job segregation, 20, 29, 61-67 passim, 70-72; in reform proposals (USSR), 17-22 passim, 39-40; and sex stereotyping, 35, 62, 63; in skills and wages, 27, 29, 30, 34, 35, 38, 61; and "social feminist" logic, 30; vs. working women, 14, 20, 21, 31, 136-38, 140. *See also* Affirmative action; Equality vs. equity; Equality under socialism; Labor legislation in U.S.; Labor legislation in USSR; Labor productivity, and female job segregation; Pronatalism

Inflation, 59, 65, 89-90, 101, 113, 114

Institute of Economics (Academy of Sciences, USSR), 14

Institute of Sociology (USSR), 21

Intergovernmental Personnel Administration, 91

"Intermittents," 75, 76

International Labor Office (ILO), 4, 5

International Workers' Movement Institute (USSR), 21

Invalids. *See* Handicapped, The
Iowa State Employment and Training
    Council, 66

Jackson, Jesse, 102
Jackson-Vanik amendments, 134
Jancar, Barbara, 140
Japan, 107
Job discrimination. *See* Inequities, and
    discrimination
Job Pressure Days, 109
Jobs programs, 90, 127, 128, 142. *See
    also* CETA
Joint resolution (USSR), 13, 40, 52, 53
"Just pay," 28. *See also* Comparable
    pay; Equal pay

Kanaeva, I. N., 20n
Kanter, Rosabeth Moss, 105, 106, 118
Khrushchev, Nikita, 10, 35
Kishinev, 10
Kotliar, A. E., 27, 54
Kuleshova, L., 19n
Kvasha, A. Ia., 23, 24, 25n

Labor, Department of (DOL), 66, 69,
    81, 97, 99, 103. *See also* Bureau of
    Apprenticeship and Training (BAT);
    Employment and Training Adminis-
    tration; Labor Statistics, Bureau of
Labor code (USSR, 1971), 11. *See also*
    Labor legislation in USSR
Labor force: changes in attitudes of, 91,
    104-6, 112 (*see also* "New breed"
    workers); composition of women
    in, 32-35, 68 (*see also* Inequities,
    and discrimination; Inequities, and
    job segregation; Inequities, and sex
    stereotyping); growth in, 89, 90-91;
    ineffective use and underutilization
    of, 25, 33, 43, 45, 59, 88; optimal
    utilization of, 50-51; proportion of
    on alternative work schedules, 73.
    See also Education of workers;
    Labor productivity; Skilled workers;
    Unskilled workers

Labor legislation in U.S.: and civil rights
    legislation, 98-99; and federal em-
    ployee unions, 122n; laws of 1978,
    54-55, 74-86, 101, 125, 143; pro-
    posed reforms in, 87, 102-3, 114-16;
    and retirement, 90-91. *See also* Af-
    firmative action; Hearings on labor
    legislation (U.S. House and Senate,
    1977-78); Humphrey-Hawkins Full-
    Employment Act (1978); Work
    environment
Labor legislation in USSR: and discrim-
    ination vs. women, 17, 19-20; and
    labor protection laws, 29, 30; and
    part-time proposals, 47-49, 51-52;
    prospects for reforms in 1980s, 141-
    42; reforms of 1970s, 11-16 passim,
    20-21; and status of women, 138.
    See also Economic growth, and pro-
    posals to increase
Labor productivity: declines in, 12n,
    25, 37, 40-41, 88, 107, 129, 136;
    and female job segregation, 61;
    increases in with part-time employ-
    ment, 10-11, 82, 101, 120, 122,
    141-42; and labor problems, 6, 7;
    limitations in, 23, 33; and under-
    utilization, 59-63 passim. *See also*
    Economic growth, proposals to
    increase; Labor shortages; "New
    breed" workers; Work environment
Labor shortages: alleviation of with
    part-time employment, 10, 11, 41;
    and low birthrates, 23; of skilled
    workers, 42, 43, 50, 51; in Western
    Europe, 6; and work reforms, 28.
    See also Pronatalism
Labor Statistics, Bureau of (Depart-
    ment of Labor), 60
Lapidus, Gail, 140
"Latch-key" children, 57, 58
League of Women Voters, 87n
Leave without pay. *See* Labor legisla-
    tion in USSR, and reforms of 1970s
Legislation. *See* Labor legislation in
    U.S.; Labor legislation in USSR

Leisure-sharing, 5, 137. *See also* Voluntary Reduced Hours program
Levitan, Sar, 89
Lex, Louise, 66
Life-work expectancy, 60
Litvinova, G. I., 23, 24
Livingston, Gene, 89, 95, 97
"Lordstown syndrome," 104, 106
"Lump of labor" explanation, 60

Mainstreaming. *See* CETA
Management: and labor relations, 3, 57, 126; and opposition to part-time employment, 43-47, 122-24, 131; and support for compressed time, 125-26. *See also* Trade unions
Manevich, Ye. L., 24
Market socialism, 49
Massachusetts, 73, 82, 85
Maternity leave, 14, 22, 23, 25, 47, 52
McAuley, Alastair, 16, 19
McDonald's, 73
Medvedeva, T. N., 23
"Mental" occupations, 35, 36
Messerschmidt Research and Development Center (Munich), 73
Miller, Joyce, 86, 111
Mills, James, 89
Minority groups. *See* Handicapped, The; Older workers; Racial minorities; Students; Women in U.S.; Women in USSR
Mitterand, François, 5
Moldavia, 10, 16, 19
Motivation of workers. *See* Work environment
Motorola, 103
Motor Vehicles, Department of (California), 94
Multinational corporations, 5-6

National Association of Retired Federal Employees, 84
National Center for Labor Productivity and the Quality of Work Life, 108-9

National Commission on Employment Policy, 62
National Commission on Working Women, 61
National Congress for Community Economic Development, 87
National Council for Alternative Work Patterns (NCAWP), 5, 74, 91, 110, 126
National Federation of Federal Employees (NFFE), 122n, 125, 126
National Governors' Association, 91
National Organization for Women (NOW), 87
National Urban Coalition, 87n
National Urban League, 102
National Women's Political Caucus, 76
NCAWP. *See* National Council for Alternative Work Patterns
Neo-conservatives, 99
New breed liberals, 142
"New breed" workers, 92, 105-6, 121
New Right, 82, 88
Night shifts, 14, 27-28
Norton, Eleanor Holmes, 87, 89, 98, 101, 102
Novitskii, A., 22
Novosibirsk Academy of Sciences, 31
NOW. *See* National Organization for Women

Occupational Safety and Health Administration (U.S.), 29n
OFCCP. *See* Office of Federal Contract Compliance Programs
Office of Federal Contract Compliance Programs (OFCCP), 29n, 66, 68, 69
Office of Management and Budget (OMB), 75, 77, 83, 85, 130
Office of Personnel Management (OPM), 74, 75, 77, 78, 83, 85, 101
Older workers, 65, 84, 112-13, 115-16, 116n. *See also* Pensioners
OMB. *See* Office of Management and Budget
Output. *See* Labor productivity

Overemployment, 89
Overtime, 74
Owens, John D., 73

Pacific Telephone and Telegraph, 94
Pan American Airlines, 94
"Parental leave." *See* Sweden
Part-time employment in U.S.: broad advantages of, 101-4 (*see also* Older workers); and equality for women, 70, 81 (*see also* Inequities, efforts to eliminate); and federal employees, 55, 75-78 passim, 83; as incremental change, 73, 82, 83; and innovations in states, 73 (*see also* California; Short-Time Unemployment Compensation [STC]; Voluntary Reduced Hours program); official responses to, 77, 83, 85, 95 (*see also* Trade unions, responses to labor reforms of); opposition to, 120, 126-27, 129, 131 (*see also* Management, and opposition to part-time employment; Trade unions, opposition to alternative work schedules of); as policy issue, 7-9, 54-57 (*see also* Unemployment, as policy issue); proportions in workforce on, 20, 73; as response for economic efficiency, 76, 136 (*see also* Economic growth; Quality of Work Life [QWL]; Unemployment, and efforts to reduce); and sex roles, 58, 78, 117; types of, 3-4; as women's issue, 82, 102 (*see also* Feminism). *See also* Alternative work schedules; Compressed time; Flexitime; Labor legislation in U.S.; Work-sharing
Part-time employment in USSR: as advantage to women, 10, 12, 22, 26-27, 39, 51, 129 (*see also* Maternity leave); broad advantages of, 12 (*see also* Pensioners); experiments in, 10-13, 44; as incremental change, 137, 139, 140; official responses to, 21, 50-51 (*see also* Management, and opposition to part-time employment); as policy issue, 7, 10-22 (*see also* Labor legislation in USSR, and part-time proposals; Labor legislation in USSR, and reforms of 1970s; "Social feminist" logic; Unemployment, as policy issue); proportions in workforce on, 15-16; and reform discrimination vs. women, 19-21, 50-52, 139 (*see also* Inequities, in reform proposals (USSR); Inequities, vs. working women; Pronatalism; Selective unemployment); as response for economic efficiency, 14-15, 26, 41-42, 50, 88-89, 140-42 (*see also* Economic growth; Unemployment, and efforts to reduce); and skilled workers, 131-32; types of, 3-4; and vocational advancement, 14, 20; as women's issue, 52; women's responses to, 9, 15-21 passim, 26, 42, 46, 48, 139. *See also* Alternative work schedules; Compressed time; Flexitime; Work-sharing
Pensioners, 11, 12, 13, 16, 41. *See also* Older workers
Perevedentsev, V. A., 22, 23
Phased retirement, 76, 78. *See also* Older workers; Pensioners; Social security system
Piece-work. *See* "Homework"
Piskunov, V. P., 18
Planovoe khoziaistvo, 26
Poland, 49
Policy formation, 1-2. *See also* Alternative work schedules; Labor legislation in U.S.; Labor legislation in USSR; Part-time employment in U.S.; Part-time employment in USSR
Post Office and Civil Service Subcommittee (U.S. House of Representatives), 83, 85
Prejudice. *See* Inequities
Presidential Commission on Pension Policy, 114, 115

"Prime sponsors" (CETA), 65n, 66
Productivity. *See* Economic growth; Labor productivity
Professional personnel. *See* Skilled workers
Pronatalism, 14-15, 18, 22-25, 51-53, 89, 135
Proposition 13 (California), 5, 95-96
Protestant work ethic, 104, 117, 132
Public Interest, 99
Public sector, 125, 129. *See also* Federal employees (U.S.)

"Qualitative" dimensions of labor reserves (USSR), 23, 24, 25, 36
Quality circles, 109
Quality of life, 88, 89, 91, 92, 105, 117. *See also* "New breed" workers; Work environment
Quality of Work Life (QWL), 106-8, 121
QWL. *See* Quality of Work Life

Rabochii klass i sovremennyi mir, 21
Racial minorities (U.S.), 63-64, 76, 78, 90, 92, 102. *See also* CETA; Inequities, and discrimination
Ramsay, Arch, 78, 81
Rational-comprehensive approach (USSR), 31-32, 33, 138
Reagan, Barbara, 62
Reagan, Ronald, 99, 114, 116, 129, 134; and affirmative action, 68, 69n; and part-time employment, 102-3, 142
Recessions (U.S.), 63, 64, 93, 97, 99, 100, 101
Reduced work. *See* Part-time employment
Reforms. *See* Labor legislation in U.S.; Labor legislation in USSR; Pronatalism; Work environment
Republican Party, 99
Reserved quotas, 14
Reserve workers, 17, 44, 46
Retail trade sector, 59

Retirement. *See* Labor legislation in U.S., and retirement; Older workers; Pensioners; Phased retirement
Retirement benefits. *See* Fringe benefits
Riabushkin, T. V., 23, 24
Round-table conference (USSR, 1978), 15, 31, 32, 33, 47, 138
Russian republic, 15
Russian Republic State Committee on Labor Resource Utilization, 11

Safety conditions. *See* Hazardous work (USSR); Work environment
Salaries. *See* Wages and salaries
Sales sector, 110, 111
San Mateo County (California), 93
Santa Clara County (California), 93
Sarbanes, Paul, 142
Sawhill, Isabel, 62, 89
Schroeder, Patricia, 83, 131; work-sharing bill of, 97-98, 102, 103
Segregation. *See* Inequities, and job segregation
Select Committee on Aging (U.S. House of Representatives), 84
Select Committee on Investment Priorities and Objectives (California Senate), 93
Selective unemployment, 50, 51
Senate. *See* Committee on Government Affairs (U.S. Senate); Committee on Labor and Human Resources (U.S. Senate); Hearings on labor legislation (U.S. House and Senate, 1977-78); Social security system; Subcommittee on Aging (U.S. Senate)
Senior citizens. *See* Older workers; Pensioners
Service sector, 12, 12n, 41, 59, 110, 111, 113
Sex roles. *See* Alternative work schedules, and sex roles; Part-time employment in U.S., and sex roles
Sex stereotyping. *See* Inequities, and discrimination

Sexual discrimination. *See* Inequities

Sexual equality. *See* Inequities; "Social feminist" logic

Shared Work Unemployment Benefits. *See* Short-Time Unemployment Compensation (STC)

Shchekino reform, 43

Shishkan, N. M., 19n

Short-Time Unemployment Compensation (STC), 95-97, 101, 103, 127-28, 130-31, 142

Single mothers, 17-18, 19

Skilled workers, 16-17, 33, 36-37, 44, 51, 92. *See also* Labor shortages, of skilled workers

Slavic ethnic groups, 15, 23-25 passim, 51, 89, 135, 138. *See also* Pronatalism

Smith, Ralph, 62, 64

"Social feminist" logic, 30-31, 32

Socialism and equality. *See* Equality under socialism

Social Security Act (1978), 113, 114

Social security system, 113-15, 130-31

Solarz, Stephen (bill of), 84, 85, 125

Solidarity, 49

Sonin, M. Ia., 14, 15, 36, 62

Spellman, Gladys, 83

Stagflation, 90

Staggered work hours, 3

Stagnation. *See* Economic growth

State Committee on Labor (USSR), 29

State furloughs, 4. *See also* Short-Time Unemployment Compensation (STC)

STC. *See* Short-Time Unemployment Compensation

Stern, Barry A., 89, 105, 106, 118

Steshenko, V. S., 18

Students, 12, 44, 76

Subcommittee on Aging (U.S. Senate), 84

"Subtle revolution," 59

Sweden, 2, 2n, 30, 72

Taganrog study, 19, 20

Tallinn, 10

Tatarinova, N. I., 39, 62

Taylorism, 106

Technological advance: constraints against, 26, 37, 43, 135; and dehumanization, 109; effects on women of, 42, 62, 89; revolution in, 89-90, 91-92. *See also* "Qualitative" dimensions of labor reserves (USSR); Work environment

Temporary federal workers (U.S.), 75, 81

Thurow, Lester, 65

Tkachenko, A. A., 23, 24

Trade sector. *See* Retail trade sector. *See also* Service sector

Trade unions: declines in membership of, 110; opposition to alternative work schedules of, 74, 120-29; and reduced work contracts, 5; responses to labor reforms of, 84, 94, 107, 114; and women, 86, 110-12. *See also* AFSCME; Coalition of Labor Union Women (CLUW); Communications Workers of America (CWA); Management; United Automobile Workers (UAW)

Tsongas, Paul, 142

Turchaninova, S. Ia., 27, 54

Turnover rates, 38, 41, 44, 48, 105

Turovsky, Fyodor, 46

Twenty-Fifth Party Congress, 15

Twenty-Sixth Party Congress, 13, 52

UAW. *See* United Automobile Workers (UAW)

Underemployment, 7, 14, 25, 62, 63

Unemployment: efforts to reduce, 4-6, 89, 93-98, 136, 139, 142; increases in, 56, 90-91; as policy issue, 88-104; and social security, 113. *See also* Selective unemployment

Unemployment compensation. *See* Fringe benefits

Unions. *See* Trade unions

United Automobile Workers (UAW), 107, 108, 121, 129. *See also* Trade unions

United Kingdom, 2

Unskilled workers: as drag on growth, 14, 24-26, 37, 89, 135, 141; effects of part-time employment on, 14, 16, 20, 75; proportion of women among, 33-36 passim, 89. *See also* Labor productivity, declines in; Technological advance

Urban Institute, 59, 62

Urban League, 87n

Urlanis, B. Ts., 22, 23, 25

U.S. House of Representatives. *See* Hearings on labor legislation (U.S. House and Senate, 1977-78); Post Office and Civil Service Subcommittee (U.S. House of Representatives); Select Committee on Aging (U.S. House of Representatives)

U.S. Senate. *See* Committee on Government Affairs (U.S. Senate); Committee on Labor and Human Resources (U.S. Senate); Hearings on labor legislation (U.S. House and Senate, 1977-78); Social security system; Subcommittee on Aging (U.S. Senate)

Vacation time. *See* Fringe benefits

Veterans, 65

Vishnevskii, A. G., 23

Viveros-Long, Anamaria, 74-75

Voluntary Reduced Hours program, 93-94

Wages and salaries: disparities among workers of, 14, 33, 34, 62-63; and education, 61; and flexitime, 121; and premium pay, 27, 29, 124-25. *See also* Equal pay; Inequities, in skills and wages; "Just pay"

Washington Star, 94

Watts, Glen, 109

Welfare policy (USSR), 19, 49

Western Electric Company, 94

Western Europe, 4, 6, 73, 96, 124

West Germany, 2, 4, 107

White-collar workers. *See* "Mental" occupations; Skilled workers

Wilensky, Harold L., 2n

Winston, Kathryn Teich, 21

Wisconsin, 73, 82, 94

"Woman question," 30

Women and Russia, 138

Women in U.S.: full-time vs. part-time employment for, 57-58; and job counseling, 62; and job safety, 29n; as policy focus, 2-3, 99; proportions in workforce of, 56, 59-61, 66-69, 90, 117, 134; and recessions, 60, 63-64, 101; responses to alternative work schedules of, 54; support for 1978 labor legislation of, 122n. *See also* Alternative work schedules, and sex roles; Coalition of Labor Union Women (CLUW); Education of workers; Federally Employed Women (FEW); Feminism; Inequities; Part-time employment in U.S., and equality for women; Part-time employment in U.S., and sex roles; Part-time employment in U.S., as women's issue; Temporary federal workers (U.S.); Trade unions, and women; Wages and salaries; Women's advocacy groups; Women's movement

Women in USSR: advantages of part-time work for, 11-15, 19n, 119 (*see also* Maternity leave; Part-time employment in USSR, as advantage to women); generational differences among, 34-35; and job safety regulations, 28-30 (*see also* Hazardous work [USSR]); as policy focus, 2-3, 52, 138 (*see also* EKO; "Social feminist" logic); positive attributes in workforce of, 38-39; proportions in labor force of, 32-37 passim, 134 (*see also* Selective unemployment;

Unskilled workers, as drag on growth); and vocational mobility, 14, 34. *See also* Inequities; Part-time employment in USSR, women's responses to; Pronatalism; Single mothers

Women's advocacy groups, 55, 66, 85, 102, 139. *See also* Feminism

Women's Congressional Caucus, 83

"Women's issues." *See* Women's movement

Women's Lobby, 82n

Women's movement, 86-88. *See also* Feminism

Women's Work Force, 87n

Work, concept of in U.S., 116-17, 118

Work environment, 6, 26, 28-29, 105-7, 109, 120. *See also* Labor legislation in USSR, and labor protection laws

Work-sharing: and affirmative action, 101-3; and CETA, 70; definition of, 3-4; experiments in, 5, 94-98; as norm in U.S., 73; opposition to, 120, 126-29, 131; vs. unemployment, 136, 142; in Western Europe, 4, 96. *See also* Short-Time Unemployment Compensation (STC); Voluntary Reduced Hours program

Yankelovich, Daniel, 92, 106

JOEL C. MOSES is Professor of Political Science, Iowa State University. He received his Ph.D. degree from the University of Wisconsin-Madison in 1972. He has taught as a visiting faculty member at Cornell University and the University of California, San Diego. He is the author of *Regional Party Leadership and Policy-Making in the USSR* (New York, 1974), *The Politics of Female Labor in the Soviet Union* (Ithaca, 1978), and several articles on Soviet politics in journals and symposiums.

INSTITUTE OF INTERNATIONAL STUDIES
UNIVERSITY OF CALIFORNIA, BERKELEY

215 Moses Hall   Berkeley, California 94720

CARL G. ROSBERG, *Director*

Monographs published by the Institute include:

RESEARCH SERIES

1. *The Chinese Anarchist Movement.* R.A. Scalapino and G.T. Yu. ($1.00)
7. *Birth Rates in Latin America.* O. Andrew Collver. ($2.50)
15. *Central American Economic Integration.* Stuart I. Fagan. ($2.00)
16. *The International Imperatives of Technology.* Eugene B. Skolnikoff. ($2.95)
17. *Autonomy or Dependence in Regional Integration.* P.C. Schmitter. ($1.75)
19. *Entry of New Competitors in Yugoslav Market Socialism.* S.R. Sacks. ($2.50)
20. *Political Integration in French-Speaking Africa.* Abdul A. Jalloh. ($3.50)
21. *The Desert & the Sown: Nomads in Wider Society.* Ed. C. Nelson. ($5.50)
22. *U.S.-Japanese Competition in International Markets.* J.E. Roemer. ($3.95)
23. *Political Disaffection Among British University Students.* J. Citrin and D.J. Elkins. ($2.00)
24. *Urban Inequality and Housing Policy in Tanzania.* Richard E. Stren. ($2.95)
25. *The Obsolescence of Regional Integration Theory.* Ernst B. Haas. ($4.95)
26. *The Voluntary Service Agency in Israel.* Ralph M. Kramer. ($2.00)
27. *The SOCSIM Microsimulation Program.* E. A. Hammel et al. ($4.50)
28. *Authoritarian Politics in Communist Europe.* Ed. Andrew C. Janos. ($3.95)
29. *The Anglo-Icelandic Cod War of 1972-1973.* Jeffrey A. Hart. ($2.00)
30. *Plural Societies and New States.* Robert Jackson. ($2.00)
31. *Politics of Oil Pricing in the Middle East, 1970-75.* R.C. Weisberg. ($4.95)
32. *Agricultural Policy and Performance in Zambia.* Doris J. Dodge. ($4.95)
33. *Five Classy Computer Programs.* E.A. Hammel & R.Z. Deuel. ($3.75)
34. *Housing the Urban Poor in Africa.* Richard E. Stren. ($5.95)
35. *The Russian New Right: Right-Wing Ideologies in USSR.* A. Yanov. ($5.95)
36. *Social Change in Romania, 1860-1940.* Ed. Kenneth Jowitt. ($4.50)
37. *The Leninist Response to National Dependency.* Kenneth Jowitt. ($4.95)
38. *Socialism in Sub-Saharan Africa.* Eds. C. Rosberg & T. Callaghy. ($12.95)
39. *Tanzania's Ujamaa Villages: Rural Development Strategy.* D. McHenry. ($5.95)
40. *Who Gains from Deep Ocean Mining?* I.G. Bulkley. ($3.50)
41. *Industrialization & the Nation-State in Peru.* Frits Wils. ($5.95)
42. *Ideology, Public Opinion, & Welfare Policy: Taxes and Spending in Industrialized Societies.* R.M. Coughlin. ($6.50)
43. *The Apartheid Regime: Political Power and Racial Domination.* Eds. R.M. Price and C. G. Rosberg. ($12.50)
44. *Yugoslav Economic System in the 1970s.* L.D. Tyson. ($5.50)
45. *Conflict in Chad.* Virginia Thompson & Richard Adloff. ($7.50)
46. *Conflict and Coexistence in Belgium.* Ed. Arend Lijphart. ($7.50)

47. *Changing Realities in Southern Africa.* Ed. Michael Clough. ($12.50)
48. *Nigerian Women Mobilized, 1900-1965.* Nina E. Mba. ($12.95)
49. *Institutions of Rural Development.* Eds. D. Leonard & D. Marshall. ($11.50)
50. *Politics of Women & Work in USSR & U.S.* J.C. Moses. ($9.50)
51. *Zionism and Territory.* Baruch Kimmerling. ($12.50)
52. *Soviet Subsidization of Trade with Eastern Europe.* M. Marrese & J. Vanous. ($14.50)
53. *Voluntary Efforts in Decentralized Management.* L. Ralston et al. ($9.00)
54. *Corporate State Ideologies.* C. Landauer. ($5.95)
55. *Effects of Economic Reform in Yugoslavia.* J. Burkett. ($9.50)
56. *The Drama of the Soviet 1960s.* A. Yanov. ($8.50)
57. *Revolutions and Rebellions in Afghanistan.* Eds. M.N. Shahrani & R.L. Canfield. ($14.95)
58. *Women Farmers of Malawi.* D. Hirschmann & M. Vaughan. ($8.95)

POLITICS OF MODERNIZATION SERIES

1. *Spanish Bureaucratic-Patrimonialism in America.* M. Sarfatti. ($2.00)
2. *Civil-Military Relations in Argentina, Chile, & Peru.* L. North. ($2.00)
9. *Modernization & Bureaucratic-Authoritarianism: Studies in South American Politics.* Guillermo O'Donnell. ($8.95)

POLICY PAPERS IN INTERNATIONAL AFFAIRS

1. *Images of Detente & the Soviet Political Order.* K. Jowitt. ($1.25)
2. *Detente After Brezhnev: Domestic Roots of Soviet Policy.* A. Yanov. ($4.50)
3. *Mature Neighbor Policy: A New Policy for Latin America.* A. Fishlow. ($3.95)
4. *Five Images of Soviet Future: Review & Synthesis.* G.W. Breslauer. ($4.50)
5. *Global Evangelism Rides Again: How to Protect Human Rights Without Really Trying.* E.B. Haas. ($2.95)
6. *Israel & Jordan: An Adversarial Partnership.* Ian Lustick. ($2.00)
7. *Political Syncretism in Italy.* Giuseppe Di Palma. ($3.95)
8. *U.S. Foreign Policy in Sub-Saharan Africa.* R.M. Price. ($4.50)
9. *East-West Technology Transfer in Perspective.* R.J. Carrick. ($5.50)
10. *NATO's Unremarked Demise.* Earl C. Ravenal. ($3.50)
11. *Toward Africanized Policy for Southern Africa.* R. Libby. ($7.50)
12. *Taiwan Relations Act & Defense of ROC.* E. Snyder et al. ($7.50)
13. *Cuba's Policy in Africa, 1959-1980.* William M. LeoGrande. ($4.50)
14. *Norway, NATO, & Forgotten Soviet Challenge.* K. Amundsen. ($3.95)
15. *Japanese Industrial Policy.* Ira Magaziner and Thomas Hout. ($6.50)
16. *Containment, Soviet Behavior, & Grand Strategy.* Robert Osgood. ($5.50)
17. *U.S.-Japanese Competition-Semiconductor Industry.* M. Borrus et al. ($7.50)
18. *Contemporary Islamic Movements in Perspective.* I. Lapidus. ($4.95)
19. *Atlantic Alliance, Nuclear Weapons, & European Attitudes.* W. Thies. ($4.50)
20. *War and Peace: The Views from Moscow and Beijing.* Banning N. Garrett & Bonnie S. Glaser. ($7.95)